Lectionary Worship Workbook

Soul Motion

Series IV, Cycle C

Julia Ross Strope

CSS Publishing Company, Inc., Lima, Ohio

Appreciation for my friends:
Colleague, Jim Dollar, who wrote the foreword
Greensboro artist, Melanie Basset, who prepared the visuals
Musician daughter, Leandra Merea Strope, who drew the Celtic knot and suggested hymns

Copyright © 2009 by
CSS Publishing Company, Inc.
Lima, Ohio

Some scripture quotations are from the *Good News Bible*, in Today's English Version. Copyright American Bible Society 1966, 1971, 1976. Used by permission.

Some scripture quotations are from the New Revised Standard Version of the Bible, copyright 1989 by the Division of Christian Education of the National Council of the Churches of God in the USA. Used by permission.

For more information about CSS Publishing Company resources, visit our website at www.csspub.com or email us at csr@csspub.com or call (800) 241-4056.

Cover design by Leandra Merea Strope and Barbara Spencer

ISSN: 1938-5560

ISBN-13: 978-0-7880-2624-0
ISBN-10: 0-7880-2624-9

PRINTED IN USA

Table Of Contents

Season 6 - Early Pentecost — Promotion

Season 7 - Late Pentecost — Slow Motion

Additional Materials

Foreword

Humans have always sought to express our experience of the Holy with words, music, and action. We cannot contain that experience. It demands expression, response. In certain instances, the expression of the experience can become a vehicle of the experience, and a feedback loop is created where experience and expression is one thing. The European cathedrals, the monoliths at Easter Island, and the cave drawings at the Cave of Chauvet-Pont-d'Arc in France, are places where the expression of our response to the experience of the Holy engenders the experience. Holy places lend themselves to Holy encounters.

The language of response and the structure that shapes it and gives it form can also serve to create the experience it expresses. Gregorian chants and the responses of the Taizé community, and that of Iona, have the capacity to carry participants to deeper (or higher, if you prefer) levels of the understanding, the knowing, which connect us with the essence of spiritual reality.

The words we use in worship can create the experience that the words are used to express when they meet a certain quality of readiness, or openness, in the worshiper. There are no magical phrases, no enchanted formulas, no charmed incantations. We cannot be carried against our will into an encounter with the Holy, either by word, or music, or sacred space. Some people, it seems, will always mistake the voice of God for thunder rolling. And, at various points in our lives, it can be said of us all that we "have eyes and do not see, ears and do not hear."

At the same time, words can block the flow of Spirit to spirit and prevent the experience of connection with the Holy. It is the peculiar genius of the crafters of liturgy to assist the movement of soul and to amplify the sounds of the heart, the sighs too deep to be spoken. Julie Strope has the gift of being able to carry us beyond where we have been in opening up new ways of seeing by subtly (and sometimes not so subtly) changing what we say in approaching the Holy.

One of the 10,000 Spiritual Laws states, "There is no intimacy apart from vulnerability." We cannot come to know God without exposing ourselves in the process. As we say who we are and how it is with us, we see it, perhaps, for the first time. It is the effort at articulation that expands awareness, that deepens consciousness. This volume of liturgical forms and responses shapes our seeing by leading us to say things we may not have said before. The movement of soul is based upon the openness of heart and our willingness to hear more than has been said.

The movement of soul and the openness of heart carry us through an infinite progression of identity, integrity, vision, purpose, clarity, and awareness. At the center of this process is the presence of the Holy, and our capacity to sense that presence, respond to it, and align ourselves with it. Liturgical forms are age-old ways of shaping our response to the experience of the Holy, even as they provide the structure for a continuing experience of Holy Presence.

With this resource, Dr. Strope provides an invaluable aid for the expression of our response to the sacred dimension, to the Mystery of life and being. The language is real, not ecclesiastical; of the twenty-first century, not inherited from, along with the baggage of, the past, and inclusive of feminine and masculine, and provides a wonderful means for the response to, and the experience of, that which is Holy and among us.

Jim Dollar
Church of the Covenant, PCUSA
Greensboro, North Carolina

Motions Of The Soul

Hands
Hands that won't and hands that do
Hands manicured and open wide
We have hands to still and reach

Hands
Hands that receive and hands that give
Hands to curl and crawl
We have hands to raise and wait

Hands
Fingers that point and palms that tingle
Hands to create silence, beauty, and music
We have hands that shake and sing

Hands
Hands that slap and hands that clap
Hands to work and caress
We have hands to heal and bless

Hands
Hands lithe to dance and meditate
Hands to rest and hope
We have hands to reject and invite

Hands
Hands colored with warts and kinky digits
Hands old, young, and in between
We have hands that touch and weave

Hands
Like magnets or vices
Like wrappings and bandages
Hands manifest divine dance and dealings
For all to see

Introduction

Faith in God is an opening up, a letting go, a deep trust, a free act of love....
God's hat was always unraveling. God's pants were falling apart.
God's cat was a constant danger.
God's ark was a jail. God's wide acres were slowing killing me.
God's ear didn't seem to be listening ...
[Yet] God would remain a shining point of light in my heart. I would go on
  loving.

— Yann Martel, *Life of Pi*

Since Abraham, perhaps, words have been the primary medium for communicating with The Other, with animals, and with humans. Since Augustine and Constantine, Aquinas and Kierkegaard, the perceived *D'bar* of the Holy has dominated academic and church conversations. During the last century, humans stretched the previous boxes of thought about the universe and human roles; here are some of the changing ideas I hear discussed at church suppers:

- evolution invited humans to consider themselves part of a whole universe unfolding;
- cosmology removed a tiered universe and introduced black holes and an expanding universe;
- women voted and moved to the public arena;
- research and experimentation expanded the understanding of human sexuality and the ability to shape and control reproduction;
- the Holy became imminent and an intrinsic part of Creation (instead of external);
- the divide between poverty and wealth widens in every nation while technology brings nations together as a global village;
- economics of one nation now affect the whole planet; and
- religions are tools in the hands of the powerful, pitting tribes and countries against one another.

Ideas have changed so drastically that fearfulness and discomfort catapult individuals into two disparate positions:

- those who set aside previous conceptions of religion and the Holy to assemble a new system that nurtures personal spiritual longings; and who turn more doggedly to the "faith of the fathers."

Those people in between are often silent, many not attending to spiritual/soul yearnings or finding avenues outside the church. Though church growth materials suggest that they are just waiting to be invited to join a faith community, "a field white unto harvest," these people often resist involvement in organized religion.

Consequently, this workbook is an attempt to be a resource for people designing worship events in a manner that people can visit a sanctuary, gather to rest, and connect with others while being aware of the Holy Presence and get some of their needs met. John Calvin's seventeenth concern encourages us to be "ever reforming." In this attitude of "ever reforming," the awareness of continuing human development suggests that what was workable for the last generation is not adequate for new generations. Individuals, too, explore, change, and grow. At this point in my life, guides on my journey to the Holy include Karen Armstrong, Matthew Fox, Caroline Myss, Parker Palmer, Houston Smith, and John Shelby Spong.

Worship in this workbook is people gathering to feel included and affirmed as they quiet the culture's claims and invite the Holy to inspire, give peace, and motivate them to do goodness. Thanksgiving and exploration of cultural issues such as poverty, child abuse, health care, drugs, and violence as entertainment, *en masse* is energizing. Expression of current issues and current awareness in current language is also energizing/empowering. As people experience the Holy, they share their journeys with one another, encouraging honesty, questions, and non-judgmental conversations. Language is inclusive and contemporary.

In the worship format, there is no "invocation" since I experience God as already present. Prayer in this workbook is awareness of the Holy Presence, time for two-way conversation with the transcendent. Prayer brings to consciousness the good and the less-than-good; it becomes an opportunity to let go of whatever is incongruent and inconsistent within one's emotions, thought, and relationships. Prayer relaxes the ego and makes room for God. The "confession" is an acknowledgment, a declaration, admitting what is. I have rarely included a "word of grace" and no "assurances of pardon" since I believe that God alone gives "assurance." Since the word "God" carries so much baggage in our culture, I use words that describe the Holy One like The Divine, Sacred, Mystery, Awesome, and others.

The Bible is the source book of stories that reveal the developing consciousness of humankind in the beginning of recorded history. Bible stories illuminate the human desire to be in relationship and connected to creative energies, to God. We see ourselves mirrored in many of the ancient stories. Our received scriptures are early dialogue with Yahweh God in a cosmology that supports warfulness, one-upsmanship, destruction of the planet, and abuse of women and children. We look to the New Testament, to Jesus of Nazareth who challenged that ancient system. He is our hero, the Christ, who says that life abundant (John 10) is possible for every person and tribe; the kingdom of heaven, the reign of God, is for everyone! So in a cosmology that includes black holes, magma, and space travel, our concept of the Holy expands; we seek to understand the word of God in ways that do not diminish life nor deny scientific evidence.

Since the global economy is designed for profit and not to promote justice, people who believe the reign of God is coming to earth need one another and must take responsibility for the dream of life abundant and fairness for all peoples. In community, we acknowledge

- the Holy Spirit among and within us,
- the inconsistency between words and attitudes, and
- the encouragement by companions so we can change our incongruent ways.

We gather to express our gratitude, our disappointments, our questions, and our hopes. With all our senses we sing, pray, dance, meditate, listen, and talk with one another in our own language. We are attentive to the Holy Presence, inspiring, encouraging, and empowering.

This workbook for each Sunday of the liturgical year (plus several feast days) explores the lectionary texts, using contemporary language. When I turned to scripture, I usually read Today's English Version but the use of scripture is paraphrased. If you prefer a different version of the Bible, please feel free to substitute your preferred version. Some of the elements such as "A Contemporary Affirmation" are repeated as whole units or with variations for a particular week's emphasis. Material spoken by "people" is bold face and can be lifted easily to most bulletins. The contemporary quotes are provided for intellectual stimuli. The charcoal hands depicting the motions of the spiritual journey reproduce well on bulletins and newsletters.

The traditional church year is divided into seven "motions" of spiritual journey. Season one (Advent) is named **In Motion**. The calendar cycle begins again. The time that is past is intentionally set aside and attention is given to a fresh cycle. People are *in motion*, busy preparing for a new child, a God-child, and for enjoying family and friends.

Season two (Christmas) is named **Commotion**. When the anticipated moment is realized, commotion erupts! Food and stories, gifts and memories are integral and satisfying parts of the *commotion*.

Season three (Epiphany) is named **Locomotion**. As the commotion subsides, people integrate their gifts into their closets and lifestyles. They move about, mindful that the God-child grows up and teaches ways to manifest the Holy in a culture that thrives on flexible truth, profit, and power hoarding. People choosing to follow the teachings of Jesus of Nazareth "locomote," finding ways to practice the "Reign of God" principles.

Season four (Lent) is named **No Motion**. After the flurry of activity during **In Motion**, **Commotion**, and **Locomotion**, people can now reflect on what works and what doesn't, what satisfies the soul and what doesn't. **No Motion** gives people time to consider what the Divine Voice is challenging them to be and to do. **No Motion** is a period of time for people to prepare to make changes in their attitudes, expectations, and uses of time.

Season five (Easter) is called **Emotion**. The time of reflection, **No Motion**, erupts into new options. Resurrection is a reality as the story of Jesus suggests. Transformation in all areas of life at every developmental stage are possible. Creativity is seen and felt in the natural world and in the soul.

Season six (early Pentecost) is named **Promotion**. Now the period of activity, inner empowerment, is projected to the external world. Energy and ideas are apparent as people are mindful of interior contentment. There is an impulse to tell others about one's own inner journey to God and to invite them to nurture a similar experience. Passion is contagious and often shows up in creative activities decked in bright colors. The psyche projects much energy into external arenas; it *promotes* justice.

Season seven (late Pentecost) is called **Slow Motion**. As with agricultural cycles, after producing beauty and food, rest is necessary, while still being mindful of both internal and external needs to participate with God's Reign. Activity slows; passion is less visible; the wisdom gleaned from experience manifests as accommodation, tolerance, synergy, generosity, gratitude, and gentleness. Again, there's awareness of a cycle ending so a new generative period — a fresh pregnancy, vital evidence of Divine Presence with humanity, can begin.

In this resource book, we are wordsmyth, artist, and musician. We provide oral, visual, and aural materials to inspire and encourage planners of faith events, worship, and intergenerational occasions. Thanks to Becky Allen and CSS for shaping this workbook for people who have a passion for creating events with Great Mystery! Our task, our pleasure, is to enjoy God and one another!

Julia Ross Strope
Church of the Covenant (PCUSA)
Greensboro, North Carolina

Musician's Notes

The knot is an ancient symbol of unity, of both binding and loosening, of the labyrinthine nature of a spiritual journey. The shape of this particular knot (Celtic) shown on the cover was inspired by the cross, a symbol of both balance and salvation; the star, a light in the darkness, and symbol of divine guidance; the thorny crown, a symbol of the pain essential to growth; and the circle that represents the unity and connectedness of all things.

Hymns are an essential part of congregational worship. Singing hymns together is a powerful act in that it unifies our voices and gives us a way to participate directly in harmony. Hymns ground and center us together; they provide a container for our emotions. It is important that the congregation feels connected to the music, that they know the hymns, and be able to sing them lustily. At the same time, it is important to be intentional about the words we sing, and congregations who sing only the old hymns will never come to know and love the new ones. In my own church work, I seek a balance between the new and the familiar, while always being intentional to choose texts that work with the liturgy and are sensitive to the issues with which the congregation grapples.

The liturgy in this book hopes to be broadly inclusive, to deal openly and honestly with issues that we face today in our daily lives. In choosing hymn suggestions to accompany this liturgy, I have drawn primarily from *The United Methodist Hymnal* (1989, The United Methodist Publishing House), *The Presbyterian Hymnal* (1990, Westminster/John Knox Press), and *Chalice Hymnal* (1995, Chalice Press). Many of the hymns were written recently, many are older; many of the new texts have familiar tunes. I have attempted to be true to the understanding of who we are as Christians and to also provide options that will be readily available and even familiar to many congregations.

There is an ever-growing number of wonderful texts and tunes being written; many denominations compile these into hymnal supplements. Abingdon Press publishes the *Abingdon Press Hymn Series*, a delightful collection of new hymns in small volumes.

My congregation occasionally enjoys the challenge of hearing styles of music that are radically different from our norm, including modern avant-garde and early-Renaissance polyphony. Poets in my congregation enjoy writing hymn texts to celebrate church anniversaries and other special events. Yours may, too.

Leandra Merea Strope
Minister of Music
The Olin T. Binkley Memorial Baptist Church
Chapel Hill, North Carolina

Season 1
Advent

In Motion

Advent 1

Jeremiah 33:14-16   1 Thessalonians 3:9-13
Psalm 25:1-10   Luke 21:25-36

The truth, Dumbledore sighed.
It is a beautiful and terrible thing and
Therefore should be treated with great caution.
                                    — *Harry Potter And The Sorcerer's Stone*

This is what Dumbledore sends his defender!
A songbird and an old hat!
Do you feel brave, Harry Potter?
Do you feel safe now?

                                                   (Tom Riddle to Harry)
                                    — *Harry Potter And The Chamber Of Secrets*

Greeting

It's a new season in the life of the faith, and we are confronted again with truths about Divine Presence and the stories we have learned that pass along those truths. How does the truth of Jeremiah shape our lives in a new millennium on a different continent? What does the birth of Jesus of Nazareth have to do with us?

Our minds ask these questions and our souls are moving through gestation with fresh ideas of the Eternal, of embodying truth, and seeking new understandings of abundance and privilege.

Call To Worship
(Includes the lighting of the Advent Wreath)

Leader: Already, the year is behind us and we are counting the days until Christmas — the eldering for one set of reasons and the young for another. We've come here to enjoy the festivities of December and to tell again the stories that encourage us to be God-bearers in our world.

People: The scriptures say that God has made promises of safety and prosperity to people who are willing to be loyal bearers of goodness and grace, mercy and hospitality.

Leader: In every generation, leaders emerge who love the Holy One and promote righteousness and beauty.

People: When events of living seem overwhelming, we are glad for the reminder that God is near and will not desert us during political upheaval, natural disasters, and family disputes.

Leader: We are expecting God to come among us in new ways; we are expecting to birth holiness right here!

People: Ring the bells! Clap your hands! Our hearts rejoice.

Leader: Make a circle. Light a fire. Sing a song of love.

People: We know the stories of the past — priests and prophets, too.

Leader: Now for us this candle brings a vision of our hope ...
People: that God will move among us with strength and peace!
(One purple candle on the Advent Wreath is lit.)

Prayer Of Thanksgiving (Leader)

Living God — with gladness we see stars; we hear angels; we remember old stories. Here, together, we thank you for the images surrounding us, pointing to you. Thanks, too, for the talents assembled in this place, for we are aware that all good things come from you. Amid the beauty, we give you our undivided attention. Amen.

Call To Confession (Leader)

Quiet the chatter in your minds.

Let the Spirit refresh you with awareness of how you might be whole and how you can be available for others with contagious joy.

Let's recite the printed confession and then listen in silence for the Divine Voice.

Community Confession (Unison)

**Loving God — Christmas comes but once a year; thank you for being active in our
     lives all year long!**
Reveal the negative aspects of our behaviors and free us from their hold on us.
Let us feel your empowering love sending us with peace into the world. Amen.

Word Of Grace (Leader)

Like the wreath, God encircles us with divine grace; like the flame, God warms our hearts; like the candle, God lights our darkness. In a baby, we see hope of a future and our fears vanish in the newborn Christ. Hallelujah!

Congregational Choral Response   Canticle of Mary, *Magnificat* (v. 1, modified)

My soul gives glory to our God; my soul sings forth its praise;
God immerses us in loveliness in many marvelous ways.

Sermon Idea

Amid the merchandizing in our culture, we hear the cries of the hungry, the lonely, and the war-weary. Though we are surrounded with the excitement of joyful surprises and family gatherings, we still are aware of life's disappointments and suffering. A sturdy faith that God is present in all the ups and downs allows us to move through the stages of life with some sense of purpose and reach out with a cup of tasty soup and a glass of good water, a listening ear and a compassionate heart. Gestation, birthing, maturing, eldering, and dying are all motions of the body and soul throughout life. This season gives us opportunity to notice how we allow the Holy to work and play with us.

Contemporary Affirmation (Unison)

We experience God among us as the creative Spirit working through our thoughts, our hands, and our feet to make a bit of heaven on earth.

We believe God is among us — vulnerable and strong, loving and sustaining each one who welcomes the Holy.

We know God is in this world; we dream of fresh political structures that are fair, respectful, and inclusive.

We trust that God is reconciling families and nations and resurrecting the God-image in all people.

Through every part of our human journey, God is with us; we are not alone. Hallelujah!

Offertory Statement (Responsive)

Leader: We work to pay our mortgages, to buy things for our homes, to put nutritious food on our tables, and to entertain ourselves.

People: And then the world takes so much from us.

Leader: At the same time, there are men and women in our town who need basic supplies for their survival.

People: We will give our time, talents, and moneys to support this place and to provide for people in need.

Doxology   While Shepherds Watched Their Flocks (v. 6)

All glory be to God on high, And to the earth be peace;
Good will to all from highest heaven
Begin and never cease! Begin and never cease!

Prayer Of Thanksgiving (Leader)

For all we have, for all we are becoming, thank you, God. For money, for families, for this church home, we are grateful. Amen.

Intercessory Prayers (Leader or Readers)

Energy of the Universe — see this world and its pains; look at the violence and the suffering that rain on innocent children and adults. Like a mother and a father pregnant with new life, we pray for gentleness and strength and divine protection for our own children and for all the children in our global village. Stop the terror that rattles houses and souls; halt the war that maims and kills.

Lover of the World — come among your creatures, our brothers and sisters, with passion that counters greed. Come to your people with wisdom for a sustainable economy. Come to your people with wisdom to provide work that pays, health care that leads to wellness, and foods that nurture the body. Come among your creatures with love, which gives birth to a new way to be in relationships with ourselves and with others around this planet.

Maker and Shaker of our Humanity — body and soul, we are yours. You know how strong and how fragile we are. Hold us when the pain seems unbearable; soothe us when our losses leave us empty; befriend us when loneliness curdles our hearts; where we feel broken, mend us; when we cry in despair, move us to new awareness of sufficiency.

Dreamer of a New Reign — let your peace and your heaven come to earth. Set in motion human mercy and hospitality that reach into our own towns and around the world; set in motion economic possibilities for all peoples; set in motion a transparent honesty, which erases corruption; set in motion a contentment with life and things so that we are not caught in voracious buying.

Thank you for Jesus who moved through birth, childhood to adulthood, and shared your wisdom and your grace with all the world. Refresh us with love to give away. Amen!

Benediction (Leader)

May the beauty of a sleeping baby fill you with wonder, the curiosity of a toddler dance in your toes, the anticipation of a lover carry you into tomorrow, the peace of Christ soothe your mind, and the joy of Holy Spirit brighten your whole day and night! While we are absent from this place, know that you are cradled by the living God!

Music

Come Down, O Love Divine
 Words: Bianco of Siena (15th century); tr. Richard F. Littledale, 1867, alt.
 Music: Ralph Vaughan Williams, 1906
 DOWN AMPNEY

Gracious Spirit, Dwell With Me
 Words: Thomas T. Lynch, 1855, alt.
 Music: Charles F. Gounod, 1872; harm. A. Eugene Ellsworth, 1994
 LUX PRIMA

Love Divine, All Loves Excelling
 Words: Charles Wesley, 1743
 Music: John Zundel, 1870
 BEECHER

One Candle Is Lit
 Words: Mary Anne Parrott, 1988
 Music: William J. Kirkpatrick, 1895
 CRADLE SONG

People Look East
 Words: Eleanor Farjeon, 1928
 Music: Traditional French Carol; harm. Martin Shaw, 1928
 BESANÇON

Toda la Tierra (All Earth Is Waiting)
 Words: Catalonian text by Alberto Taulè, 1972; English tr. Gertrude C. Suppe, 1987
  (Isaiah 40:3-5)
 Music: Alberto Taulè, 1972; harm. Skinner Chávez-Melo, 1988
 TAULÉ

Advent 2

Malachi 3:1-4   Philippians 1:3-11
Luke 1:68-79   Luke 3:1-6

The truth, Dumbledore sighed.
It is a beautiful and terrible thing and
Therefore should be treated with great caution.
                   — Harry Potter And The Sorcerer's Stone

This is what Dumbledore sends his defender!
A songbird and an old hat!
Do you feel brave, Harry Potter?
Do you feel safe now?

                        (Tom Riddle to Harry)
                   — Harry Potter And The Chamber Of Secrets

Call To Worship
(Includes the lighting of the Advent Wreath)

Leader: Already, the year is behind us and we are counting the days until Christmas — the eldering for one set of reasons and the young for another. We've come here to enjoy the festivities of December and to tell again the stories that encourage us to be God-bearers in our world.

People: The scriptures say that God has made promises of safety and prosperity to people who are willing to be loyal bearers of goodness and grace, mercy and hospitality.

Leader: In every generation, leaders emerge who love the Holy One and promote righteousness and beauty.

People: When events of living seem overwhelming, we are glad for the reminder that God is near and will not desert us during political upheaval, natural disasters, and family disputes.

Leader: We are expecting God to come among us in new ways; we are expecting to birth holiness right here!

People: Ring the bells! Clap your hands! Our hearts rejoice.

Leader: Make a circle. Light a fire. Sing a song of love.

People: We know the stories of the past — deserts, flowers, too.

Leader: Now for us this candle brings a vision of sprightly breeze ...

People: that God will move among us with strength and peace!

(Two purple candles on the Advent Wreath are lit.)

Prayer Of Thanksgiving (Leader)

Living God — with gladness we see stars; we hear angels; we remember old stories. Here, together, we thank you for the images surrounding us, pointing to you. Thanks, too, for the quiet of this moment and the companionship among us gathered here. Amid the beauty, we give you our undivided attention. Amen.

Call To Confession (Leader)

Quiet the chatter in your minds.

Let the Spirit refresh you with awareness of how you might be whole and how you can be available with contagious joy for others.

Let's recite the printed confession and then listen in silence for the Divine Voice.

Community Confession (Unison)

Loving God — Christmas comes but once a year; thank you for being active in our lives all year long!

Reveal the negative aspects of our behaviors and free us from their hold on us.

Let us feel your empowering love sending us with peace into the world. Amen.

Word Of Grace (Leader)

Like the wreath, God encircles us with divine grace; like the flame, God warms our hearts; like the candles, God lights our darkness. In a baby, we see hope of a future and our fears vanish in the newborn Christ. Hallelujah!

Congregational Choral Response   Canticle of Mary, *Magnificat* (v. 1, modified)

My soul gives glory to our God; my soul sings forth its praise;

God immerses us in loveliness in many marvelous ways.

Sermon Idea

The images in Malachi, a strong soap that washes clean and a fire that polishes silver, appeal to the senses of smell, sight, and touch. God's presence with us is like that — appealing to all our senses! When our whole selves are saturated with the Holy, then we will be what God intends. In Philippians, the image that stands out is the connectedness we have with one another; the ribbons that circle us flow from Jesus and their goal is to honor God. The final section of Luke 1 is (father to John and Uncle to Jesus) Zechariah's ecstatic delight with the prospect of fresh, unmistakable activity of God on behalf of oppressed creatures.

The Luke story is told in the hymn "Song Of Zechariah." If there are male dancers in the congregation, this can be a powerful and masculine choreographed presentation.

The Luke story works well as a choral reading. Four readers, each with a microphone, can stand/sit in various sections of the gathering space.

Reader 1: After John is born to Elizabeth, father Zechariah is overcome with gratitude and feels the Holy Spirit ablaze within.

Reader 2: Praise God! The God who walked with our fathers and mothers!

Reader 3: God has come to the help of oppressed people and has set them free!

Reader 1: The Holy One has provided a mighty hero, a Savior.

Reader 2: Prophets of ancient times have told us again and again that God would not desert us — that we would be delivered from enemies!

Reader 3: As we look back, we see how God has been with our ancestors, showing mercy and comfort.

Reader 2: God appeared to Abraham and Sarah and they heard the divine affirmation of progeny, property, and holy presence.

Reader 3: Without fear, people could honor God with righteous living every day!

Reader 1: Then, Zechariah has a blessing for his son:

Reader 4: You, John, my child, will be a spokesperson for the Most High God. You will show others how to experience forgiveness from sin, how individuals might experience the mercy and tenderness of God. Your humility will welcome God like a bright dawn with salvation to shine from heaven on all who live in dark shadows. You, my son, John, will prepare the way for paths of peace.

Reader 1: John grew up, maturing in body and spirit.

Reader 2: He lived in the desert until he was ready to be a public leader among the people of Israel.

Reader 3: While John and Elizabeth celebrated the birth of their child, John, later dubbed "The Baptist," Cousin Mary and Joseph were expecting their first child to be named "Jesus," later called "the Christ."

Contemporary Affirmation (Unison)

We experience God among us as the creative Spirit stimulating our thoughts, working through our hands and our feet to make a bit of heaven on earth.

We believe God is among us — vulnerable and strong, loving and sustaining each one who welcomes the Holy.

We know God is in this world; we dream of fresh political structures that are fair, respectful, and inclusive.

We trust that God is reconciling families and nations and resurrecting the God-image in all persons.

Through every part of our human journey, God is with us; we are not alone. Hallelujah!

Offertory Statement (Responsive)

Leader: We work to pay our mortgages, to buy things for our homes, to put nutritious food on our tables, and to entertain ourselves.

People: And then the world takes so much from us.

Leader: At the same time, there are men and women in our town who need basic supplies for their survival.

People: We will give our time, talents, and moneys to support this place and to provide for people in need.

Doxology   While Shepherds Watched Their Flocks (v. 6)

All glory be to God on high, And to the earth be peace;
Good will to all from highest heaven
Begin and never cease! Begin and never cease!

Prayer Of Thanksgiving (Leader)

For all we have, for all we are becoming, thank you, God. For money, for families, for this church home, we are grateful. Amen.

Intercessory Prayers (Leader or Various Readers)

Energy of the Universe — thank you for setting us free from soul-threatening tyrannies. Continue to inspire us with words and actions of peace. Thank you for John the Baptist who calls us to open ourselves to your creating love. Thank you for Jesus the Christ who challenges us to imagine a godly way to be in the world as peace-makers, justice-workers, and mercy-carriers. Live in us as gratitude, passion, and joy.

Lover of the World — can you see through the dark actions and thoughts of humankind? Do you weep at the terror and war that invades the psyche and destroys the body and mind? Do you grieve at the destruction of the earth's land, air, and water? Save this world from self-destruction. Raze human greed and sow seeds of collaboration on fertile hearts of politicians and warlords; raise government and business responsibility from profit to meaningful work and healthcare for all children and adults. Guide us all to paths of honest communication, curious seeking, and satisfying relationships.

Maker and Shaker of our Humanity — like good soap, bathe us in goodness. Like refiner's fire, polish our expectations. Like a physician, encourage us to be available to the wholesomeness in our environment. Like an artist, recolor our pains and griefs until light shines through.

Dreamer of a New Reign — let your peace and your heaven come to earth. Set in motion human mercy and hospitality that reach into our own towns and around the world; set in motion economic possibilities for all peoples; set in motion a transparent honesty that erases corruption; set in motion a contentment so that we are not caught in voracious buying.

Thank you for Jesus who moved through birth, childhood to adulthood, and shared your wisdom and your grace with all the world. Refresh us with love to give away. Amen!

Benediction (Leader)

May the beauty of a sleeping baby fill you with wonder; the curiosity of a toddler dance in your toes; the anticipation of a lover carry you into tomorrow; the peace of Christ soothe your mind; the joy of Holy Spirit brighten your whole day and night! While we are absent from this place, know that you are cradled by the living God!

Music
Awake! Awake, And Greet The New Morn
    Words and Music: Marty Haugen, 1983
    REJOICE, REJOICE

Blessed Be The God Of Israel
    Words: Michael Perry, 1973
    Music: Hal Hopson, 1983
    MERLE'S TUNE

Like A Child
    Words and Music: Dan Damon, 1992
    LIKE A CHILD

"Sleepers, Wake!" A Voice Astounds Us
    Words: Philipp Nicolai, 1599; tr. Carl P. Daw Jr., 1982
    Music: attr. Philipp Nicolai, 1599; harm. J. S. Bach, 1731
    WACHET AUF

Advent 3

Zephaniah 3:14-20   Philippians 4:4-7
Isaiah 12:2-6   Luke 3:7-18

> *The truth, Dumbledore sighed.*
> *It is a beautiful and terrible thing and*
> *Therefore should be treated with great caution.*
>   — *Harry Potter And The Sorcerer's Stone*

> *This is what Dumbledore sends his defender!*
> *A songbird and an old hat!*
> *Do you feel brave, Harry Potter?*
> *Do you feel safe now?*
>
>   (Tom Riddle to Harry)
>   — *Harry Potter And The Chamber of Secrets*

Call To Worship
(Includes the lighting of the Advent Wreath)

Leader: Already, the year is behind us and we are counting the days until Christmas — the eldering for one set of reasons and the young for another. We've come here to enjoy the festivities of December and to tell again the stories that encourage us to be God-bearers in our world.

People: The scriptures say that God has made promises of safety and prosperity to people who are willing to be loyal bearers of goodness and grace, mercy and hospitality.

Leader: In every generation, leaders emerge who love the Holy One and promote righteousness and beauty.

People: When events of living seem overwhelming, we are glad for the reminder that God is near and will not desert us during political upheaval, natural disasters, and family disputes.

Leader: We are expecting God to come among us in new ways; we are expecting to birth holiness right here!

People: Ring the bells! Clap your hands! Our hearts rejoice.

Leader: Make a circle. Light a fire. Sing a song of love.

People: We dream the future and we hope for joy — joy that makes our lives full and satisfying.

Leader: Now for us these candles illuminate the possibility of joy ...

People: that God will move among us with strength and peace.

(Two purple candles on the Advent Wreath are lit and then the pink one, making three glowing lights — hope, peace, and joy.)

Prayer Of Thanksgiving (Leader)

Living God — with gladness we see stars; we hear angels; we remember old stories. Here, together, we thank you for the images surrounding us, pointing to you. Here, we sing and express our joy. Here, there is no reason to be afraid. Amid the beauty, we seek truth so we give you our undivided attention. Amen.

Call To Confession (Leader)
Quiet the chatter in your minds.
Let the Spirit refresh you with awareness of how you might be whole and how you can be available for others with contagious joy.
Let's recite the printed confession and then listen in silence for the Divine Voice.

Community Confession (Unison)
Loving God — Christmas comes but once a year; thank you for being active in our lives all year long!
Reveal the negative aspects of our behaviors and free us from their hold on us.
Let us feel your empowering love sending us with peace into the world. Amen.

Word Of Grace (Leader)
Like the wreath, God encircles us with divine grace; like the flame, God warms our hearts; Like the candles, God lights our darkness. In a baby, we see hope of a future and our fears vanish in the newborn Christ. Hallelujah!

Congregational Choral Response   Canticle of Mary, *Magnificat* (v. 1, modified)
My soul gives glory to our God; my soul sings forth its praise;
God immerses us in loveliness in many marvelous ways.

Sermon Idea
The primary theme for the third Sunday in Advent is joyful living. In Zephaniah, people are told that there is no reason to be afraid (3:15), that God's love will give new life (3:17), and that God will be joyful with them (3:17-18). In Isaiah, the idea of being unafraid shows up along with the image that "fresh water brings joy to the thirsty" (12:3). At the other end of the continuum, John the Baptist berates the people as "snakes" and assures them that punishment is sent from God (Luke 3:7). While "guilt trips" worked well back then, they don't today. So the question the people ask is vital, "What are we to do?" (3:10). In our culture, if we desire to "rejoice and think about worthwhile things" (Philippians 4), then we must find activities that caress our souls — meditation, varying kinds of prayer, dancing our emotions (joy, anger, sadness, fear), inspiring conversations, resisting addictions to media interpretations of the world....

Contemporary Affirmation (Unison)
We experience God among us as creative Spirit stimulating our thoughts, working through our hands and our feet to make a bit of heaven on earth.
We believe God is among us — vulnerable and strong, loving and sustaining each one who welcomes the Holy.
We know God is in this world; we dream of fresh political structures that are fair, respectful, and inclusive.
We trust that God is reconciling families and nations and resurrecting the God-image in all persons.
Through every part of our human journey, God is with us; we are not alone. Hallelujah!

Offertory Statement (Leader)

With joy, we share what we have — food, money, clothes, hope, and passion.

Doxology   While Shepherds Watched Their Flocks (v. 6)

All glory be to God on high, And to the earth be peace;
Good will to all from highest heaven
Begin and never cease! Begin and never cease!

Prayer Of Thanksgiving (Leader or Unison)

Eternal God — we are thankful for the many ways *good news* is passed along. Use our moneys, our space, and our energies to make heaven a possibility. Amen.

Intercessory Prayers (Leader or Readers)

Energy of the Universe — we pray for ourselves and for the whole planet. As our ancestors prayed for Jerusalem, we pray for the United States of America and for Israel; we pray for Pakistan and India, for Iraq and Egypt, for England and Ireland, for Mexico and China. Sometimes we confuse loyalty and justice, equality and affluence as we seek high-paying jobs, great health care, and top-notch education. During this season of "hawking wares," help us discern what is vital to birthing God; clarify with us a midwife's joy; bless us with fearlessness; let us hear your affirmation.

Lover of the World — we pray for this planet and its children. Somehow, nastiness makes its way to hurt the earth and to scar children. Let good news and helpfulness overcome violence and mean-spiritedness. Protect children from poverty, hunger, sexual abuse, and soul-violence. Let the joy we sing about at Christmas actually pervade the goings and comings in the world.

Maker and Shaker of our Humanity — we are keenly aware that life is not all "roses and light." Our bodies ache; our hearts grieve; our minds are cluttered; our souls are often hungry. Heal us from hair to toenail, from finger to finger. Strengthen us to endure skinned knees, bruised elbows, fractured lumbar discs, and fatiguing nights. Let joy come again and surprise us as fresh water delights the thirsty and moon rises inspire good dreams.

Dreamer of a New Reign — let your peace and your heaven come to earth. Set in motion human mercy and hospitality that reach into our own towns and around the world; set in motion economic possibilities for all peoples; set in motion a transparent honesty that erases corruption; set in motion a contentment so that we are not caught in voracious buying.

Thank you for Jesus who moved through birth and childhood to adulthood, and shared your wisdom and your grace with all the world. Refresh us with love to give away. Amen!

Benediction (Leader)

May the beauty of a sleeping baby fill you with wonder; the curiosity of a toddler dance in your toes; the anticipation of a lover carry you into tomorrow; the peace of Christ soothe your mind; the joy of Holy Spirit brighten your whole day and night! While we are absent from this place, know that you are cradled by the living God!

Music

Lift Up Your Heads, Ye Mighty Gates
    Words: Georg Weissel, 1642; tr. Catherine Winkworth, 1855
    Music: Thomas Williams, 1789; harm. Lowell Mason (1792-1872)
    TRURO

On Jordan's Bank The Baptist's Cry
    Words: Charles Coffin, 1736; tr. John Chandler, 1837, alt.
    Music: Musikalisches Handbuch, 1690; harm. William Henry Monk, 1847, alt.
    WINCHESTER NEW

Prepare The Way
    Words: Mikael Franzen (1771-1847); adapt. Charles P. Price, 1980, alt. 1989
    Music: Then Swenska Psalmboken, 1697; arr. American Lutheran Hymnal, 1930
    BEREDEN VÄG FÖR HERRAN

Savior Of The Nations, Come
    Words: Sts. 1-2 Martin Luther, 1523; tr. William Reynolds, 1851; sts. 3-5 Martin L. Seltz,
        1969
    Music: Enchiridion Oder Handbüchlein, 1524; harm. J. S. Bach, alt.
    NUN KOMM, DER HEIDEN HEILAND

Advent 4

Micah 5:2-5a   Hebrews 10:5-10
Luke 1:47-55 or Psalm 80:1-7   Luke 1:39-45 (46-55)

The truth, Dumbledore sighed
It is a beautiful and terrible thing and
Therefore should be treated with great caution.
                                        — *Harry Potter And The Sorcerer's Stone*

This is what Dumbledore sends his defender!
A songbird and an old hat!
Do you feel brave, Harry Potter?
Do you feel safe now?

                                                (Tom Riddle to Harry)
                                        — *Harry Potter And The Chamber of Secrets*

Call To Worship
(Includes the lighting of the Advent Wreath)

Leader: Good morning! We've gathered for various reasons; some of us are dreading being alone during this season; some of us to enjoy the holiday music and decorations. Most of us anticipate remembering the Christmas story with its holy family.

People: **Yes, we love the Christmas story and the images that remind us we too carry God into the world.**

Leader: We will sing and pray, dance and sing the old story of God coming into the world as a baby — a vulnerable baby!

People: **Like Mary and Elizabeth, we will serve God and we will pray that God will keep us safe in a topsy-turvy world. Like Zechariah, we name our children, encouraging them to use their talents for God.**

Leader: Ring the bells! Clap your hands! Our hearts rejoice.

People: **We make a circle and light candles! We sing of love!**

Leader: Listening for truth and passing it along with joy is an awesome task. We have received the good news that God, the Holy One, comes to us in unexpected forms. We receive the divine and invite holiness to be at home in us!

(Light two purple candles on the Advent Wreath; light the pink one and then the third purple candle. All four candles burn brightly.)

Prayer Of Thanksgiving (Leader)

Living God — we thank you for John and Jesus. We recognize people who make the way easier for us like John did for Jesus. We recognize teachers whose wisdom follows us all our lives — like Jesus' Sermon on the Mount and his vivid parables. We are grateful for God's coming to earth and for the care that Mary and Joseph gave to Jesus. During this hour, we listen for fresh ways to embody the Holy and to receive the love offered us. Amen.

Call To Confession (Leader)

Sin separates us from God and from one another — whether it be action, attitude, or things left undone. Sin for you might be wrong thoughts about the right thing or right thoughts about the wrong thing. Now is your opportunity to reflect and work out with God changes that will give you peace and freedom. Pray with me the printed prayer and then continue your conversation in silence with God.

Community Confession (Unison)

Loving God — we don't offer you burnt offerings; we offer you a home on earth — our minds, bodies, and souls.

Our thoughts and behaviors, our loves and our hates, quite different from the first century, get in the way of our being satisfied with living.

Help us be aware of the behaviors that bring disempowering consequences to us.

Renew us with deep peace so that we carry goodness into the world. Amen.

Word Of Grace (Leader)

Like a lovely dawn, God moves over us and sets us free from guilt and shame. You can be like the sun filling the darkness! Hallelujah!

Congregational Choral Response   Canticle of Mary, *Magnificat* (v.1, modified)

My soul gives glory to our God, my soul sings forth its praise;
God immerses us in loveliness in many marvelous ways!

Sermon Idea

There are so many Bible stories about relationships and places that still affect history today, even our daily lives. John and Jesus were cousins and at least the men looked for some sort of tension between them. But neither John nor Jesus set about to compete for the greatest number of followers. Palestine and Israel today torment each other as did Ishmael and Isaac, Esau and Jacob thousands of years ago. It's difficult to use some of the symbols of the Christmas story without feeling sad about the events in the Holy Land. Nevertheless, we can rejoice with the idea that we are fetus-people, nurtured in the womb of God as Jesus was nurtured by Mary. A vital fetus is always moving and the mother at some point is ready to birth the baby into the world to grow on its own. Our understanding of human maturation and of God changes as we grow. I suspect Jesus matured, too, perceiving God differently as his experiences with the Divine expanded. A title/theme might be: Symbols of the Divine for our times.

Contemporary Affirmation (Unison)

We experience God among us as creative Spirit stimulating our thoughts, working through our hands and our feet to make a bit of heaven on earth.

We believe God is among us — vulnerable and strong, loving and sustaining each one who welcomes the Holy.

We know God is in this world; we dream of fresh political structures that are fair, respectful, and inclusive.

We trust that God is reconciling families and nations and resurrecting the God-image in all persons.

Through every part of our human journey, God is with us; we are not alone. Hallelujah.

Offertory Statement (Leader)

Our bodies are the homes we have for ourselves and for God. We take care of them and we reach out to others, encouraging them to care for their bodies, too. With our money, our talents, and our skills, we do provide food for hungry people, chairs for tired people, and help for homeless people. Let's combine resources so we can minister here and in other places.

Doxology   While Shepherds Watched Their Flocks (v. 6)

All glory be to God on high, And to the earth be peace;
Good will to all from highest heaven
Begin and never cease! Begin and never cease!

Prayer Of Thanksgiving (Leader)

Everliving God — we are thankful for money and jobs, talents and skills that make life together good and provide for others. If only no one would go to bed at night hungry! If only everyone would have a roof overhead! We pray for your reign to manifest on earth. Amen.

Intercessory Prayers (Leader or Readers)

Creating Spirit — we read the Christmas story and imagine how it might have been for pregnant Mary and anxious Joseph, how it might have been to birth a first child without the comforts of hot water and soft mattresses; without numbing drugs for the pushing pains. We imagine people waiting and watching for new leadership. And we realize that we are the shepherds and the magi; we are the citizens being counted and taxed. There are people around us who find signs that say, "Sorry, no room." We pray for humankind. Create among us all a mind and passion for justice and kindness.

Birthing Spirit — no matter how old we are, we long to be held and rocked, loved, and touched. Within each of us is that child who seeks wholeness and strength. Within each of us is the hope that you labor us into the world so that when the time is right, we labor you into the world.

Healing Spirit — no matter how old we are, our bodies feel pain; our psyches receive wounds, and our relationships come apart. Overcome us with wholeness; overpower us with grace, and let us feel peace and comfort from head to toe.

Spirit of Peace — we pray for this planet. Some say it is abused and sick; some say, so what. We pray for the tribes that still live by the laws of retaliation. We pray for children who are maimed by adults. We pray for adults who hurt other adults. We pray for our government and our leaders; give them wisdom, courage, and skill. We long for peace and prosperity for all peoples — without deception, greed, and hoarding. We pray for peace everywhere.

Spirit of Christ — you are birthed again into our minds and into our world. Help us give you room to be and to grow. Amen.

Benediction (Leader)

Like the shepherds, sing and dance with each other;
Like the magi, be curious about nature;
Like Mary and Joseph, nourish the Divine;
As your own authentic self, use your hands and your feet, your voice and your mind, to make plenty of room for your own loved ones and for those in need.
And as a Christmas gift to satisfy yourself —
Want what you have, do what you can, and be who you are!
                                    — Forrest Church, *Love & Death* (Boston: Beacon Press, 2008)

Music

Come, Thou Long-Expected Jesus
    Words: Charles Wesley, 1744
    Music: Rowland Hugh Prichard, 1831
    HYFRYDOL
    (Alt. tune: STUTTGART)

Jesus Comes With Clouds Descending
    Words: Charles Wesley, 1758, alt.
    Music: Thomas Olivers, 1763; harm. Ralph Vaughan Williams, 1906
    HELMSLEY

Lo, How A Rose E'er Blooming
    Words: German carol (15th century); tr. Theodore Baker, 1894
    Music: Traditional melody; arr. Michael Praetorius, 1609
    ES IST EIN ROS

O Lord, How Shall I Meet You?
    Words: Paul Gerhardt, 1653; tr. Catherine Winkworth and others, 1863, alt.
    Music: Melchior Teschner, 1614; harm. William Henry Monk, 1861
    VALET WILL ICH DIR GEBEN

The Angel Gabriel From Heaven Came
    Words: Para. Sabine Baring-Gould (1834-1924)
    Music: Basque carol, arr. Edgar Pettman and John Wickham
    GABRIEL'S MESSAGE

To A Maid Engaged To Joseph
    Words: Gracia Grindal, 1984
    Music: Rusty Edwards, 1984
    ANNUNCIATION

Watchman, Tell Us Of The Night
    Words: John Bowring, 1825, alt. 1972
    Music: Joseph Parry, 1879
    ABERYSTWYTH

Season 2
Christmas

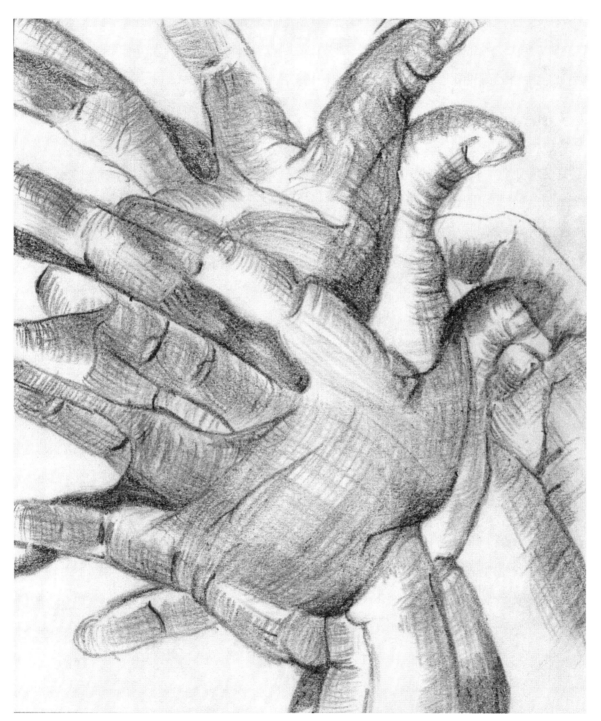

Commotion

Christmas Eve

Isaiah 9:2-7   Titus 2:11-14
Psalm 96   Luke 2:1-4 (15-20)

> *The wonderful cycle of the year,*
> *with its hardships and periods of joy is celebrated ...*
> *continue in the life of the human group.*
> — Joseph Campbell, *The Hero With a Thousand Faces*

If there are children in the congregation and adults who enjoy "performing," invite them ahead of time to pantomime the Luke 2 story. *(Everyone can wear slacks and a turtleneck shirt.)* Designate the lead adult angel (Gabriel), lead adult shepherd, adult Mary, and adult Joseph several weeks prior to Christmas Eve.

Since there is no rehearsal, ask the lead characters to arrive fifteen minutes early in costume and go over space, props, and costumes for other participants. Masking tape on the floor, labeled for each role, is helpful. A manger can be set in the chancel as a visual focal point. A doll can be hidden close by. *(If you do not want the mess of straw, use some colorful blankets of fabric.)*

Haloes, shepherd staffs, and toy sheep can be laid out on the back pew to be picked up as children and adults enter the worship space. At the time of the Luke 2 reading, people leave their pews and "embody" their parts of the story. The reader must have a good sense of pacing. *(Live sheep dogs add a magical touch to the story.)*

Call To Worship
(Includes the lighting of the Advent/Christmas Wreath.)

Leader: The night we've been waiting for! Christmas Eve with lots of creative commotion! I'm glad we've gathered here to celebrate the season and to read again from the ancient prophets who talked of God's coming to them with salvation, mercy, and prosperity. We are expecting God to come among us in new ways; we are expecting creative holiness to be birthed right here!

People: Ring the bells! Clap your hands! Our hearts rejoice.

Leader: Make a circle. Light a fire. Sing a song of love.

People: We know the stories of past miracles — a newborn baby cradled in a manger, a young mother, angels, and shepherds, too!

Leader: We dream a future and we hope for joy — the joy of God birthed in us anew!

People: Light the candles! Three purples ones for hope, peace, and truth; light the pink one for joy!

(Someone lights the Advent candles.)

Leader: Light the white one, too.

People: Light the Christ candle, the one in the center: Christ is light for the world! Hallelujah!

(Someone lights the Christ candle.)

Prayer Of Thanksgiving (Leader)

Living God — we are excited! We are glad for bright stars and angels. We're glad for observant shepherds and a young woman birthing a child who has challenged the whole world to experience your love as salvation, peace, and justice. Here, together, we thank you for the images surrounding us, pointing to you. Thank you for birth, life, and hope! Amid the poinsettias and evergreens with commotion in our childlike hearts, we are listening for and responding to your enthusiastic presence. Amen.

Congregational Choral Response   Canticle of Mary, *Magnificat* (v. 1, modified)

My soul gives glory to our God; my soul sings forth its praise;
God immerses us in loveliness in many marvelous ways.

Twentieth-Century Reading

All this was a long time ago, I remember,
And I would do it again but set down
This set down
This: were we led all that way for
Birth or Death? There was a Birth, certainly,
We had evidence and no doubt. I had seen birth and death,
But had thought they were different; this Birth was
Hard and bitter agony for us, like Death, our death.
We returned to our places, these kingdoms,
But no longer at ease here, in the old dispensation....

— T. S. Eliot, "The Journey of the Magi"
Printed in *Watch for the Light*, Plough Publishing House, 2001

Carol   Silver Bells

Available in *The Reader's Digest Merry Christmas Songbook*, eighteenth printing, page 66.

Twentieth-Century Reading

A people in darkness: Today I see before me the millions imprisoned, the exiled, the deported, the tortured, and the silenced ... on them the divine light now shines. People in darkness: How that cries out today from the Third World in Africa and Asia and from the Third World in our own country — cries for liberation and human rights! The struggle for power and for oil and for weapons ruins the weak, enriches the wealthy, and gives power to the powerful. This divided world is increasingly capable of turning into a universal prison camp. And we are faced with the burning question: On which side of the barbed wire are we living and at whose cost? The people in darkness see a great light. To this people — to them first of all — the light shines in all its brightness.... Do we belong to this people or do we cling to our own interpreters of the signs of the times...? The new human being has been born and a new humanity will be possible.... This is God's initiative on behalf of betrayed and tormented humanity....

— Jürgen Moltmannn, *The Disarming Child*
Printed in *Watch for the Light*, Plough Publishing House, 2001

Carol   To A Maid Engaged To Joseph

Contemporary Reading
    This is the irrational season
    When love blooms bright and wild.
    Had Mary been filled with reason
    There'd have been no room for the child.

                        — Madeleine L'Engle, *The Irrational Season*

Carol   The Angel Gabriel From Heaven Came

Scripture   Luke 2:1-20 (as a dramatic playlet)

Narrator 1:   I want to tell you an old story. A long time ago, when the Roman empire existed, the Emperor, Augustus ordered a census — a counting of all the people who were part of the empire. Quirinius was the governor of Syria. Everyone was ordered to go to the place of his birth and register. This meant that many people had to do some traveling. Our assumption is that only men were counted. But Joseph, who lived in Nazareth had to walk about seven miles south to Bethlehem.

(Mary and Joseph slowly wander through the congregation toward the manger area.)

                Bethlehem was the birth place of the famous King David. Since Joseph was a descendant of David — way down the line, or way out on a life tree limb, whichever way you wish to describe it, he had to make that trip. Joseph took Mary with him on the journey. She was very pregnant.

Narrator 2:   When they arrived in Bethlehem, all the motels were full. So Joseph and Mary ended up making do in a barn with a room full of animals.

(Mary and Joseph are at the manger by now.)

Narrator 1:   While Joseph and Mary were in Bethlehem, the time came for her to have the baby. She birthed her first son!

(A real baby is a wonderful "prop"; otherwise, a doll will do.)

Narrator 2:   She wrapped him in a blanket! She swaddled him and laid him in the manger.

(Mary and Joseph spend a few moments wrapping the baby.)

Narrator 1:   That same awesome night when Mary was birthing her son, some shepherds were in the fields taking care of their sheep. All was well.

(Shepherds move to their designated place.)

(Angel shows up — stand on stool/pew/ladder to add height.)

Narrator 2:   But then, an angel appeared in the sky!

(Other angels gather around.)

Narrator 1:   Messengers from God! The whole sky was bright!

Narrator 2 or   Don't be afraid! I am here with good news for you —
Angel Gabriel: news that will bring joy to all kinds of people!
                     This day, this very day in David's town, your Savior was born —
                     Christ the Lord!

Narrator 1:   Here's proof: You will find a baby lying in a manger, all wrapped in cloth.

Narrator 2:   Suddenly, there were lots of angels singing *(can be sung by a choir, or spoken in unison by the angels or said by the narrator)* Glory to God in the highest heaven and peace on all the earth!

Narrator 1:   Then all the angels went back to heaven. *(angels exit, using all the aisles)* The amazed shepherds looked at each other. One of the them said *(narrator or lead shepherd)* "Let's go to Bethlehem and see if the angel was truthful."

(Shepherds meander to stand behind the manger, facing the congregation, not blocking the baby.)

Narrator 2:   The shepherds hurried into the town.

Narrator 1:   Sure enough. The shepherds found Mary and Joseph. They looked into the manger and there was a baby! The shepherds were so excited!

(Mary and Joseph can hold the child for their admiration; or give the child to the lead shepherd for cuddling. A soloist sings "Away In A Manger.")

Narrator 2:   When they calmed down, the shepherds told Joseph and Mary about the visiting angels. They reported what the angel said about their child!

Narrator 1:   Can you imagine the excitement in Bethlehem? The people who saw the angels were amazed by what the shepherds said.

Narrator 2:   Eventually, the shepherds returned to their sheep on the hillside. They were still excited, so they sang "joy-songs" to God. I wonder if anyone else heard their "joyful noise"?

Narrator 1:   Luke, the story writer, says Mother Mary remembered all these unusual things; Luke doesn't tell us whether Joseph remembered them, too.

Narrator 2:   It's a wonderful story. We hope you "ponder" it as Christmas Eve turns into Christmas Day — the birth day of Jesus of Nazareth, Mary's and God's son!

(Everyone freezes in place until the congregation begins singing the next carol.)

Carol   C-H-R-I-S-T-M-A-S

Available in *The Reader's Digest Merry Christmas Songbook*, eighteenth printing, page 70.

(All the story pantomimers return to their seats during this song.)

Meditation Idea

When unexpected things happen, often an uproar breaks loose. When darkness hinders people seeing clearly, confused commotion is the result. Darkness, in the gospels, is a state of mind, an attitude of heart. When unexpected light brings clarity to a situation, joyful commotion erupts in the environment. Both Isaiah and John speak of light in darkness. Jesus offers light for our darkness and ways to be active in our world.

Scripture (Unison)   Isaiah 9:2-3a, 6 (modified)

We have walked in darkness; Now we see a bright light!
We have walked in shadows; But now the shadows are gone.
God gives us joy and we are happy.
A child is born! We call this child, Wonderful Counselor,
Mighty God, Bringer of Peace!

(Lights can be extinguished; leaders can light their candles from the Christ candle and pass the flame to the person at the end of each row who in turn passes it to the next person. Enjoy the candlelight amid the darkness for a moment, then sing the next carol.)

Carol   Silent Night (*a cappella*, vv. 1 and 3)
                                                   (add Night Of Silence by John Rutter)

(Extinguish all the candles after the last stanza has concluded. Lights need to come up quickly.)

Benediction (Leader)

In Bethlehem, in New York, and in *(insert name of your town)* there are people searching for love. In your heart and mind, in your body and psyche, love and light are bouncing around! You leave here with more than enough to share! Now — may the beauty of a sleeping baby fill you with wonder; the curiosity of a toddler dance in your toes; the anticipation of a lover carry you into tomorrow; the peace of Christ soothe your mind; the joy of the Holy Spirit brighten your day and night! While we are absent from this place, know that you are cradled by the living God! Merry Christmas!

Music

Any Christmas carols

Christmas Day

Isaiah 62:6-12   Titus 3:4-7
Psalm 97   Luke 2:(1-7) 8-20

Gathering music   Christmas medley

(Light the Christ candle.)

(Invite adults, children, and youth ahead of time to bring a favorite gift for a one-sentence show and tell.)

Greeting

Leader: Merry Christmas!

People: Merry Christmas!

Leader: Settle your Christmas gifts on the pew beside you and find the space within your minds and hearts to sing, pray, listen, and talk.

People: We've been counting the whole year and today is finally here! How glad we are for God's coming to earth in human form! How glad we are for the family and friends with whom we share this joy!

Leader: "Incarnation" is the big word we use to describe how the Holy One was in Jesus of Nazareth and how the Holy Spirit lives in us.

Carol   Joy To The World

Prayer (Leader or Unison)

Living God, we celebrate with you the goodness of creation and your home among human-kind. In these moments together, we thank you for the gift of life in Jesus and in one another. In our conversations, overflow your love for the world and for us. May our loyalty to you be audible; may your presence be visible in our thoughts and actions. Amen.

Silence For Reverie

(Five minutes; ring in the silence with a bell or prayer bowl; close the silence with a bell or prayer bowl.)

Leader: Consider what has been good and satisfying this past week; notice what you would do differently. Be grateful for God's sustaining grace.

Congregational Response   Savior Of The Nations, Come (v. 4)

(After five minutes of silence and the striking of a bell, the accompanist plays meditatively and then the congregation sings.)

Brightly does your manger shine, Glorious is its light divine.
Let not sin o'ercloud this light; Ever be our faith thus bright.

Scripture   Isaiah 9:2-7

Carol   Born In The Night Mary's Child

Scripture   Luke 2:1-20

Hymn   All My Heart Today Rejoices

Meditation   Shared Gifts
    Minister or leader reflects briefly on the hopes of humankind for a savior. Then s/he talks about "gifts" of God including Jesus of Nazareth as a baby to Mary and Joseph and to all humankind as a teacher. Mention might be made of the gifts to the baby: gold, frankincense, and myrrh. S/he can show and tell her/his special Christmas gift, such as, "Today, this is my special gift because...." Then s/he invites members of the congregation to share their gifts.

Hymn (Congregation or Ensemble)   Joyful Christmas Day Is Here, tune: KURISUMASU

Offertory Statement (Leader)   'Twas In The Moon Of Wintertime (v. 1)
(Can be spoken or sung)
    O children of the forest free ...
    The Holy Child of earth and heaven Is born today for you.
    Come kneel before the radiant boy Who brings you beauty peace and joy.

Gift Of Music   'Twas In The Moon Of Wintertime, Silent Night,
(might be instrumental)   or The Snow Lay On The Ground

Doxology   Angels We Have Heard On High (Refrain)
    Gloria, in excelsis Deo!

Thanksgiving Prayer
    God of Jesus and Mary — thank you for our minds that think and for our hearts that feel compassion and love. For these moneys, for talents, and for time to be intentional about making your kingdom visible and tangible here and throughout the global village, we are grateful. Amen.

An Affirmation (Leader)
    There are many ways to articulate our faith story. Poets and essayists, artists and choreographers, theologians and apologists down through the ages have left us a large repertoire of words, melodies, paintings, and movements. In the nineteenth century, Cecil Frances Alexander wrote a poem that was given a melody in 1849 by Henry John Gauntlett, one year after the lyrics were written. Today, we sing this carol as our affirmation of the Christmas story — "Once In Royal David's City."

Benediction
Leader: We've counted the days and Christmas is here!
People: We are grateful God chose humankind as "home."
Leader: Show that gratitude in the ways you are with one another today and every day. Demonstrate your thankfulness with words and actions.
People: We leave here determined to live the truths of the Christmas story!
Leader: Merry Christmas!

Congregational Response   Go, Tell It On The Mountain (v. 3 with refrain)

Down in a lowly manger the humble Christ was born,
and God sent us salvation that blessed Christmas morn.
Go, tell it on the mountain, over the hills and everywhere;
go, tell it on the mountain, that Jesus Christ is born!

Music

Any Christmas carols

Christmas 1

1 Samuel 2:18-20, 26   Colossians 3:12-17
Psalm 148   Luke 2:41-52

> *The wonderful cycle of the year,*
> *with its hardships and periods of joy is celebrated ...*
> *continued in the life of the human group.*
> — Joseph Campbell, *The Hero With a Thousand Faces*

Call To Worship

(Includes the lighting of the Christ candle in the Advent/Christmas Wreath; wreath may need to be refreshed; all candles are gone except the center large Christ candle. The Advent/Christmas tree can be left in place also, showing the symbols of the holy days and slowing down the culture's hurry to the next buying season.)

Leader: Happy New Year! 20?? is on the next calendar page! Christmas symbols are still here — until Epiphany when our images change to depict a maturing Jesus. During these last four weeks, we've told our faith stories and our family memories; we've given gifts, as the magi gave gifts to the Christ Child and as God has given divine presence in Jesus of Nazareth.

People: From him we learn to be God-bearers in this world.

Leader: Our expectations have been met: God is among us in new ways.

People: Like angels, we sing to God; like shepherds, we honor God and all creation.

Leader: Praise God! Hallelujah!

People: Light the Christ candle again to remind us that Christ is light for the world and banishes our own darkness!

(Someone lights the Christ candle.)

Prayer Of Thanksgiving (Leader or Unison)

Living God — how awesome you are, Creator of the cosmos! Mountains and trees, birds and reptiles all indicate your imagination! Thank you for making us creative like you. Thank you for our imaginations that impel us to express our love for you in many ways! We are grateful for the Christmas season and the gift of the Divine Child, Jesus. In this hour, our hearts and minds await your inspiration. Amen.

Call To Confession (Leader)

Wise men and women in our pasts have followed bright stars. Like the magi so long ago, we look for signs and symbols to guide us toward holiness. In these few moments, we consider the visual and aural artifacts that we allow in our space. Reflect on activities for your body and soul as you move from 20?? to 20??. Pray with me the printed prayer and then listen in silence for the Divine Voice.

Community Confession (Unison)

Loving God — as we look back over this last year, we are aware of things we wish we had done differently.

Sometimes we have not been hospitable; sometimes we have been stingy; sometimes we have spoken unkindly; sometimes we have been nasty.

Relieve us of guilt and help us be aware of the opportunities when we can manifest your goodness in our homes, in our neighborhoods, and in our church.

Empower us with newly birthed delight and go with us as peace into the world. Amen.

Word Of Grace (Leader)

The magi did not travel alone. Nor do we. In community we see our best and our worst selves. With one another, we experience the seasons of the year and our own developmental processes. It is good news that we are not isolated but journey together through periods of joy and hardship. We are a gift from God to one another. In fact, we are people of God; God loves us and we clothe ourselves with compassion, kindness, humility, gentleness, patience, and tolerance. Hallelujah!

Congregational Choral Response   As With Gladness, tune: DIX (v. 4)

Holy Jesus, every day, keep us in the narrow way;
And when earthly things are past, bring our ransomed souls at last
Where they need no star to guide, where no clouds thy glory hide.

Sermon Idea

The Christmas epic is told as family events and as a tribal event. Luke leaves out the story of visiting wise men and proceeds to name, circumcise, and present the baby at the temple where we hear Simeon bless him in the presence of his parents. The details of Jesus' life are sketchy but today's gospel story reports the family going to Passover festival annually. The episode today presents a savvy twelve-year-old who revels in intellectual, theological, and political dialogue with adults in positions of authority. We see the child in conflict with his parents over what he perceives to be his life call. The stage is set for tension between Jesus and people in power. Individuals responding to the Spirit today run into the shoulds and oughts of previous empires as Jesus did in the first century. Nevertheless, we are to be about growing in wisdom and peaceableness topped with large doses of compassion.

Contemporary Affirmation (Unison)

We wait and seek; we search and journey until God meets us in stables and on streets, in our backyards, and at computers.

The Holy meets our humanity in the commotion of birth and birthday parties.

The Christ shines like a star to bless and guide our wanderings.

Holy Spirit lives through us as masculine and feminine gestures manifesting a bit of heaven here on earth.

All nature announces the imagination of the Creating God! Hallelujah!

Offertory Statement (Leader)

With our tithes and offerings, with our talents and money, we honor God.

Doxology   What Star Is This With Beams So Bright? (v. 4)
                                                               tune: PUER NOBIS NASCITUM

To God the Father, God the Son, and Holy Spirit — three in one,
May every tongue and nation raise an endless song of thankful praise.

Intercessory Prayers (Leader or Readers)

Light of the World — thank you for the goodness we experience. When tomorrow's path is unclear, help us to be patient.

Mothering God — thank you for these holidays, for all the activities that make us happy and tired. When we ache, touch us with patient wholeness. Nurture our souls and bodies so we are healthy as we manifest your hospitality in the world.

Fathering God — thank you for your presence. We appreciate your love and creative energies. Expand our imaginations so we can participate in your reign on this earth.

Keeper of Time and Eternity — thank you for the blessings of this past year, for varied adventures with your Spirit, for new opportunities to know ourselves and others. Thank you for the men and women, century after century, who passed along the stories of your birth among humankind. Help us midwife your goodness in our neighborhoods. Thank you for our children. Keep them safe and hopeful.

Dreamer of a New Reign — this is a season of peace, we like to think. When we are honest, we see that peace is a long way off, a long time coming. But like shepherds and young parents in every generation, we pray for peace throughout the global village, in our families, and in our minds. We wish the beauty of Eden and the tranquility of the stable would surround the whole cosmos. Overflow your creativity through us so that you are loose and lively in the world. Amen!

Benediction (Leader)

May the beauty of a sleeping baby fill you with wonder;
The curiosity of a toddler dance in your toes;
The anticipation of a lover carry you into tomorrow;
The peace of Christ soothe your mind;
The joy of the Holy Spirit brighten your whole day and night!
While we are absent from this place, know that you are cradled by the living God!
Happy New Year!

Music
Any Christmas carols

Christmas 2

Jeremiah 31:7-14   Ephesians 1:3-14
Psalm 147:12-20   John 1:(1-9) 10-18

Let us awaken from the soul-crushing allures
Of sophisticated resignation and cynical chic,
To savor instead the world of abundance and possibility
That awaits just beyond the self-imposed limits of our imagination.
— Forrest Church, *Love and Death*

Call To Worship
Leader: Welcome to this sanctuary, this place of tranquility and celebration, this place of safety and hope. God is here; God is our source of life!

People: **God existed before the world and this sanctuary were made!**

Leader: People have walked this earth before us; their words and their lives are recorded in books around the world.

People: **We look to Jesus, the God-Man and teacher, to his cousin, John, and to the friends of Jesus for wisdom about relationships and decisions.**

Leader: In Jesus we see God and we hear God. God has made a home with humankind!

Prayer Of Thanksgiving (Unison)
Holy One — we celebrate your coming to earth, your incarnating in Jesus of Nazareth! We are grateful that our bodies are homes for you as well. Though the world is chaotic, we trust your presence to sustain us and to give us a spot of internal peace. Thank you for this time and this place of listening and responding to words, music, and silence. Amen.

Call To Confession (Leader)
We make time to reflect on what is running around in our heads and hearts. When we find something that is disturbing, we frequently need to make amends with ourselves, with others, or with God. Now is time to consider your own awareness of living. Pray with me the printed confession and then continue your conversation silently with God.

Community Confession (Unison)
Creating God — sometimes cynicism retards our responses to your goodness.
Sometimes we disregard the treasures around us.
Sometimes we find it difficult to envision a kingdom of peace and equality, of justice and abundance.
We are not like the first-century shepherds nor sky gazers like the Zoroastrian priests.
Free our senses from the literalization of good old stories; free our minds from the clutter of our culture so that we can participate with your twenty-first-century reign in this world.
Let us be co-creators with you. Amen.

Sermon Idea

The biblical passages are all texts of hope — *Via Positiva.* We know from psychological and spiritual observations that people create their own futures with their attitudes about life. The Judeo-Christian religion emphasizes positive thinking, hopeful attitudes. Today's texts demonstrate this. For many twenty-first-century friends of Jesus, the question is how we can continue to hope when the truth of tangible reality is far from the hope of exquisite poetry in Jeremiah, Psalms, John, Ephesians, and others. The images we use at Christmas of a welcoming Jerusalem belonging to the great nation of Israel are difficult to use when we listen to international news. The equality of men and women is hard to visualize when we hear about African warriors maiming girls and drugging boys. The peace we long for internally and externally seems impossible with the huge population of the planet vying for land, food, water, and clean air. Yet, the poetry is beautiful and hopeful.

For many, the hype of the Christmas buying-selling season produces a "blue" feeling, a down sensation — *Via Negativa.* Of course, there are other biblical stories that emphasize the sorrows of humankind — the story of Jesus' crucifixion, Stephen's stoning, and so on. For people who have experienced the death of a loved one during a Christmas season, there is dread that prohibits them from enjoying the reds and greens, silvers and golds of the holidays. These lectionary Bible texts for today challenge the preacher to notice the difference between the poetry of hope thousands of years ago and the reality of the global village — *Via Creativa!* Spiritually and psychologically, many people evade the noise of the malls, the expense of gift-giving, and the scratchy music using the images Christianity has loved and found helpful on the human journey; they make time for solitude or small group intimate sharing. Church holiday planners can take the needs of these people into account when they make the calendar by providing time/events for honest sharing of their experiences with the "blue downside of Christmas." We might imagine with them the "downside" for the Holy Family in an occupied country — physical pain, emotional trauma, financial fears ... twelve days of Christmas can provide opportunities to address many contemporary doubts, fears, and yearnings.

A title/theme might be "The Word We Hear" or "Light for Our Astigmatism" — attempting to articulate the presence of God in our culture and how we find inspiration and avoid cynicism: spend time with literature that promotes noble behavior; spend time with people who seek psychological/spiritual satisfaction/salvation; establish an aesthetically pleasing environment using images that acknowledge the ups and the downs of life; meditate/pray; push the boundaries of received traditions; articulate your journey with the Holy Spirit/Word/God/Christ, using words, water colors, yarn, clay, or beads.

Contemporary Affirmation (Unison)

We believe that God is and was embodied by Jesus of Nazareth.

We believe that Jesus lived and taught a personal and corporate lifestyle that honored God, self, and others.

We believe that God is present as the Holy Spirit, as a Creating Spirit within us.

We believe that we are expected to be helpful to one another, to our neighbors near and far, and to behave in ways that do not abuse the planet.

We believe that Christmas and all holy days are opportunities to remember the stories of Jesus and to consider the decisions we have made.

In our living and in our dying, God is with us. Amen. Let it be so.

Offertory Statement (Leader)

We have opportunity to create beauty, to maintain this space, to share food with hungry people, and to work toward the end of homelessness. It takes money, creative planning, talents, and skills. Let us give as we can.

Doxology   While Shepherd Watched Their Flocks (v. 6), tune: CHRISTMAS

All glory be to God on high
And to the earth be peace;
Good will to all from highest heaven
Begin and never cease!

Thanksgiving Prayer (Leader)

God of then and now — we are thankful people, blessed with enough for today and probably for tomorrow. We sing our gratitude; we marvel at the natural world; we enjoy one another. Thank you for what we have and for your empowering presence. Amen.

Intercessory Prayers (Leader or Readers)

We look to you, Holy One, for healing of our broken hearts and our aging bodies. We look for bandages to hold our minds and souls together when we feel fragmented. We look to you for music when our songs have become scrambled. We look to you for moisture for our lands and for our psyches.

As the new year matures, Holy One, we pray for our elected leaders. Rain wisdom on them; grow their thoughts toward making peace here and among all nations. Shine through them so corruption is revealed and blown away. Radiate through them until no one is hungry and weapons are replaced by tools.

As Christmas fades into Epiphany and Lent, Holy One, let us receive divine guidance, unmistakable and plain. As we tell the old stories of human experience with you, let us make new stories of how we are sustained by your presence in this era of technology and scientific exploration. Let our stories tell how you heal our blind spots and clear up our hearing; let our stories tell how you gather people with peace. Let our stories have plots that resolve into people being neighborly and respecting those who are different.

We pray for our children and grandchildren. We are glad for the next generation. Impress them with your love and generosity, Holy One. Protect them from cruelty. Help them to care for the earth as well as for their own bodies. May they learn the teachings of Jesus and embody them.

Satisfy those who long to feel close to you, Holy One. Take our griefs and our disappointments and mold them into experiences that let us be at peace in your presence. Amen.

Benediction

Leader: Tradition says this is the Christmas season.

People: Our bodies and souls have set this time to tell the stories of hope, joy, and relationships.

Leader: We have told the stories of Jesus and John, of Mary and Elizabeth; we have remembered the curiosity of shepherds and the insights of sky watchers. We have sung like angels!

People: We go from sanctuary into the world with ideas that stretch our thinking, with images that soothe our emotions, and with lyrics that enrich our interactions with others.

Leader: God is with you. Live fully! Make peace! Do justice! Let it be so. Amen.

Music
Any Christmas carols

Season 3
Epiphany

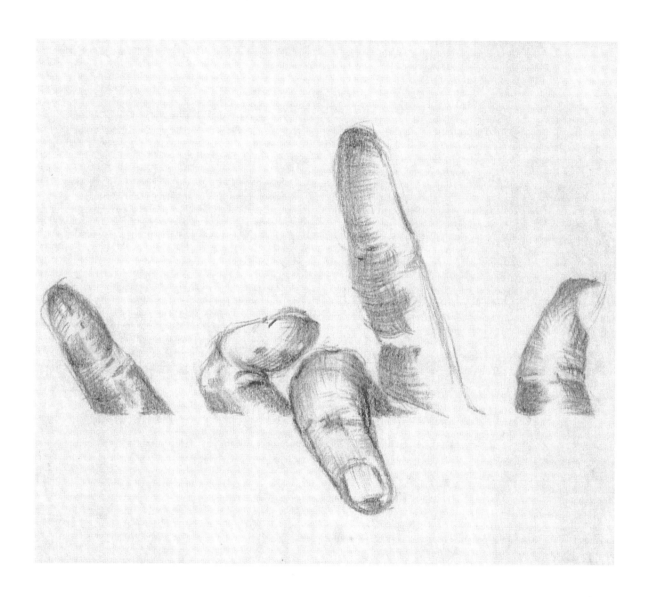

Locomotion

The Epiphany Of Our Lord

Isaiah 60:1-6   Ephesians 3:1-12
Psalm 72:1-7, 10-14   Matthew 2:1-12

The light of truth is in the skies. Or it may be only a shadow.
The ways of God are strange and cause conflicts of faith and impulses of love,
opportunities or temptations. Is not love the light of the soul?
— Henry van Dyke, *The Other Wise Man* (paraphrased)

Call To Worship

Leader: I'm so glad we're here together! Today's the day we want to be wise and know just where to locate God.

People: This is Epiphany, the day when we are magi and bring our best gifts to God.

Leader: God quite clearly is here —

People: in each of us!

Leader: We have hopes that when the stars shine just right, we will find the baby who grows up to be our teacher and guide.

People: We will search like the ancient men and women until we find some tangible evidence of God being at home with us!

Leader: We know the story: Around 4 CE, astrologers and astronomers read into the movement of the stars the hopes of God being ruler and savior on this earth.

People: They followed the star until it stood over a certain place in Bethlehem. There they found a baby, named Jesus, with Mary, his mother. They gave their gifts of gold, frankincense, and myrrh. Those scholars understood the baby to be their future king.

Leader: Let us be joyful wise people in this age, searching, singing, and sharing the goodness of God!

Prayer Of Thanksgiving (Leader)

God of yesterday and today — thank you for all of nature that makes your creativity visible to us. Thank you for stories that help us understand our search for you and your seeming absence. We are grateful that every now and then, we have an epiphany — a clear experience of your presence and your activity with us. Let us be wise as we journey from now until eternity. The gift we give this hour is our undivided attention. We anticipate being enthused by your Spirit with words, silence, and music. Amen.

Call To Confession (Leader)

Do you feel confused? Empty? Burdened? Ecstatic? Now is time to consider gifts not given. Or maybe unkind words and actions directed toward someone. Or maybe soul wounds that are not healing. After our spoken prayer, make your own in silence to God. Join me.

Community Confession (Unison)
Spirit for us who seek — guide us to find you, to be surprised by the clarity with which
you show up to heal us and to cleanse us from shame and guilt.
Lift our eyes from the problems of our lives to see ways you make us whole. Amen.

Word Of Grace (Leader)
The God who came in Jesus comes to us. The One who was recognized by wise men looking at stars long ago is available to all our senses. Be alert for the Creator in your environment! And be at peace in your mind and your emotions.

Sermon Idea
A title/theme might be Clearly Hidden — God in our World. It is no secret that God has created humankind. It is no secret that humans can relate to the transcendent. But it is not clear how God works or why God sometimes uses the divine strong right hand (protective) and at other times uses the strong left hand (violent). The hope for a unified and peaceful Jerusalem is clear. The reality of tribal conflicts centuries old is also clear. We humans need to hope, need to trust that tomorrow will be better than today. With God's Spirit, Holy Spirit, we can make anything happen, even family peace and peace in Jerusalem. The *how* is not clear.

Two of the Epiphany lectionary texts have secrets! The secret in Ephesians and Matthew seems to be that there are many more of God's children than contained in Israel, more than just Jews! The magi are not Jews, yet they know the ancient prophecies and receive dream messages from the same God that Paul later experiences as inspiring. Their secret is that they are to protect the baby. At the same time, Herod is afraid of losing power and, according to Matthew, immediately begins to protect his future but keeps his fears and his dreadful plans secret.

Two texts (Psalms and Isaiah) are right out front with their message! No secret for them! God will someday fix Jerusalem; it will be so well ruled and so beautiful that everyone will praise God. People's needs will be met and rulers will be benevolent. The prophet and the poet are blatant in their optimistic expectations that Yahweh would intervene in human affairs. God's action would be obvious and everyone would be delighted. Each person alert for the Holy One would have an epiphany! For some, it is difficult to entertain the idea that Divinity steps into human time and sets things right. Nevertheless, we know the whole story: Jesus, as an adult, taught that we should work for and expect justice and peace.

The sky gazers, attuned to the movement of the stars and their own dreams, guard the baby and their hope. Epiphany means to see clearly. God is clearly seen at work in the sky and with the magi who knew the scriptures well enough to look for a new leader — a leader sent by the Creator of the stars. Van Dyke's tale of *The Other Wise Man* is a nice story to consider. (Google it for audio.) In van Dyke's imagination, the One to be sought and served is not clearly manifest. One magi misses his date with the others and his opportunity to see the baby; he spends his life looking for the One. He is in Jerusalem the day Jesus is crucified and realizes he is too late. In this story, God is "clearly hidden" in people who desperately need life's necessities.

Contemporary Affirmation (Unison)
The Bible story of the wise men seeking a king is our story; we seek Divine affirmation and guidance.
The baby they found is our vulnerable and growing experience with the Holy.
The secret they kept is our personal promises to the invisible Spirit.
The gifts they offered are our talents, our resources, and our loyalty.

Their journey back to their own cities is our journey across this earth, aware of being surrounded by Holy Spirit and desiring to make this world a kinder place.

We are not alone. God surrounds us and we are content as we walk with the Holy One. Amen. Let it be so!

Offertory Statement (Leader)

Wise people still follow stars and sing with angels! Wise people are good neighbors and generous with their resources. Wise people participate with the Spirit for the goodness of all people. It may not be gold, frankincense, or myrrh that we put in the offering plates. But whatever your gift is, it is acceptable.

Doxology
While Shepherd Watched Their Flocks (v. 6), tune: CHRISTMAS

All glory be to God on high and to the earth be peace;
Good will to all from highest heaven begin and never cease!

Prayer Of Thanksgiving (Leader)

For all the gifts that are ours, for the strength to make a difference in our community, we thank you. Amen.

Intercessory Prayer (Leader or Readers)

God of Dreamers — look at this world. See the messes we have made with our greed. See the children who are sold into slavery. See the poverty in America and in Africa and in every nation. We need dreams to compel leaders and ourselves to find a way to feed all the hungry and house all the homeless. We need wisdom to empower us to act now to bring something of your kingdom to earth. Move our elected leaders and the leaders of the whole world to lead the way to justice and peace.

God of Star Watchers — we like to think ourselves among the wise and gifted. So we turn to you for light for our darkness; we turn to you for healing for our bodies and souls. Let us be alert for epiphanies! Let us use our gifts to provide nurture and companionship to those bereft of loveliness.

God of Secrets — we are glad you have not withheld yourself from humankind. We are grateful you have made our bodies homes for your Spirit. As we recognize the systems of nature, we are glad that you have not kept secret your imagination for we see it everywhere in the universe! We do not understand how evolution continues to change this planet, but we do know that we have been negligent with the waters, the air, and the land. Work in us until we demand that industry develop a conscience and protect the hills and forests, waters and air.

God of Life — we pray for peace throughout this global village. Show yourself to violent people as the resource for neighborliness and benevolent power. May guns and rockets, land mines and hand grenades be turned into tools for every one to grow food. Give solace to families whose children and parents have been killed or maimed in war. Let all humankind be makers of peace. Amen.

Benediction (Leader)

May the Creator of stars light your way;
May angels sing with you sad and joyful;
May you hear the voice of the Holy Spirit whispering guidance;
May you be wise enough to protect the Holy within you.

Go from this place feeling at peace with yourself and with God who keeps divine intentions secret but continually demonstrates love for you.

Be who you are, do what you can, and want what you have. Amen.

Music
God Of Our Life
        Words: Hugh T. Kerr, 1916, alt., 1928
        Music: Charles Henry Purday, 1860; harm. John Weaver, 1986
        SANDON

I Am The Light Of The World!
        Words: Jim Strathdee, 1969, in response to a Christmas poem by Howard Thurman
        Music: Jim Strathdee, 1969
        LIGHT OF THE WORLD

Sing Of God Made Manifest
        Words: Carl P. Daw Jr., 1989
        Music: Jacob Hintze, 1678; harm. Johann Sebastian Bach
        SALTZBURG

Spirit Of God, Unleashed On Earth
        Words: John W. Arthur, 1972, alt.
        Music: Attr. Elkanah Kelsay Dare, as in Pisbury's United States Harmony, 1799
        KEDRON

There's A Spirit In The Air
        Words: Brian Wren, 1969
        Music: Medieval French melody; harm. Richard Redhead, 1853
        ORIENTIS PARTIBUS

This Is A Day Of New Beginnings
        Words: Brian Wren, 1978, rev. 1987
        Music: Carlton R. Young, 1984
        BEGINNINGS

What Was Your Vow And Vision
        Words: Brian Wren, 1975, rev. 1994
        Music: Southern Harmony, 1835; harm. Hal H. Hopson, 1986
        COMPLAINER

The Baptism Of Our Lord
Epiphany 1
Ordinary Time 1

Isaiah 43:1-7   Acts 8:14-17
Psalm 29   Luke 3:15-17, 21-22

> *A single song is being inflected through all the colorations of the human choir.*
> *The way to become human is to recognize the lineaments of God in all the won-*
> *derful modulations of the face [of humankind].*
> — Joseph Campbell, *The Hero With a Thousand Faces*

Call To Worship

Leader: Happy New Year! With new determination we listen for the voice of God and we desire to respond happily.

People: We also listen with new care for the promises of scriptures, which might make our lives prosperous and easier.

Leader: We are here together, then, to pay attention to the ways men and women have honored the holy.

People: And to hear again about the life and teachings of Jesus of Nazareth.

Leader: Today we celebrate the baptism of Jesus.

People: We long for an experience with God that is life-shaping;
we want the Holy Spirit to come upon us;
we want to hear divine affirmation —
we want to feel the pleasure of God.

Leader: God has made us and all creatures! God has looked and declared,
"It is good."
With that knowledge, we join our voices to rejoice and to be thankful.

Prayer Of Thanksgiving (Unison or Leader)

God of the past and present — we've turned the calendar page. With our whole selves mind, body, and soul — we thank you for your presence with us and among all peoples. Sprinkle us with your grace; renew again our connections with one another and with your Spirit. Speak clearly so we do not mistake your affirmation with the "sweet talk" of our society. Amen.

Call To Confession (Leader)

The past is done; the present is now. Now is the moment to be freed from old baggage and sin; now is the moment to receive fresh direction for your days and nights. Let's pray in unison and then make our personal commitments to God.

Community Confession (Unison)
Living God — disappointments and betrayals clutter our minds.
Nasty words and bitterness hamper our relationships.
Belligerent attitudes get in the way of your guidance.
We regret all these thoughts and behaviors and we pray for freedom from guilt and shame.
As this new year matures, transform us to live fully aware of your beguiling love. Amen.

Word Of Grace (Leader)

You are an offspring of God. Rejoice and live appropriately — gently, contentedly, hospitably, and generously. The heavens do open; the Spirit does declare that God is with you. Receive this good news and live as a bold disciple of Jesus the Christ.

Sermon Idea

The rite/ritual of baptism in the new year is a powerful image of new intentions and new awarenesses for each person's current stage of development. A cedar branch dipped into the baptismal font waters and sprinkled over people is a way to immediately get people's attention! From the *slow motion* of waiting/expecting through the *commotion* of new birth to the *spiral motion* or *locomotion* of loss-of-innocence to coming-of-age, our perceptions of the Holy morph as does our sense of self in the world. Our hands and our thoughts move sometimes randomly. Questions to consider might be:

- What difference does it make that we are in church together baptized?
- How do our behaviors and attitudes change when we say that the Holy Spirit anoints us?
- What happens in our souls/spirits as we receive fresh blessings?
- How do we participate in the "human choir" after we are refreshed?

Contemporary Affirmation (Unison)
Throughout nature we see the imagination of the creating God.
In Jesus the Christ we learn how to be in relationship with the Holy.
With the Holy Spirit, we are empowered to embody divine love and mercy.
In community, we experience belonging and receive the encouragement to live as faithful
    disciples of Jesus and to struggle for justice and peace for all creatures.
Together, we have an insistent voice, proclaiming that there is a "kingdom of heaven."

Offertory Statement (Leader)

The new page of the calendar reminds us that few things in life are sure.
We sit here in space heated and cooled, painted and carpeted.
Our psyches are coached with music and ministers, with books and supplies.
For sure, our culture demands money in exchange for things that are important to us.
So we pass plates that receive your contributions to maintain this building, to refresh these accoutrements and to reach out to those in need.

Doxology   Now Thank We All Our God, tune: NUN DANKET ALLE GOTT
    Now thank we all our God with hearts and hands and voices,
    Who wondrous things hath done in whom this world rejoices;
    Who from our mothers' arms hath blessed us on our way
    With countess gifts of love and still is ours today.

Prayer Of Thanksgiving (Leader)

For the wonders of life together and the challenge to make the world better, we thank you. Amen.

Intercessory Prayers (Leader or Readers)

Dependable God — our mortality greets us as we prepare for sleep and as we wake; our fragility shows up when disease clobbers us. We long to feel your healing presence; we yearn for reassurance that this life is not all there is. We look for signs of your work among us; we make time to be still and to be aware that you are sustaining Holiness in the clamor of earning our keep in society. Thank you for the rituals that take us through each day.

God of Tomorrow — time dangles before us and still peace has not come to this universe. The year is young and we pray for peace among adults so the children can grow up to know gentleness, sanity, collaboration, and compromise. We pray for peace between nations whose place in the world market is dependent upon every other nation. Let wisdom come to leaders and followers in dreams and in lucid conversations. Let the wishes of Christmas be realized in our homes and in the world.

God of Stillness and Motion — we do our dervishes and feel the dizziness of your divinity completing our humanity. When our pace seems to be a dawdle, you greet us in good food, in beautiful pictures, in stimulating conversations, in bright babies, and in our own mirrors. In the quiet and in the fierceness of our days and relationships, you breathe, "It is good," reminding us that we co-create with you the possibilities of Christ walking here in our town and on our street corner. Thank you for the variety in our thoughts and activities, on the land, in the waters, and in the sky. Amen.

Benediction/Charge (Leader)

As you leave the sanctuary, be alert for all the colors of humanity; listen for songs beginning low and swelling to a great "Hooray!" Watch for the modulations of souls — your own and others, move about wearing some sign of God-within, reaching with unmistakable goodness to those close by. Most of all, may the God of today and tomorrow enliven your days and nights through this new year!

Music

God Of Our Life
    Words: Hugh T. Kerr, 1916, alt., 1928
    Music: Charles Henry Purday, 1860; harm. John Weaver, 1986
    SANDON

I Am The Light Of The World!
    Words: Jim Strathdee, 1969, in response to a Christmas poem by Howard Thurman
    Music: Jim Strathdee, 1969
    LIGHT OF THE WORLD

Sing Of God Made Manifest
    Words: Carl P. Daw Jr., 1989
    Music: Jacob Hintze, 1678; harm. Johann Sebastian Bach
    SALTZBURG

Spirit Of God, Unleashed On Earth
    Words: John W. Arthur, 1972, alt.
    Music: Attr. Elkanah Kelsay Dare, as in Pisbury's United States Harmony, 1799
    KEDRON

There's A Spirit In The Air
    Words: Brian Wren, 1969
    Music: Medieval French melody; harm. Richard Redhead, 1853
    ORIENTIS PARTIBUS

This Is A Day Of New Beginnings
    Words: Brian Wren, 1978, rev. 1987
    Music: Carlton R. Young, 1984
    BEGINNINGS

What Was Your Vow And Vision
    Words: Brian Wren, 1975, rev. 1994
    Music: Southern Harmony, 1835; harm. Hal H. Hopson, 1986
    COMPLAINER

Epiphany 2
Ordinary Time 2

Isaiah 62:1-5   1 Corinthians 12:1-11
Psalm 36:5-10   John 2:1-11

> *A single song is being inflected through all the colorations of the human choir.*
> *The way to become human is to recognize the lineaments of God in all the won-*
> *derful modulations of the face [of humankind].*
> — Joseph Campbell, *The Hero With a Thousand Faces*

Call To Worship

Leader: Welcome! Together we will explore ancient stories about a wedding, a city, and our life together.

People: **We've come to thank God for the gift of life and to ask for help when our paths are difficult.**

Leader: Then let our thanks begin — in music, in conversation, and in prayer; let our time together be pleasing to God and to one another.

Prayer Of Thanksgiving (Leader)

Gracious God — the year seems fresh and we want to hope that goodness and peace bless us all. We are grateful for the opportunities that come to us and for the ways we can be your voice and your justice in our neighborhoods. During this time, we offer you our undivided attention so that your Spirit can minister to us as we worship you. Amen.

Call To Confession (Leader)

God's love is constant and dependable. Like birds, we find ourselves "snuggling" for protective grace. We take these moments as opportunity for introspection. Pray with me the prayer printed in your bulletins. Then name for yourself and God the unmerciful and inhospitable, the unrighteous attitudes and behaviors that block your wholeness.

Community Confession (Unison)

Living God — we want to be good people. We want to do what is right.
We want to be known as disciples of Christ.
Yet we do not do what we ought.
We do not love you with our whole selves nor care for our neighbors as we care for ourselves.
Straighten our thinking; inspire our actions; free us from last year's errors.
Let us exhibit your presence wherever we are. Amen.

Sermon Idea

In the Isaiah text, we can recognize our roots in Judaism. We have prayed for Jerusalem — Jerusalem as an image of a perfect community and as a contemporary city claimed by Jews,

Muslims, and Christians. We are still praying for peace as did the prophets before Jesus himself grieved over its divisions. We can anticipate Passover as we look at the psalm and prophet; the sermon could consider the images of scriptures — Psalm 36 as well as Isaiah 62 — compared with the literal ways they have been read. The interpretation might also look at contemporary politics and globalization and ask how we can accommodate ancient stories. Likewise, the issues of "costly show weddings" and alcoholism might be addressed as quite different from the gospel of John in 30 CE. The epistle texts for today and the next two Sundays are so familiar that they have little impact on the people sitting in pews. Perhaps the image of the body functions could be dramatized by leaders whose roles in the congregation are clear and visible, for example, the person who serves as a long-range planner — we might say she serves our Body Politic as *brain*; another member enjoys growing zucchinis and is adamant about caring for the earth — he serves our Body Politic as hands that share what he grows and as a voice in local government for clean water and sheltering the homeless. Another congregant may hold lots of balls in the air without getting stressed and still keeps a clear head — we might say she is a *big toe*, helping us as Body Politic keep our balance.

Another way to look at all the lections as a whole is: a society that is civil and hospitable feels good about itself and has a far-reaching good reputation.

Contemporary Affirmation (Unison)
Throughout nature we see the imagination of the Creating God.
In Jesus the Christ we learn how to be in relationship with the Holy.
With the Holy Spirit, we are empowered to embody divine love and mercy.
In community, we experience belonging and receive the encouragement to live as faithful
disciples of Jesus and to struggle for justice and peace for all creatures.
Together, we have an insistent voice, proclaiming that there can be a "kingdom of heaven."

Offertory Statement (Leader)
With tithes and offerings, with money and talents, we care for this building and reach out to neighbors with joy and kindness.

Doxology   Now Thank We All Our God, tune: NUN DANKET ALLE GOTT
Now thank we all our God with hearts and hands and voices,
Who wondrous things hath done in whom this world rejoices;
Who from our mothers' arms hath blessed us on our way
With countless gifts of love and still is ours today.

Prayer Of Thanksgiving (Leader)
Thank you, God, for what we have and who you are shaping us to be. Amen.

Intercessory Prayers (Leader or Readers)
God — we pray for peace — peace now — peace tomorrow — peace within and peace external to our psyches.

God — we pray for strength — strength in our decisions — strength in our bodies — strength in our souls.

God — we pray for others. With unmistakable tenderness, make yourself and your grace palpable to people who seek wholeness.

God — we thank you for revealing yourself in Jesus of Nazareth. We want to live as his disciples. Amen.

Benediction/Charge (Leader)

As you leave the sanctuary, be alert for all the colors of humanity; listen for songs beginning low and swelling to a great "Hooray!" Watch for the modulations of souls — your own and others, move about wearing some sign of God-within; reach with unmistakable goodness to those close by. Most of all, may the God of today and tomorrow enliven your life through this new year!

Music

Come, Holy Spirit, Our Souls Inspire
    Words: Attr. Rabanus Maurus, 9th century; trans. John Cosin, 1627, alt.
    Music: Plainsong, Mode VIII; arr. Healey Willan (1880-1968)
    VENI CREATOR SPIRITUS

Immortal, Invisible, God Only Wise
    Words: Walter Chalmers Smith, 1867, alt.
    Music: Welsh folk melody
    ST. DENIO

Many Are The Lightbeams
    Words: De unitate ecclesiae, Cyprian of Carthage, 252; tr. Anders Frostenson, 1972, 1986
    Music: Olle Widestrand, 1974; harm. A. Eugene Ellsworth, 1994
    MANY ARE THE LIGHTBEAMS

Who Is My Mother, Who Is My Brother?
    Words: Shirley Erena Murray, 1991
    Music: Jack Schrader, 1991
    KINDRED

Epiphany 3
Ordinary Time 3

Nehemiah 8:1-3, 5-6, 8-10   1 Corinthians 12:12-31a
Psalm 19   Luke 4:14-21

A single song is being inflected through all the colorations of the human choir.
The way to become human is to recognize the lineaments of God in all the won-
derful modulations of the face [of humankind].
— Joseph Campbell, *The Hero With a Thousand Faces*

Call To Worship

Leader: Welcome! Together we'll explore ancient stories about a public reading, the awe-someness of Creation, satisfying life together, and we will claim our God-given abilities.

People: We've come to thank God for the Holy Spirit, for the wonders of nature, and for the gifts given to humankind. And we've come to ask for help in the rough, dark spots of our journey.

Leader: Then let our conversations and our songs acknowledge Divine Presence; let our activities express our needs and joys.

Prayer Of Thanksgiving (Leader)

Gracious God — thank you for today and for the multifaceted ways you are with us. For this place we call "Church Home" and for these companions we call the "Body of Christ," we are grateful. We're glad to be called "Beloved" and "God-Pleasing," glad for our *life together*. For this hour, we relax in your inspiring presence, listening for ideas that will sustain us during the coming week. Amen.

Call To Confession (Leader)

We learn about God as we look at Creation, for nature reveals God's creativity and orderliness. Let us take time to reflect on our souls and minds, so we learn about ourselves. Join me in the Community Confession.

Community Confession (Unison)

Living God — disappointments and betrayals clutter our minds. Nasty words and bitterness hamper our relationships.

Belligerent attitudes get in the way of your guidance. We regret these thoughts and behaviors and we pray for freedom from guilt and shame.

As this new year matures, transform us to live generously with the gifts of your Spirit. Amen.

Word Of Grace (Leader)

In the light of God, we can see our errors; open to the Spirit, we can recognize hidden faults and be freed from them. Our words and our thoughts are acceptable to God! Hallelujah! Jesus the Christ leads us to a dynamic relationship with the living God!

Sermon Idea

The 1 Corinthians passage continues the theme of last week. Today, the preacher/speaker might consider asking how a well-functioning Body of Christ will interact with nature, with the city, and with government. The first six verses of the lectionary psalm might lead the way into ecological issues: clean skies, fresh air, planet atmosphere, and awareness of nature at different places: North Pole, South Pole, Australia, desert, wet lands, and so on. Verses 7-14 suggest that good government honors justice more than profit, happiness more than wealth, and fairness more than personal power. Verses 12 and 13 speak of needing one another as well as self-reflection in order to see clearly since we can rarely see our own faults. Given the downward turn of the economy, will church communities support one another? Will faith families actually share what individuals have so that houses are not lost, medical care is available, and food is on every table? Will disciples of Jesus practice loving one another?

Contemporary Affirmation (Unison)

Throughout nature we see the imagination of the creating God.

In Jesus the Christ we learn how to be in relationship with the Holy.

With the Holy Spirit, we are empowered to embody divine love and mercy.

In community, we experience belonging and receive the encouragement to live as faithful disciples of Jesus and to struggle for justice and peace for all creatures.

Together, we have an insistent voice, proclaiming that there can be a "kingdom of heaven."

Offertory Statement (Leader)

We each have roles in our *life together*. One role we share is to be benevolent supporters of the ministry of Christ in this place.

Doxology   Now Thank We All Our God, tune: NUN DANKET ALLE GOTT

Now thank we all our God with hearts and hands and voices,
Who wondrous things hath done in whom this world rejoices;
Who from our mothers' arms hath blessed us on our way
With countless gifts of love and still is ours today.

Prayer Of Thanksgiving (Leader)

This is your world, Holy One. Thank you for loving and sustaining it. Thank you, too, for the opportunity to be co-creators with you. Amen.

Intercessory Prayers (Leader or Readers)

Eternal God — thank you for your undeniable presence. Where there is dis-ease among us, free us from it. Where there is retaliation and vengeance among tribes and nations, dismiss the grudges that hold people captive. Where there is war and terror, give people a new sense of what it means to be a nation within a global environment.

Mothering God — we are a part of the Body of Christ. With our skills and thoughts, nurture this place and this whole community. Help us each to play our part eagerly and happily.

Fathering God — our Body of Christ is a small part of the whole. As we work with one another for goodness and beauty here, inspire us develop justice and mutuality, lodging and food, education and hope for all peoples.

God of Body and Soul — touch us with healing in our psyches and in our bodies. Guide us to wholeness and happiness. Give us strength sufficient for each day; free us from pain. Sustain us on our journey to you. Amen.

Benediction/Charge (Leader)

Fingers and toes, tongue and thoughts —
It is our privilege to use them to benefit many people.
Go from here with ideas for the week ahead;
Be loving and gentle at home and at work, at school and at play.
Take time to enjoy the Holy.

Music

All Beautiful The March Of Days
    Words: Frances Whitmarsh Wile, 1911
    Music: English folk melody; arr. Ralph Vaughan Williams, 1906
    FOREST GREEN

In Loving Partnership
    Words and Music: Jim Strathdee, 1983
    PARTNERSHIP

Live Into Hope
    Words: Jane Parker Huber, 1976
    Music: Thomas Williams, 1789; harm. Lowell Mason (1792-1872)
    TRURO

The Heavens Above Declare God's Praise
    Words: Christopher L. Webber, 1986
    Music: Scottish Psalter, 1635; harm. The English Hymnal 1906, alt.
    CAITHNESS

Epiphany 4
Ordinary Time 4

Jeremiah 1:4-10   1 Corinthians 13:1-13
Psalm 71:1-6   Luke 4:21-30

A single song is being inflected through all the colorations of the human choir.
The way to become human is to recognize the lineaments of God in all the won-
derful modulations of the face [of humankind].
— Joseph Campbell, *The Hero With a Thousand Faces*

Call To Worship
Leader: Welcome to this place where we can speak like humans and angels!
People: **Ah — but we know that if we are not compassionate we're like noisy whistles!**
Leader: Welcome on this winter day to this place where love is part of our mission statement.
People: **Hmm. We know that the spiritual journey with God requires more than words in an official document.**
Leader: Welcome to this sanctuary where love is a divine gift and our human goal.
People: **Great! We are glad to be here; for one hour, we feel protected from the world's cynicism and profiteering gaze.**
Leader: But love is not confined to one hour each week!
People: **Right. Here we are refreshed in spirit so we can be patient and kind, not jealous or conceited. We lose all desire to be ill-mannered and selfish. We lose the need to keep a record of others' wrongs. We choose to be truthful and happy, never giving up on faith and hope.**
Leader: Love is eternal, a treasure from God —
People: **A treasure we carry inside to share with others.**

Prayer Of Thanksgiving (Leader)
Living God — so many gifts you give us — opportunity to gather in this place, to mature together in faith, hope, and love. Thank you for encouraging us day after day to practice love, charity, friendship, and compassion. Amen.

Call To Confession (Leader)
We learn about God as we look at Creation, for nature reveals God's creativity. When we take time to reflect on our souls and minds, we learn about ourselves. Pray the printed prayer with me, then you and God have a private conversation.

Community Confession (Unison)
Living God — disappointments and betrayals clutter our minds. Nasty words and bitterness hamper our relationships.
Belligerent attitudes get in the way of your guidance.
We regret all these thoughts and behaviors and we pray for freedom from guilt and shame.

As this new year matures, transform us to live generously with the gifts of your Spirit. Amen.

Word Of Grace (Leader)

In the light of God, we can see our errors; open to the Spirit, we can recognize hidden faults and be freed from them. Our words and our thoughts are acceptable to God! Hallelujah! Jesus the Christ leads us to a dynamic relationship with the living God!

Sermon Idea

How many essays and sermons have people heard about love and compassion? How many brides and grooms use 1 Corinthians 13? Tsunamis and hurricanes and all natural disasters tug at our hearts and purse strings. Terrors and malevolence by humans push our anger buttons. War scenes repulse us. Poverty displays jerk our gag reflexes. Faith-based initiatives have laid societal burdens on people who take seriously 1 Corinthians 12 and 13. Where does adequate funding come from for alleviating worldwide poverty? (In 2005, the UN said the biggest problem facing humanity is global poverty.) Do governments make decisions with 1 Corinthians 13 in mind? Should they? Do educators work with children on the basis of 1 Corinthians 13? Should they? As Christians, can we minimize the "-isms," which plague our culture by using the ethics and behaviors suggested in 1 Corinthians 13? At town meetings? At soccer games? With international family planning?

Contemporary Affirmation (Unison)

Throughout nature we see the imagination of the Creating God.
In Jesus the Christ we learn how to be in relationship with the Holy.
With the Holy Spirit, we are empowered to embody divine love and mercy.
In community, we experience belonging and receive the encouragement to live as faithful disciples of Jesus and to struggle for justice and peace for all creatures.
Together, we have an insistent voice, proclaiming that there is a "kingdom of heaven."

Offertory Statement (Leader)

We can make our appreciation for this place and the nurturing we do tangible with our money and our time.

Doxology   Now Thank We All Our God, tune: NUN DANKET ALLEGOTT

Now thank we all our God with hearts and hands and voices,
Who wondrous things hath done in whom this world rejoices;
Who from our mothers' arms hath blessed us on our way
With countless gifts of love and still is ours today.

Prayer Of Thanksgiving (Leader)

Generous God, there are so many kinds of riches, only one of them is money. Thank you for wealth that comes to us in relationships, in creation, and by the Spirit. Thank you, too, for money to make our way in the world. Amen.

Intercessory Prayers (Leader or Readers)

Lover of our Souls — we say you are the Creator of all that is; we say you invite us to be co-creators with you. Empower us to embody patience and kindness with strangers as well as with friends, with the ecosphere, and with animals.

Artist of the Universe — move among us and through this planet home; brush governments and citizens with the colors of civility and respect. Bring an end to the ugliness of war and terror. Bring young and old, gay and straight, black and white, male and female, rich and poor under a rainbow of bright hope for justice and "enough" for all creatures.

Architect of the Cosmos — be clear with us in synchronicity and in happenstance so we may participate in caring for the land and sky; the water and air all around this globe. Open our eyes to the Christ in others; project the light of Christ through us so all who come near us recognize your Spirit. Work through the Body of Christ to restore sanity and wholesomeness to manufacturing, to chemicals used in foods, to nuclear research, and to human exploitation of reproduction.

Engineer of Humanity — we live and die, feeling connected to your energy and grace. Fill our cracks with curiosity, soothe our aches, inspire our thinking, heal our dis-eases, and make us whole.

Holy One — thank you for Jesus and his teachings. Help us to walk this earth as creative thinkers following his example. Amen.

Benediction (Leader)

As you leave the sanctuary, be alert for all the colors of humanity; listen for the songs beginning low and swelling to a great "Hooray!" Watch for the modulations of souls — your own and others, move about wearing some sign of God-within; reaching with unmistakable goodness to those close by. Most of all, may the God of today and tomorrow enliven you with joy!

Music

The Gift Of Love (Though I May Speak)
    Words: Hal H. Hopson, 1972
    Music: Traditional English melody; adapt. Hal H. Hopson, 1972
    GIFT OF LOVE

Gracious Spirit, Holy Ghost
    Words: Christopher Wordsworth, 1862
    Music: Jane Manton Marshall, 1985
    ANDERSON

I Cannot Dance, O Love
    Words: Jean Janzen, 1991, based on the writing of Mechthild of Magdeburg
    Music: Swedish folk tune; harm. Lahrae Knatterud, 1983
    BRED DINA VIDA VINGAR

Love Divine, All Loves Excelling
    Words: Charles Wesley, 1743
    Music: John Zundel, 1870
    BEECHER

Not For Tongues Of Heaven's Angels
    Words: Timothy Dudley-Smith, 1985
    Music: Peter Cutts, 1969
    BRIDEGROOM

Ubi Caritas Et Amor (Live In Charity)
    Words: Latin (9th century); tr. Taizé community
    Music: Jacques Berthier (20th century)
    UBI CARITAS

Womb Of Life
    Words: Ruth Duck, 1986, 1990
    Music: Traditional Dutch melody; arr. Julius Roentgen, 1906
    IN BABILONE

Epiphany 5
Ordinary Time 5

Isaiah 6:1-8 (9-13)   1 Corinthians 15:1-11
Psalm 138   Luke 5:1-11

> *A single song is being inflected through all the colorations of the human choir.*
> *The way to become human is to recognize the lineaments of God in all the won-*
> *derful modulations of the face [of humankind].*
> — Joseph Campbell, *The Hero With a Thousand Faces*

Call To Worship (Leader)

We are in sanctuary — together, removed from the world, secluded for a while.

We have brought with us our burdens and anxieties.

We've come here with our hopes and thanksgivings.

For one hour, we can intentionally, consciously set all this aside knowing we can pick it up again as we return to our worlds.

Make space in your mind and psyche for the Spirit — space for changing systems, for rising energy, and for flaming audacity.

Listen for the God of grace and laughter.

Listen for new rhythms calling to you.

Prayer Of Thanksgiving (Leader)

God of this Century — we are aware that the images our ancestors used to make you "real" for themselves don't open our imaginations to you. There must be a myriad of ways we can experience your empowering presence, a million ways we can perceive you with all our senses! Our minds are alert; our souls are eager. We sing and pray, listen and speak our appreciation for your dynamic presence. We are ready to imagine you for our times. Amen.

Call To Confession (Leader)

Newness of life is available to us as we let go of burdensome memories and painful replays of what might have been. In these few moments, we can reflect on who we are and where we are going. Pray with me and then carry on your conversation with God.

Community Confession (Unison)

God of Today — disappointments and betrayals clutter our minds. Nasty words and bit-terness hamper our relationships.

Belligerent attitudes get in the way of your grace.

Injustice and prejudices cloud our national priorities.

We regret these thoughts and behaviors; free us from guilt and shame.

Transform us individually and as a nation so our words and actions are consistent with your love. Amen.

Sermon Idea

When we wonder what enriches and satisfies the twenty-first-century soul, it is difficult to use Isaiah 6 as a model for gathered or private worship. The cosmology and anthropomorphism don't translate well for the technologically educated mind. A sermon title/theme might be: *Soul Update*. What symbols and images impel us to say, "Yes, I will be an active, hospitable home for the Holy," and "Yes, I will work for justice and mutuality in my home, my church, my nation, and the global village."

A satellite dish? Archetypal dreams? Athletic and movie images often have components that do not fit with Jesus' "commandments" to love yourself, your neighbor, your enemy, and the stranger. Technological games and sports often consume time and energy we might otherwise use for meditation or service activities. If resurrection is to be among our experiences, we must be open to non-traditional, non-classical options of inviting God to make us new.

Contemporary Affirmation (Unison)

God was in the beginning.

God is still present — present for us 21st century people! We will learn to recognize God's creating, inspiring, and empowering in post-modern images.

God is imaginative beyond our human guidelines!

Jesus taught in the first century and was murdered for confronting government and religious authorities. His teachings continue to challenge us.

Holy Spirit is a divine presence within human beings and in the cosmos.

We gather as seekers attempting to understand humanity and divinity. We care for each other so we are not alone. Amen!

Offertory Statement (Leader)

The exchange of energies within your body and soul is between you and God.

The exchange of money from our wallets to the church budget is between us and God, too; together we support ministry on this street corner.

Doxology   As A Chalice Cost Of Gold (v. 4), tune: INWARD LIGHT

When I dance or chant your praise, when I sing a psalm or hymn,

When I teach your loving ways, let my heart add its Amen.

Let each cherished outward rite thus reflect your inward light.

Prayer Of Thanksgiving (Leader)

Great God — in gratitude for your loving presence, we give you our whole selves! Use us and our talents and our money to make your grace tangible on our street. Amen.

Intercessory Prayers (Leader or Readers)

Thank you, Creating God, for the mysteries of the universe. Help us participate with you in protecting them from human greed and debris.

Thank you, Creating God, for the multiple nations and religions throughout the global village. May our words and our actions be consistent with your love.

Thank you, Eternal God, for creating us in your image. Stop the terror that ravishes our bodies and souls. Halt the wars that maim our children and devastate the land. Stop the injustice that breeds poverty, disease, and discontent.

Thank you, Healing God, for sufficient strength to endure each day, to learn new things, to hold on to goodness, and to let go of unhelpful ideas. Satisfy our hearts. Amen.

Benediction/Charge (Leader)

As you leave the sanctuary, be alert for all the variations of humankind. Listen for songs and laughter, tears and groans. Watch for the modulations of your own soul. Be aware that the living God cradles you and all creation! Serve with joy!

Music

Here I Am, Lord
    Words: Daniel L. Schutte, 1981
    Music: Daniel L. Schutte, 1981; harm. James Snyder, 1994
    HERE I AM, LORD

How Clear Is Our Vocation, Lord
    Words: Fred Pratt Green, 1981
    Music: C. Hubert H. Parry, 1888
    REPTON

I Will Give Thanks With My Whole Heart
    Words: Christopher L. Webber, 1986, 1988
    Music: Cantionale Germanicum, 1628; arr. J. S. Bach, c. 1708
    HERR JESU CHRIST

Jesus Calls Us
    Words: Cecil Frances Alexander, 1852
    Music: William H. Jude
    GALILEE

Renew Your Church
    Words: Kenneth L. Cober, 1960, alt.
    Music: American folk melody, c. 1840
    ALL IS WELL

Sois La Semilla (You Are The Seed)
    Words: Cesareo Gabraín, 1979; tr. Raquel Gutiérrez-Achon and Skinner Chávez-Melo
    Music: Cesareo Gabraín, 1979; harm. Skinner Chávez-Melo, 1987
    ID Y ENSEÑAD

Tú Has Venido A La Orilla (Lord, You Have Come To The Lakeshore)
    Words: Cesário Gabaráin, 1979; tr. Gertrude Suppe, George Lockwood, and Raquel
        Achón, 1988, alt.
    Music: Cesário Gabaráin; harm. Sinner Chávez-Melo
    PESCADOR DE HOMBRES

We Are Living, We Are Dwelling
    Words: Arthur C. Coxe, 1840, alt.; st. 2 adapt. Ruth Duck, 1995
    Music: Thomas J. Williams, 1890
    EBENEZER

Epiphany 6
Ordinary Time 6

Jeremiah 17:5-10   1 Corinthians 15:12-20
Psalm 1   Luke 6:17-26

A single song is being inflected through all the colorations of the human choir.
The way to become human is to recognize the lineaments of God in all the won-
derful modulations of the face [of humankind].
— Joseph Campbell, *The Hero With a Thousand Faces*

Call To Worship
Leader: Good morning! I'm glad we're together again! The busy-ness of Christmas and
          New Year are behind us. But I see Valentine's Day and Ash Wednesday right around
          the corner.
People: All the holidays remind us that life is good.
Leader: That's true — for all the rituals that hold time and the challenges of living.
People: We are grounded in faith, in the teachings of Jesus, and we are happy people.
Leader: Or as the psalmist said, "We are happy because we are planted by streams of living
          water!"
People: Yes!

Prayer Of Thanksgiving (Leader)
Energy of the Universe — thank you for the tranquil beauty and the vital energy of this
place.
    The culture, the environment, and our bodies are changing so fast!
    We are grateful for this time to sit and think, to listen for your voice, to sing and pray.
    Thank you for your dependable presence and your sturdy love.
    We are eager to participate with your Spirit. Amen.

Call To Confession (Leader)
The past is done; the present is now. Now is the moment to be freed from haunting memories and sin. Now is the moment to receive fresh direction for your days and nights. Let's pray
in unison and then make our personal commitments to God.

Community Confession (Unison)
Living God — disappointments and betrayals clutter our minds. Nasty words and bitter-
    ness hamper our relationships.
Belligerent attitudes get in the way of your guidance.
We regret these thoughts and behaviors and pray for freedom from guilt.
As this year matures, transform us to live fully aware of your indwelling love. Amen.

Sermon Idea

Social events as well as employment events are times when others are observing us — our conversation style, the beverages we hold in our hands, our ability to listen/hear. As friends of Jesus, we also exhibit the gifts of the Spirit. Is there a reward for our good behavior? What is our satisfaction? Where do we get encouragement to be faithful to Jesus' teachings when we are in situations that do not value our lifestyle? Are Christians known by the ways they care for each other?

Contemporary Affirmation (Unison)
Throughout nature we see the imagination of the creating God.
In Jesus the Christ we learn how to be in relationship with the Holy.
With the Holy Spirit, we are empowered to embody divine love and mercy.
In community, we experience belonging and receive the encouragement to live as faithful
  disciples of Jesus and to struggle for justice and peace for all creatures.
Together, we have an insistent voice, proclaiming that there is a "kingdom of heaven."

Offertory Statement (Leader)

Student, teacher, CEO, grocery store bagger — we each have talents that enrich our *life together*.

Money pays our electricity and water bills.
Money sends food to Urban Ministry.
Money pays salaries.
Give as you can.

Doxology   Now Thank We All Our God, tune: NUN DANKET ALLE GOTT
Now thank we all our God with hearts and hands and voices,
Who wondrous things hath done in whom this world rejoices;
Who from our mothers' arms hath blessed us on our way
With countless gifts of love and still is ours today.

Prayer Of Thanksgiving (Leader)

Thank you, Living God, for the talents and skills that make each of us significant to this faith family.

Thank you for sufficient money to pay our way in this world. Amen.

Intercessory Prayers (Leader or Readers)

God of Body and Soul — we devote ourselves to be in harmony with your Spirit. Heal us from head to toe, inside and out. Synchronize our "I can" with your hopes for humankind.

God of Insight — many of us weep for we have lost someone or something important. Comfort us and renew our strength.

God of Gentleness — how rigid we have become! Open us to the splendor of creation. Soften our harshness and work through us to make our homes and neighborhoods safe.

God of Justice — integrate our sense of right, peace, and justice. Work through us to reconstruct a society that values the multicolors of humanity, the weak, and the lonely. Plant peace with our hands and hearts.

God of Mercy — shower the global village and all its tribes with compassion. Heal ancient grudges and birth hospitality in every religion and in every person. Radiate goodness between nations. Help us to recognize and confront untruth and corruption so everyone everywhere can envision abundant life! Amen.

Benediction (Leader)

As you leave the sanctuary, be alert for all the colors of humanity; listen for songs beginning low and swelling to a great "Hooray!" Watch for the modulations of souls — your own and others, move about wearing some sign of God-within; reaching with unmistakable goodness to those close by. May the God of today and tomorrow enliven you with joy!

Music

Cristo Vive (Christ Is Risen)
    Words: Nicholas Martinez, 1960; trans. Fred Kaan, 1972
    Music: Pablo Sosa, 1960, alt.
    ARGENTINA (Sosa)

Come, Ye Faithful, Raise The Strain
    Words: John of Damascus (c. 675-749); trans. John Mason Neale, 1859, alt.
    Music: Bohemian Brethren's Gesangbuch, 1544
    AVE VIRGO VIRGINUM (or ST. KEVIN; music: Arthur Seymour Sullivan [1842-1900], alt.)

Hope Of The World
    Words: Georgia Harkness, 1954
    Music: Genevan Psalter, 1551
    DONNE SECOURS

I Shall Not Be Moved
    Words and Music: African-American spiritual
    I SHALL NOT BE MOVED

Sing With All The Saints In Glory
    Words: William J. Irons, 1873
    Music: Ludwig van Beethoven, 1824; arr. Edward Hodges, 1864
    HYMN TO JOY

Epiphany 7
Ordinary Time 7

Genesis 45:3-11, 15   1 Corinthians 15:35-37, 42-50
Psalm 37:1-11, 39-40   Luke 6:27-38

A single song is being inflected through all the colorations of the human choir. The way to become human is to recognize the lineaments of God in all the wonderful modulations of the face [of humankind].
— Joseph Campbell, *The Hero With a Thousand Faces*

Call To Worship

Leader: Greetings! The year is not quite so new. But we're glad for the breath of life and for the opportunity to gather in this place.

People: We enjoy being together and we anticipate hearing God and responding with music, silence, and words.

Leader: Here we learn the teachings of Jesus, and we can practice them with each other.

People: It's easy to love one another here; it's easy to share our money and our clothes, our food and our homes.

Leader: It's not so easy, though, to practice at work and at city council Jesus' message: Love your enemies; do good to those who hate you; don't retaliate; give your shirt.

People: Nor is it easy to be kind to family members when they have betrayed us, as Joseph was with his brothers who sold him!

Leader: Thank God, we can be forgiven and try again to live the teachings of Jesus! Let's sing and pray —

People: listen and hope!

Prayer Of Thanksgiving (Leader)

Architect of the Universe — we do not understand the intricacies of living and dying or even remembering and forgiving. But we are awed with the beauty of the world and the way it works. We are grateful for companions to think and talk with about divine love, mortality, and eternity. We turn our attention to the images in this place that quiet our minds so we can hear your voice. Amen.

Call To Confession (Leader)

The psalmist expected God to intervene on behalf of people whose lifestyles conformed to religious expectations. Most of us have difficulty conforming to any set of rigid rules. The psalmist tells us not to spend our energy with concerns about others but to seek our own happiness and God will see to it that our hearts are satisfied. In these next minutes, let us explore our desires and our behaviors. If they are not aligned with God, we have opportunity to do that now. Pray with me.

Community Confession (Unison)

Loving God — we have not always been able to do to others as we want them to do to us.

We have betrayed best friends.

We have avoided whole truths.

We have even used our power to aggrandize ourselves rather than provide for people in need of companionship or life's necessities.

We know that the consequences of our behavior are guilt and sometimes shame.

Free us and give us generous and joyous attitudes that are contagious. Amen.

Word Of Grace (Leader)

It is good news that when we confess our failings, we can find our souls cleansed and healed. Internal peace is a divine gift — or as the psalmist says, "God will satisfy the desires of our hearts!"

Sermon Idea

Today's texts are reminders that though the scriptures have come to us across centuries and cultures, some destructive human behaviors hang around. Adults still sell children, make them carry weapons, and maim them. All the characters in these scriptures are male; they are concerned with other people's behavior and how some kind of justice should be meted out.

A theme/title might be: Balancing Act — Hope and Action. In Luke's Sermon on the Plain, the underlying assumption that Jesus is responding to is that God is in charge of the world and has expectations for human behavior. Luke has Jesus indicating that people of God do not judge or condemn but give and forgive. Kingdom people do not retaliate against those who attempt to victimize them. Joseph does not condemn his brothers but offers to feed them, their families, and their animals. The psalmist's assumptions about God being in charge of the world and protector of his favorite people — the Jews — are clear.

Luke's report of Jesus teaching disciples about doing to others as we would have them do to us pulls the texts toward each other. If God is in charge as the psalmist and Paul suggest, then people who are righteous will experience an easier life — Job's quandary. Joseph understands God to have been in charge of his being sold and his being the "savior" of his relatives — a cause and effect explanation. However, psychologically, Jesus' message suggests passivity and repression of physical pain and loss.

For the contemporary reader, cause and effect are not so simple; giving your shirt upon demand may impoverish one beyond sustainability. If we are living the Sermon on the Mount, if we are caring for those affected by disaster and poverty, then why spend our energy and imagination trying to figure out with Paul what lies beyond life?

The other element that is shared by today's scriptures is the articulation of hope. Humans must hope to survive — "the thing with feathers that perches in the soul," Emily Dickinson has called it. Maybe a description of hope for contemporary times is the longing for the experience of humanity being kind to each other so the world is a hospitable place and then we humans can in real time make peace.

Contemporary Affirmation (Unison)

Our senses recognize creation's beauties: we see, we hear, we touch, we smell, and we taste. God is the Designer and continues to create.

Our minds think about what we perceive and we choose to know and love God who comes to us in storms, in mountains, and in still small voices.

Our souls yearn to relate to God as a parent; we find ourselves loved.

Jesus of Nazareth was the Godbearer we relate to and to whom we give our loyalty.

The Holy Spirit, a gift promised by Jesus, lives within us and supports us as co-creators with God and as those journeying to eternity.

We are not alone. God is with us. Amen!

Offertory Statement (Leader)

Joseph in the Old Testament story made sure his brothers and their families had enough food to make it through times of famine. There are all kinds of famine around us that affect us and others in body and soul. Let us generously share what we have.

Doxology   Praise God From Whom All Blessings Flow, tune: OLD HUNDREDTH
Praise God from whom all blessings flow;
Praise God, all creatures here below.
Praise God above you heavenly hosts.
Creator, Christ, and Holy Ghost.

Prayer Of Thanksgiving (Leader)

For food and shelter in times of famine, we are grateful.

We appreciate the availability of resources and money sufficient for each day. Amen.

Intercessory Prayer (Leader or Readers)

Source of Life — we do not understand the process of living and dying. We can only imagine what happens after we take our last breath. We do understand that there are consequences to our thoughts and our actions. Help us to think and live the teachings of Jesus because they give everyone in the global village a chance to have their needs met and enjoy their time on this earth.

Healer of Body and Soul — we do know that we are mortal and that we are designed to die. How strange! We need one another to accompany us along this human journey as our bodies grow and our minds learn and our souls find peace. When we are wounded, soothe us; when we are ill, heal us; when we are sad, comfort us.

Artist of the Universe — how we marvel at blue skies and sparkling waters! How frightened we are when the wind is strong! How gentle we feel when we walk among tall trees! We want to take care of all you have created. Help us to protect the planet so our children will have a home.

God for all Nations — it is difficult to manage nations, to make laws that are fair, and to educate all children to live well in a scientific and technological world. We pray for enduring peace in every nation so that children grow up as good neighbors. We pray for peace that fills us all with hope. Help our leaders and all the world's leaders to take down fences and share resources so that all people are fed and housed. Amen.

Benediction (Leader)

Be like Joseph — compassionate with all you meet.

Be like Jesus — loving enemies and doing kindness.

Be like the psalmist — hope amid trying times that things will get better and that God walks with you, giving you strength.

Be like Paul — curious about how the body and soul work.
Go as peacemakers, wanting what you have and being your best self. Amen.

Music
Thuma Mina (Send Me Jesus)
    Words and Music: South African
    THUMA MINA

Lord, Whose Love Through Humble Service
    Words: Albert F. Bayly, 1961
    Music: attr. B. F. White, 1844; harm. Ronald A. Nelson, 1978
    BEACH SPRING

Sois la Samilla (You Are The Seed)
    Words: Caesaro Gabaraín, 1979; trans. Raquel Gutiérrez-Achon and Skinner Chávez-
        Melo
    Music: Caesaro Gabaraín, 1979; harm. Skinner Chávez-Melo, 1987
    ID Y ENSEÑAD

Epiphany 8
Ordinary Time 8

Sirach 24:4-7 or Isaiah 55:10-13   1 Corinthians 15:51-58
Psalm 92:1-4, 12-15   Luke 6:39-49

Wisdom comes from God; wisdom is with God forever.
Who can count raindrops or sand?
Who can count the days of eternity?
How high is the sky? How wide the earth?
How deep is the ocean?
Can anyone answer these questions?
To honor God is a heartfelt delight ...
To honor God is the first step to wisdom
And wisdom satisfies us completely....
— Wisdom of Jesus, Son of Sirach 1:1-13 (paraphrased)

Call To Worship

Leader: It's Sunday again! So soon! It's good to be together. It's a good day to praise God and to catch up with one another. In our scriptures today, there are verses from Sirach in the apocrypha that describe conversation: "Never praise anyone until you hear that person talk!"

People: **We talk with each other often, and we are aware that our words indicate our characters and our attitudes about life.**

Leader: We can be honest with one another about our thoughts, and we can be honest with God about our doubts!

People: **We choose not to be with people who insult others or start arguments.**

Leader: Together, we are authentic. We will listen for the Word from God, and we will respond in one way or another!

People: **Let's pray and sing!**

Prayer Of Thanksgiving (Leader)

Awesome God — we are grateful for words with which to think and communicate. We are glad you speak to make things begin and end — and continue in the middle. We are friends and neighbors, visitors and regulars; we gladly listen for your voice and respond from our heads and our hearts. Amen.

Call To Confession (Leader)

Come everyone who is thirsty. Come, God says, and I will give you life! This is an opportunity to be still and to meet God. Let's pray together and then make our individual prayers silently.

Community Confession (Unison)

Living God — how good it is to be aware of your constant love each morning!

We hear the promise of scripture that the righteous will flourish like trees.

We look inside us and realize we are not always righteous.

We do not always do what Jesus says we should do — love our enemies or reach out with a helping hand.

Free us from the angst that comes when we avoid being consistent in our following the teachings of Christ.

We do long for abundant life.

Be our strength and our joy! Amen.

Word Of Grace (Leader)

It is life we want! But in our living and in our dying, God is with us. With God's help you can feel steady and meet each day's requirements with energy. Let it be so.

Sermon Idea

Today's readings give us more Sermon on the Plain/Mount. Like last week, we are encouraged not to use our time and energy complaining or even critiquing others; rather, we are to be hospitable and gracious. A title/theme might be: Tools for Construction, because knowing the teachings of Jesus and doing them builds a life that is satisfying. Tools include fruits of the Spirit and self-discipline. Our reputations are important, too, and often precede us in social settings. We are known by how we speak and how we interact with others. Jesus says that a good person demonstrates goodness in attitudes, in conversation, and in actions. Good attitudes are tools for construction that stand even when overwhelmed by financial crises, disease, disappointment, and loss. All of today's texts talk about being steady and holding onto faith in Christ; Paul attempts to diminish fear of death but raises some issues that are contrary to real contemporary human emotion. Death may take us to our eternal home but for those left behind there is hurt. The victory in death is that suffering has ended for the one who is absent from the body. The Isaiah passage is an antidote to Paul: come everyone who is thirsty; life can be experienced. Jesus is an antidote: I have come so that you may have life. Building a lifestyle as described by Jesus in the Sermon on the Plain/Mount gives us meaning and satisfaction.

Another possible title/theme might be a local bumper sticker: Be Good for Goodness Sake. Religion (say the atheists) is not the source of moral and ethical, wise and practical information.

Contemporary Affirmation (Unison)

Words are important as we speak about God; they reveal the attitudes we hold about faith and about life.

Action is important when we claim to be disciples of Jesus; our words and our behaviors must match and demonstrate compassion.

Hospitality is important when we invite people to consider following the teachings of Jesus. Neighborliness is a requirement according to the stories Jesus tells.

In our living and our dying, we are comforted and sustained by the Holy Spirit, Divine Presence in the world. Let it be so!

Offertory Statement (Leader)

Jesus says in the Sermon on the Plain/Mount that new wine needs new containers! Old wine mellows or sours in the aging process. Our personalities are like aging wine. But our imaginations are like new wine! New containers, new options, new dreams take resources; at the same time, there are services we want to continue within our community. Let us provide the money, skills, and time.

Doxology   God, Whose Giving Knows No Ending, tune: BEACH SPRING
　　God, whose giving knows no ending, from your rich and endless store,
　　Nature's wonder, Jesus' wisdom, costly cross, grave's shattered door;
　　Gifted by you, we turn to you, offering up ourselves in praise,
　　Thankful song shall rise forever, gracious donor of our days.

Prayer Of Thanksgiving (Leader)
　　Christ, our Teacher — the images you have used inspire us — wine, bread, houses on rocks — and we are grateful. The breath of life and the resources around us help build a sturdy home for the Spirit. Let us reach out to serve our friends and our enemies. Amen.

Intercessory Prayer (Leader or Readers)
　　Holy Spirit — we hear news from around this planet. It is not news about people being kind and generous. It is not about Divine Presence making life fresh and hopeful. Peacefulness and sharing resources are not in the news, either. Something of heaven on earth doesn't show up on television airwaves. In short, the teachings of Jesus and the behaviors he suggested have not made humankind neighborly nor peaceful. We pray for leaders who are honest, insightful, and diligent about benevolent governments in our own country and throughout the global village. We pray for peace among the tribes on every continent.
　　Holy Spirit — we look around us and recognize that love has various ways of showing up. With and without legal documents, we accept those people different from ourselves. We appreciate the rainbow of skin colors and the range of sexual and gender differences. Mature us to be consistently welcoming and genuinely friendly people.
　　Holy Spirit — made in the image of God, we say; cocreators, we like to think; friends of Jesus, we assure ourselves. Expand our imaginations so we can build places and attitudes that let us glimpse the kingdom of heaven.
　　Holy Spirit — we hear the scriptures urging us to reach out to people who are experiencing difficult times. In pain and in emotional turmoil, we long for relief and healing. Stressed by jobs or joblessness, by diminishing paying power, we turn to you for guidance. We turn to one another for encouragement. Live through us as creativity, kindness, and hospitality. Amen.

Benediction (Leader)
　　Your reputation is a precious thing; keep it fresh and vibrant.
　　Your words, like the Word, make things happen; be careful how you speak.
　　Your lifestyle speaks about what is important to you; live the precepts of Jesus.
　　Your thoughts guide your behavior; may you be open minded, curious, and capable of holding opposites in balanced tension.
　　Go as peacemakers, intent on helping build the kingdom of God!

Music

Pues Si Vivimos (When We Are Living)
    Words: Stanza 1 anonymous; tr. Elise S. Eslinger, 1983; stanzas 2-4 Roberto Escamilla,
        1983; tr. George Lockwood, 1987
    Music: Traditional Spanish melody; harm. *Celebremos*, 1983
    SOMOS DEL SEÑOR

Come Down, O Love Divine
    Words: Bianco of Siena; trans. Richard F. Littledale, 1867, alt.
    Music: Ralph Vaughan Williams, 1906
    DOWN AMPNEY

God Of Grace And God Of Glory
    Words: Harry Emerson Fosdick, 1930
    Music: John Hughes, 1907
    CWM RHONDDA

We Are Called To Follow Jesus
    Words and Music: Jim Strathdee, 1978
    WE ARE CALLED

Epiphany 9
Ordinary Time 9

1 Kings 8:22-23, 41-43   Galatians 1:1-12
Psalm 96:1-9   Luke 7:1-10

They who sing pray twice.

— Saint Augustine

There are no strangers here; only friends you haven't met.

— William Butler Yeats

Call To Worship

Leader: Welcome, friends and strangers! Before the living God, we are simply human beings who gather to worship God with our thoughts, our music, and our words.

People: **We are glad for this place of prayer and for the welcome the Holy Spirit gives all of us.**

Leader: As we read the scriptures, we hear Solomon opening the new temple to people whose blood is not Jewish.

People: **And we hear Jesus saying we are to love our neighbors and our enemies — we think that includes strangers!**

Leader: Look around you. If you do not know the person next to you, share names so that you can converse after the benediction. Then, let's be united as people of God in prayer.

(Pause for people to introduce themselves to others.)

Prayer Of Thanksgiving (Leader)

Creating God — how exciting it is to gather here to listen for your voice and to meet new people! We've come with all the left-overs from last week — our sore muscles, our fears about the bank account, our anger with the neighbors.... We lay them aside and invite your Spirit to vitalize us with mercy and grace! We give you our undivided attention in our words and our thoughts. Amen.

Call To Confession (Leader)

Remember the things that trouble you. These next moments are an opportunity to give them to God and to feel free of angst, guilt, and shame.

Community Confession (Unison)

Living God — our human nature is prone to do things that are not helpful to ourselves or to others.

When we do things or plan things that violate our internal sense of right, we are uncomfortable with ourselves.

Sometimes we carry great burdens.

Take them; take them all and let us be free and creative.

Reveal to us what in us is not aligned with your Spirit.
Straighten us, we pray. Amen.

Word Of Grace (Leader)

When we have named our cacophonous ways, God straightens us and sets us free. We can sing new lyrics and a new melody for ourselves and for God.

Sermon Idea

A title/theme might be: Builder Expects Visitors to Experience the Divine, playing off the 1 Kings story where Solomon builds a temple and then prays that everyone, especially strangers, would pray and have their prayers heard. Another title/theme might be: Old Manuscripts Divulge Good News, suggesting that the ancient hope of the Davidic line was to include all ethnic groups in worship events for Yahweh throughout the Ancient Near East. What a different world Jesus would have inherited and we would be experiencing today if that hope had been realized.

The apostle Paul writes of one God, one gospel, one Christ and we know that he understood Gentiles to be included in the one God's love and grace. The psalmist talks about expressing the human emotions in music while Luke suggests that strangers expect Yahweh God to be kind and helpful because the people who worship Yahweh have the reputation of being helpful.

It's our wide, and maybe wild, dream that the teachings of Jesus will empower people to try out neighborliness rather than warfulness. Fences and guns do not give anyone security or peace. Large beautiful buildings do stand for a century or two and satisfy the human need for a sense of permanence and connectedness with the past while we look ahead.

The Lukan text could be applied to an individual's personal health. Psychology tells us that people who express their emotions are usually happier than people who repress them. And who knows — maybe God gets tired of old, complaining songs and would like to hear some new ones!

Contemporary Affirmation (Unison)

Jesus of Nazareth aligned himself with God whom he called Father.

The Holy Spirit is a divine gift that lives within us allowing us to be cocreators with God.

God is the creator of all that is; God invites us to work and pray, sing and play so that a new reign can come to earth.

We are people of God, eager to make this world a benevolent home for all creatures.
Let us take hope and wisdom into the world. Amen. Let it be so!

Offertory Statement (Leader)

Though we are eager to help the kingdom of God manifest, we need skills, supplies, and money. Let's fill the baskets!

Doxology   Great Are Your Mercies (v. 1), tune: SONG OF THE HOE

Great are your mercies, O my Maker,
Food and raiment You freely bestow.
Let me praise you always, Serve you all my days.
You the spring wind, I the grass; On me blow!

Prayer Of Thanksgiving (Leader)

We do sing — new songs and old songs, songs of joy and songs of sadness. We sing of abundance and need. We are grateful we come together to collaborate with your hopes for a new world. We are grateful for all the resources we need to make something of heaven here on earth. Amen.

Intercessory Prayer (Leader or Readers)

God of Music — there are so many songs we can sing, so many words we can speak, so many tears we shed. We are made in your image; do you too cry and rejoice? Grieve and celebrate? You know us before we are born and support us through life when we let you. We pray for people whose songs are violent and ugly, who don't have their basic life needs met. We pray for persons whose songs mourn losses we can't understand. And we pray for ourselves. Renew our songs of praise and delight; sustain our long notes and make our quick ones graceful.

God of Sacred Spaces — we believe that when and where two or three people gather to praise and pray, you are there. So we pray for loveliness and peace everywhere men and women, boys and girls turn to you. In temples, on hillsides, on playgrounds, in classrooms — let each of us feel loved and appreciated. In countries where war is the habit, find a way to let peace overwhelm the violence so that even the ground is made sacred.

God of Profane Spaces — when we think of you as Creator of all the universe, we cannot imagine any place where you would not go. In your presence, strangers can become friends over cups of tea, mothers and fathers can learn patience playing tennis, boys and girls can learn to negotiate peacefully over a chess board. Individuals seeking friends might even find them at a bar. Wherever people seek goodness and respect, be among them offering them the Spirit of love.

God of Workers — it seems that since Eden, some people have been powerful and some have been powerless. Some have learned to prosper; some have learned the art of loving; some have learned the advantages of positive thinking. Since Eden, it seems that some people are at the bottom of the pay scale and some are at the top with most of us in between. We pray for a more equal society so that everyone can have a job that is not boring and so everyone can have wholesome food on their tables. Amen. Let it be so.

Benediction (Leader)

As you leave this space, be aware that you have healing in your fingers,
    kindness on your tongue, respect in your ears
    and compassion in your thoughts.
You have received them as gifts from the Creator.
Give them to others you meet on your pathway his week and sing a new song! Amen.

Music

We Gather Together
    Words: Nederlandtsche Gedenckclanck, 1626; trans. Theodore Baker, 1894; adapt. Ruth
        Duck, 1981
    Music: Dutch melody; arr. Edward Kremser, 1877
    KREMSER

Gather Us In
    Words and Music: Marty Haugen, 1981
    GATHER US IN

God Made All People Of The World
    Words: Hyn Sul Hong, 1967; tr. David Kim and Chang Hee Son
    Music: Shin Young Ahn
    ONE WORLD

The Transfiguration Of Our Lord
(Last Sunday After Epiphany)

Exodus 34:29-35   2 Corinthians 3:12—4:2
Psalm 99   Luke 9:28-36 (37-43)

> *A single song is being inflected through all the colorations of the human choir.*
> *The way to become human is to recognize the lineaments of God in all the won-*
> *derful modulations of the face [of humankind].*
> — Joseph Campbell, *The Hero With a Thousand Faces*

Call To Worship

Leader: Greetings, this last Sunday in Epiphany!

People: The calendar says we celebrate "transfiguration" today.

Leader: "Transfiguration" — what does such an idea mean to you and me?

People: Something about "dazzling light" or "brilliant aura"!

Leader: The story says that Jesus radiated divine energy and the disciples with him on the mountain were impressed!

People: Just as the Hebrews in the wilderness were awed when they saw Moses with the Decalogue!

Leader: We, too, want an experience with the Holy so we are enlightened and can be illuminating!

People: Let's ask for that to happen:

All: Holy Spirit — we are captivated by the idea that you satisfy our minds and our souls! We know that Moses and Elijah and Jesus kindled the imaginations of their companions. Ignite us so we glisten with your presence. Amen.

Call To Confession (Leader)

Consider your body language and facial expression.

What does it say about your interior self? Take a moment to notice what is going on in your psyche and body.

Let's pray together and then continue our conversations with the Holy Mystery in silence.

Community Confession (Unison)

Light Divine — we want to reflect your creativity and hospitality in our daily activities but our minds get blurred.

Transfigure our world weariness to spirited gentleness, work, and play.

Transform our dullness into dynamic brightness.

Translate our worn images into vibrant symbols of your presence.

Transpose our habitual attitudes into harmonious lyrics and rhythms to give us and others pleasure.

Transfer our self-absorption to respect for the planet and all its creatures. Amen.

Sermon Idea

Lay the lectionary texts beside each other. All speak of an external *something* that people identified as *holy*.

Not then and not now can light, auras, and energy fields be boxed, "templed" or "museumed." They are temporary, ephemeral, transient, unstable, and unpredictable.

Yet, we long for radiance to engulf us. And when we have such an experience, we seek it again. Perhaps we can describe the experience as "being in the heart of God." Hildegard of Bingen and all the mystics wrote about being encompassed by Holy light, by the heart of God.

What images today convey the idea and the experience of an ecstatic experience with The Holy?

Contemporary Affirmation (Unison)

God is creative Energy at work throughout the cosmos.

Jesus was unified with God and radiated divine love.

Christ-light motivates us to shine goodness into moral darkness, cynicism, and poverty.

Holy Spirit keeps the light bright in us, coaxing us to be gentle, patient, kind, respectful, humble, joyful, and self-controlled.

As a community of seekers, we support each other on this journey called "Life."

Offertory Statement (Leader)

We have enough of everything to share.

Doxology   Praise God From Whom All Blessings Flow, tune: OLD HUNDREDTH

Praise God from whom all blessings flow.
Praise God, all creatures here below.
Praise God above, you heavenly hosts.
Creator, Christ, and Holy Ghost.

Prayer Of Thanksgiving (Unison)

Great Mystery — thank you for light that dazzles us unexpectedly.

Thank you for the insight to make decisions in keeping with our own integrity and sense of your presence.

Thank you for all the resources that enhance daily living.

Use us and our gifts as needed to make your love present in this world. Amen.

Intercessory Prayers (Leader or Readers)

Fascinating God — when darkness threatens, radiate your light among us. Where darkness invades streets with harmful substances and terror, glimmer hope through living wages and empowering relationships. Where past interpretations of scriptures betray your lively grace, sparkle varied images for living faithfully today. Where dogmatic attitudes circumscribe your creative imagination, shine through cracks till no rigid corners are left in any religion or in any family or in any culture.

Mesmerizing God — we long to be at rest with your contemporary Spirit! Heal our hurts; soothe our pain, comfort us in lonely hours. Help us and our children learn what is necessary to thrive in this world; integrate technology, expanding truth, and awareness of suffering into our experience with your grace. Help us look again at the teachings of Jesus and his choice to die. Give us insight for modern times and for our individual lives. Amen.

Benediction (Leader)

Our time of sanctuary is ended.

It's time to go into our worlds with the insights we've received.

Go, as collaborators, radiating the light of Holiness.

Let your aura shine so you and others have a clear path for the next day's journey!

Hallelujah!

Music

Every Time I Feel The Spirit
  Words: African-American spiritual
  Music: African-American spiritual; adapt. and arr. William Farley Smith, 1986
  PENTECOST

Jesus On The Mountain Peak
  Words: Brian Wren, 1962, 1988
  Music: Cyril Vincent Taylor, b. 1907
  MOWSLEY

O Come And Dwell In Me
  Words: Charles Wesley, 1762
  Music: Genevan Psalter, 1551; adapt. William Crotch, 1836
  ST. MICHAEL

O Holy Spirit, Root Of Life
  Words: Jean Janzen, 1991, based on the writings of Hildegard of Bingen (12th century)
  Music: Trier manuscript (15th century); adapt. Michael Praetorius, 1609; harm. George
    R. Woodward, 1904
  PUER NOBIS NASCITUR

O Wondrous Sight! O Vision Fair
  Words: Sarum Brevary, 1495; trans. John Mason Neale, 1851
  Music: William Knapp, 1738; harm. from Hymns Ancient and Modern, 1874
  WAREHAM

Swiftly Pass The Clouds Of Glory
  Words: Thomas H. Troeger, 1985
  Music: George Henry Day, 1940
  GENEVA

Transform Us
    Words: Sylvia Dunstan, 1989
    Music: Traditional French melody (17th century); harm. The English Hymnal, 1906
    PICARDY

Wind Who Makes All Winds That Blow
    Words: Thomas H. Troeger, 1983
    Music: Joseph Parry, 1879
    ABERYSTWYTH

Season 4
Lent

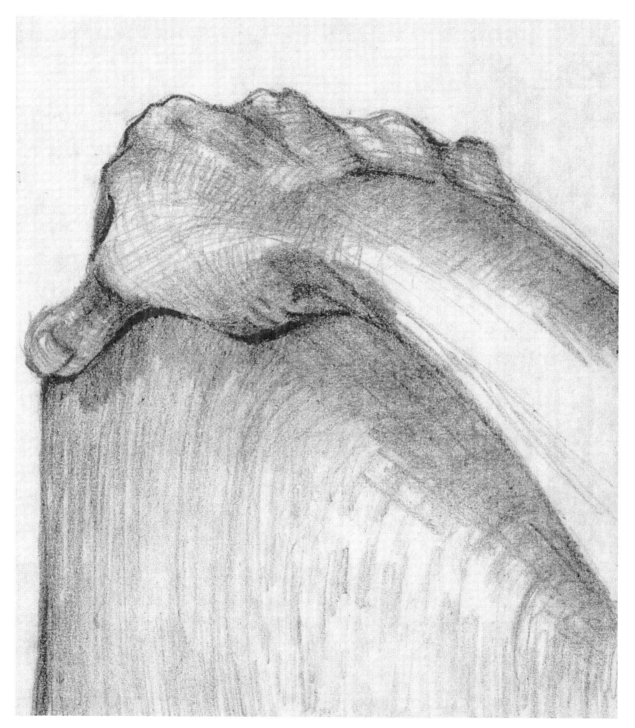

No Motion

Ash Wednesday

Joel 2:1-2, 12-17   2 Corinthians 5:20b—6:10
Psalm 51:1-17   Matthew 6:1-6, 16-21

> *A single song is being reflected through all the colorations of the human choir.*
> *The way to become human is to recognize the lineaments of God in all the won-*
> *derful modulations of the face [of humankind].*
> — Joseph Campbell, *The Hero With a Thousand Faces*

Note: This service is an abbreviated order so that people who are taking time from work can stay within their allotted time off. Also, the whole service is somber, including the music, so it ought not be too long.

Call To Worship

(During Lent, count the Sundays with a candelabrum holding six purple candles and one white candle. For Ash Wednesday, light these candles during the Call To Worship.)

Leader: Today is Ash Wednesday, following last evening's "shroving" festivities. This is a transition time; we're preparing to conclude winter activities so we can welcome spring.

People: **We are marking the passage of time by remembering that eternity is behind us and before us. In Jesus of Nazareth we see the creating God, like a mother and a father, guiding us through time to eternity.**

Leader: In this hour, we celebrate life and articulate our fascination with death.

People: **We declare again that through every season we are intentional friends of Jesus. With some dread, we anticipate the week we call "holy."**

Leader: Fortunately we know the whole story! For now, let us consider how we bear God in our international neighborhoods.

People: **We acknowledge the sign of the cross as a symbol of God reaching to us and our stretching toward one another.**

Leader: It is an ancient symbol of suffering and death.

People: **The cross is a contemporary symbol of Divine Presence with Jesus and with us in all our suffering.**

Prayer Of Thanksgiving (Leader, Unison during The Lord's Prayer)

Living God — thank you for your dependable presence. We are grateful you do not withhold information about our human journey through time. We are glad we know the whole story of Jesus' living, dying, and rising to new life. We recognize our humanity and our mortality as we remember who he was. Make real for us his prayer; inspire us as we look at the cross and wear it as a sign of our loyalty and gratitude. **Our Father who ...**

Call To Confession (Leader)

On this day/night, we make opportunity to focus on the decisions Jesus made long ago. It is opportunity, too, to consider the decisions we make day-by-day: Are they consistent with the gospel? What needs to change within our attitudes and priorities to feel God's affirmation? You are my child; I am pleased with you. Let our prayers be spoken on the right side and on the left.

Community Prayer (Antiphonal)

Left: Gracious God — thank you for Jesus of Nazareth and his willingness to challenge the systems of his day that blocked your love for humankind.

Right: Transform our *laissez-faire* attitudes that permit injustice to continue in our communities.

Left: Reshape our interpretations of bondage to include wealth and poverty.

Right: Liberate us from poverty of soul.

Left: Reconnect us with the source of meaning and purpose.

Right: Free us from guilt and shame that cloud our thinking.

All: Help us to be authentic friends of Jesus who confront inequality, miserliness, and greed. Empower us to manifest your flexible compassion. Amen.

Sermon Idea

Look at the hands throughout this book. Consider the quotes at the beginning of each section. Time is too slow or too fast for most of us on any given day. In this twenty-first century, we can imagine our DNA to be divine or our ligaments to connect with the holy. However we understand our humanness, we must be aware that we make choices and the maturing person makes those choices fully aware of the costs and the rewards. Agony and ecstasy are two ends of a continuum. Jesus made his choices. Agony seems to have been lingering. Ecstasy came later as he made breakfast for his friends and walked with them to Emmaus. Today, Ash Wednesday, asks us to declare again our loyalties. Will we live conscious of Holy Presence as we trek through each day's options? Will we speak and behave in ways consistent with Divine Presence? Will we trust that after the agony, the suffering, the pain, the loss, there will arise a newness of life? Jesus tried to prepare his disciples for impending disaster. They refused to take in his words. We must be intentional about our choices if we are to be different from those first-century friends. We know the whole story and our hands are in motion as we tell it!

Contemporary Affirmation (Unison)

We believe that the Creator of the Universe is at work with us guiding us to live by the teachings of Jesus: Judge not; make peace; be merciful....

We experience the presence of Divine Mystery as we navigate this worldly trek through sorrows and joys, choosing to align ourselves with the Holy Presence.

We believe Jesus of Nazareth walked this journey centuries ago and endured death on a cross and burial in a cave. The end of his story gives us hope: He was raised to new life!

We acknowledge that we are made from dust and to dust we will return; we also declare that we are his friends, enduring the ashes of our disappointments. Wearing the cross like a tattoo we say that we will not participate in violence but choose life!

(The Lord's Supper can be served.)

Prayer (Leader)

Eternal God — thank you for loving us and all creation and for never abandoning us. Thank you for Jesus who understood human bondage and sought to free us all. For his awareness that we all long to return to the source of good, we are grateful. For his understanding that the human situation includes wrong behaviors and dreadful consequences, we thank you.

Give us patience to be relieved of slavery to anyone or anything; give us patience to return to the soul's home; give us patience to be redirected in holy living. Amen.

Benediction (Leader)
(If darkness is preferred, all lights can be extinguished except the candelabrum. Leader invites people to come, when they are ready, to receive ashes on the hand or forehead and to return to their work/home/leisure.)

Leader: Wear the ashes as a reminder and a declaration of your determination to live consciously, aware of your times of brokenness and your times of wholeness, grateful for God's sustaining presence.

Music

Abide With Me
    Words: Henry F. Lyte, 1847
    Music: William Henry Monk, 1861
    EVENTIDE

Forty Days And Forty Nights
    Words: George H. Smyttan, 1856, alt.
    Music: Attr. Martin Herbst, 1676
    HEINLEIN

Have Mercy On Us, Living Lord
    Words: Fred R. Anderson, 1986
    Music: Hal H. Hopson, 1983
    PTOMY

How Long, O God, How Long
    Words: Thomas H. Troeger, 1991
    Music: Brent Stratten, 1993
    TAFT STREET

In The Bulb There Is A Flower
    Words and Music: Natalie Sleeth, 1986
    PROMISE

Steal Away To Jesus
    Words and Music: African-American spiritual
    STEAL AWAY

Swing Low, Sweet Chariot
    Words: African-American spiritual
    Music: African-American spiritual; arr. Bill Thomas, 1994
    SWING LOW

Lent 1

Deuteronomy 26:1-11   Romans 10:8b-13
Psalm 91:1-2, 9-16   Luke 4:1-13

You shall pass judgment on yourself. That is the hardest thing of all ...
If you succeed in judging yourself, it is because you are truly wise.
                                          (The king on a planet to the prince)
                                          — Saint Exupery, *The Little Prince*

Call To Worship

Leader: You're here! Winter is upon us and things seem very still. But we know that dormancy hides the workings of life soon to erupt into spring! Six weeks of Epiphany and transfiguration are finished, and we find ourselves with ash smudges on our heads and hands.

(Candles can be lighted to count the Sundays until Easter.)

People: **It surely does slow us down when we consider how our lives are spent and how we manifest God's loving presence! Taking seriously our own suffering and the pain of the world demands a lot of prayer and stillness.**

Leader: During the silently lengthening days, we will accentuate the goodness that lies within us. We will promote awareness of Holy Presence, and we will modify our goals and values.

People: **In the spring light, we will let go of old guilt and as Easter comes, we will relish new energies in nature and in our own psyches.**

Leader: A Divine Message comes to us in the ancient story of Jesus of Nazareth: God is One who blesses each person who seeks.

People: **We are searching to live in ways which satisfy us and serve the Holy One throughout every season of our lives.**

Prayer Of Thanksgiving (Unison)

Living God — for every goodness of every season of life, we are grateful. Thank you for being with us in times of disaster and violence, in times of upheaval and stillness. During these winter days leading to resurrection celebration, we stop our scurrying so we can be attentive to our mortality. Create in us a tip-toe breathlessness so we can take in your work. Our attention turns to you and we listen for your voice. Amen.

Call To Confession (Leader)

There are times in our lives when we struggle with what is good and what is evil. There are times when we are aimless and have difficulty balancing the goods of our culture with the truth of our own hearts. In these moments of silence, welcome the Spirit to put things in right order.

Community Confession (Unison)

Holy One — our minds are open before you.
When temptations come — for they surely will — give us clarity about your will for our lives.

When idols sneak into our thoughts and activities, remind us not to toy with your grace and power.
Nurture our souls with words and silences, with relationships and fresh opportunities.
We walk the human path Jesus walked; grant us insight to be faithful. Amen.

Congregational Choral Response Dear God And Father Of Mankind (v. 4)

Drop thy still dews of quietness Till all our strivings cease;
Take from our souls the strain and stress
And let our ordered lives confess The beauty of thy peace.

Sermon Idea

We know who our ancestors were and we know that some of them were not particularly nice. The patriarchal stories have plots, which have produced violence for women as well as for other groups. Land-grabbing and wars continue thousands of years later out of these ancient nomadic families. One bit of good news from Jesus is that we can stop replicating their plots and crimes. Harvest gifts to the temple nullified the suffering and hardship of survival. Perhaps. But presenting offerings to the church and to God do not cancel out our bribery and disrespect for one another and for the earth. Phyllis Trible's *Texts of Terror*, Anita Diamant's *The Red Tent*, and J. S. Spong's *The Sins of Scriptures* provide many ideas for developing Lenten themes of temptation, suffering, and guilt in contemporary interpretations of ancient sacred stories. In Luke 4, Jesus resists old and new arguments for self-gratification and aggrandizement. The challenge for us is to be aware of what has shaped our understandings of God and follow the Christ into new patterns for gratitude and celebration, for relationships and rituals.

Contemporary Affirmation (Unison)

The Holy comes to us in many different ways.

God continues to create in and around us, leading us to food for our souls and our bodies.

We find courage in Jesus of Nazareth who resisted the temptations that come to humankind: power over others, material wealth that obscures divine goodness, and arrogance that resists attention to divine presence.

With Holy Spirit enthusing us, we choose to live in ways that are hospitable and gracious, insightful and generous in kind deeds.

Together, we have a significant voice in our culture to demand justice for all.

In our living and in our dying, we are not alone. God is with us. Amen.

Offertory Statement (Leader)

Making the world a better place and brightening this corner of town are happening because we are blessed. Ministry in this place continues because you faithfully give money to pay the electricity, the water, and repair the walls. Ministry continues here because you give yourself to God. Our plates are big enough to receive what you can put on them.

Doxology O Love, How Deep, How Broad, How High (v. 5, modified)
tune: DEO GRACIAS

All glory to the living God for love so deep, so high, so broad;
The Trinity whom we adore forever and forever more.

Prayer For Thanksgiving (Leader)

Praise to you, Holy One, from all of us —
For dawn and dusk, for stillness and liveliness,
For time and resources enough to share.
Praise to you for grace spilling over all creatures. Amen.

Intercessory Prayers (Leader or Readers)

Fathering God — Jesus of Nazareth trusted you to bring something good out of difficult circumstances. We, too, have learned that sometimes in the midst of suffering and usually after the worst is over, some new hope, some fresh understanding emerges from our depths. Continue to work within us and this congregation so that we are bearers of fairness and equality. Continue to work among us so that children throughout this global village are educated and nourished with information and skills, civility and collaboration.

Mothering God — Jesus of Nazareth trusted you to establish a neighborly way of being in the world. We, too, want the kingdom of heaven to come to earth. Halt warring factions where they are festering. Halt behaviors that maim and starve children. Halt indoctrination that bruises souls. Bring an end to the evils that pit one country against another. Bring an end to struggles for land and water; enable all humankind to share what is available.

Majestic God — we do appreciate the mountains and oceans, the sand and rocks, the water and sky! We marvel at the whole expanding universe! And we marvel at what our bodies can and can't do. Cure us or heal us with a full awareness of your presence. Soothe our pains and give us strength to endure until our time on this human journey is complete.

Judging God — you see how voraciously we consume the earth's resources — oil, trees, waters, air ... Before it is too late, give us self-discipline and our leaders wisdom so that we might be healthy and so we pass along to the next generations full oil and gas veins, productive land, nutritious seeds, clean air, unpolluted oceans, vital forests, and bright skies. Help us resist the temptation to think someone else will fix things.

God of all — see us through this winter and bring us happily to resurrection day. Amen.

Benediction (Leader)

May the road continue smooth before you;
May there be enough light along the way;
May peace greet you at every cross road
And joy accompany you to the end.
Through whatever pain and suffering is yours to endure
Know that God is in it with you.
Amid every temptation that comes to you
Be aware that wisdom is yours for the asking.

Music

Jesus Walked This Lonesome Valley
Words and Music: American spiritual
LONESOME VALLEY

My Song Is Love Unknown
Words: Samuel Crossman, 1664
Music: John Ireland, 1918
LOVE UNKNOWN

Pues Si Vivimos (When We Are Living)
Words: St. 1 anonymous; tr. Elise S. Eslinger, 1983; sts. 2-4 Roberto Escamilla, 1983; tr.
George Lockwood, 1987
Music: Traditional Spanish melody; harm. *Celebremos*, 1983; alt.
SOMOS DEL SEÑOR

We Meet You, O Christ
Words: Fred Kaan, 1966
Music: Carl F. Schalk, 1987
STANLEY BEACH

With The Wings Of Our Mind
Words: Ik-Wham Mun, Korea; tr. Marion Pope (20th century)
Music: Don-Whan Cho, Korea, alt. Francisco F. Feliciano
TTUGOUN MAUM

Lent 2

Genesis 15:1-12, 17–18   Philippians 3:17–4:1
Psalm 27   Luke 13:31-25

You shall pass judgment on yourself. That is the hardest thing of all ...
If you succeed in judging yourself, it's because you are truly wise.

(The king on a planet to the prince)
— Saint Exupery, *The Little Prince*

Call To Worship

Leader: You're here! Winter is still holding on and things seem very still this second Sunday in Lent. Fortunately, we know that whatever is happening around us, God is with us.

(Candles can be lighted to count the Sundays until Easter.)

People: **We have no reason to be afraid. We've asked God to teach us what to do and to lead us along safe paths.**

Leader: When we look at the world, we see soldiers and terrorists; we hear of violence. Still we trust God.

People: **We take seriously our own suffering and the pain of the world, and we do a lot of praying!**

Leader: Have faith and do not despair, the psalmist says!

People: **God has been our help; the Holy One will not abandon us!**

Leader: During the silently lengthening days, we practice our faith and we accentuate the goodness of God that lies within us.

People: **As we wait for Easter, we will enjoy the days and nights; we will praise God for life!**

Prayer Of Thanksgiving (Leader)

Living God — for the goodness of every season of life, we are grateful. We are thankful for the scriptures that encourage us as we take the journey through Lent to Resurrection. For the awareness of your presence, we praise you. In times of disaster and violence, in times of upheaval and stillness, in moments of joy and delight, we can feel your grace. In this hour, our attention turns to you and we listen carefully for your voice. Amen.

Call To Confession (Leader)

With words and silence, we take note of our thoughts and activities. What do we wish would have been different this past week? What gives us reason to rejoice? In these moments, feel the Spirit soothe and bless. Pray aloud with me and then continue your conversation silently with God.

Community Confession (Unison)

Holy One — our minds are open before you.
When temptations come — for they surely will — give us clarity about your hopes for our lives.

When idols sneak into our thoughts and activities, remind us not to play games with your grace and power.
Nurture our souls with words and silences, with relationships and fresh opportunities.
We walk the human path Jesus walked; grant us insight to be faithful. Amen.

Sermon Idea

A title/theme for Luke 9:28-36 might be Talking With the Past While Looking Ahead. Another idea to play with could be Mysterious Sky Lights; another might be Personal Auras. Apparently, Peter, James, and John found it boring to stay alert for history lessons and for esoteric conversations. Jesus asked his friends to be with him emotionally and mentally as he made a journey into the past for strength. They couldn't do it. Some of us cannot accommodate our friends either; but like Peter, James, and John, and even Old Testament Orpah, we can go at least part of the way. Consequently, those disciples missed the opportunity to support Jesus and to enter into the mystery of another dimension. When they did see the effect of other-worldly presence on Jesus, Peter wanted to box it, make a museum, set up a monument.... They didn't miss out entirely because a mysterious fog surrounded James, Peter, and John, as an other-worldly voice pierced the cloud and assured them that Jesus was the Son whom God had chosen. And they had better pay attention! They didn't understand so they kept quiet about their hilltop experience. How does this story interface with twenty-first-century discipleship? There's a lot we don't understand and we must learn to ponder without forming opinions. We may have strange experiences that simply cannot be documented or explained. That's okay. Language of the spirit often is not verifiable but is true nevertheless, like a myth is true and not necessarily factual. Synonyms for *transfiguration* work better for Western culture: transformation and morphing. *Translation* might work, too, since we have the movie *Lost in Translation*. Jesus' appearance was transformed; and in hindsight, James, Peter, and John could access the power of that experience for their own ministries. Can we do the same? Perhaps for contemporary seekers, this story alerts us to the wisdom in past heroes, to the human desire to be connected with that wisdom and support, and to the momentary mystery that points to the path that is ours to follow. And we don't have to understand it! To walk in the footsteps of Christ is sufficient for our own transformations.

Contemporary Affirmation (Unison)

The Holy comes to us in many different ways. God continues to create in and around us, leading us to food for our souls and our bodies.

We find courage in Jesus of Nazareth who resisted the temptations that come to humankind: power over others, material wealth that obscures divine goodness, and arrogance that resists attention to divine presence.

With the Holy Spirit enthusing us, we choose to live in ways that are hospitable and gracious, insightful and generous in kind deeds.

Together, we have a significant voice in our culture to demand justice for all.

In our living and in our dying, we are not alone. God is with us. Amen.

Offertory Statement (Leader)

Noticing light in our culture and identifying it as goodness from God is one of our tasks.
Hearing voices that proclaim justice and living by them is our task, too.
Sharing what we have to make life better for others is also our work.
Our energies, our moneys, our talents, and our time enable us to be faithful.

Doxology   O Love, How Deep, How Broad, How High (v. 5, modified)
                                                                                 tune: DEO GRACIAS

All glory to the living God for love so deep, so high, so broad;
The Trinity whom we adore forever and forever more.

Prayer Of Thanksgiving (Leader)

We thank you for clouds that remind us that we, like Jesus, are known by you. For voices that declare your affirmation, we rejoice. With resources enough to share, we honor you. Amen.

Intercessory Prayers (Leader or Readers)

Fathering God — the psalmist trusted you no matter what. Jesus of Nazareth trusted that you would bring something good out of difficult circumstances. We trust you, too, to bring good to America and Iraq, to China and Taiwan, to Nigeria and Darfur — and to all people. Let peace come to humankind of every nation and tribe. Work through powerful leaders to minimize poverty and homelessness throughout this global village. Speak through us to demand equalization of peoples and nations, of food supplies and electricity.

Mothering God — Jesus of Nazareth worked with you to establish a neighborly way of being in the world. We, too, want the kingdom of heaven to come to earth. Halt the plague of violence that blankets so much of Israel and the lands where Jesus walked. Expose fundamentalism that bruises souls and bodies in America and throughout global marketplaces.

Judging God — how odd it seems that while we know human life depends on air, water, and soil, we permit the forests to be cut and the aquifers to be polluted and the soil to be depleted! And more than that: Some people get rich and some people lose their homes! How odd it seems that nice words are spoken but actions are not nice at all! O God, help your human creatures wise up!

Majestic God — we are awed by the human body and mind; we are amazed at what science can do to extend life. We grow pensive when we are faced with what our bodies can and can't do. Heal us with a full awareness of your presence. Help us accept mortality as the step to eternity with you. Give us strength to endure until our human journey is complete.

God of All Life — winter will soon be over; we look forward to resurrection day. Amen.

Benediction (Leader)

(The candles counting the Sundays in Lent can be extinguished.)

May the road continue smooth before you;
May there be enough light along the way;
May peace greet you at every cross road
And joy accompany you to the end.
Through whatever pain and suffering is yours to endure
Know that God is in it with you.
Amid every temptation that comes to you
Be aware that wisdom is yours for the asking.

Music

Bring Many Names
    Words: Brian Wren, 1987
    Music: Carlton R. Young, 1987
    WESTCHASE

O Love, How Deep, How Broad, How High
    Words: attr. Thomas à Kempis (1380-1471); trans. Benjamin Webb and John Mason
        Neale, 1851, alt.
    Music: "The Agincourt Song," England, c. 1415; based on E. Power Biggs, 1947; arr.
        Richard Proulx (b. 1937)
    DEO GRACIAS

Saranam, Saranam (Refuge)
    Words: Trad. Pakistani; trans. D. T. Niles, 1963
    Music: Trad. Punjabi melody; arr. Shanti Rasanayagam, 1962
    PUNJABI

We Utter Our Cry
    Words: Fred Kaan, 1983
    Music: Panderborn Gesangbuch, 1765; harm. Sydney H. Nicholson, 1916
    PADERBORN

Where Cross The Crowded Ways Of Life
    Words: Frank Mason North, 1903; adapt. Ruth Duck, 1981
    Music: William Gardiner's Sacred Melodies, 1815
    GERMANY

Lent 3

Isaiah 55:1-9   2 Corinthians 10:1-13
Psalm 63:1-8   Luke 13:1-9

You shall pass judgment on yourself. That is the hardest thing of all ...
If you succeed in judging yourself, it is because you are truly wise.
                                        (The king on a planet to the prince)
                                        — Saint Exupery, *The Little Prince*

Call To Worship

Leader: Good morning! This is the place to be if you are seeking the Holy One. This is the place to be if you long to be "at home." This is the place to praise the living God!
People: Thank God for this faith family and for this place of safety and inspiration.
Leader: Thank God for the scriptures that encourage our journey together: Come, everyone who is thirsty — here is water!
People: We are here to honor the Creator of the universe and to listen again for guidance for our days and nights.
Leader: Come, all of you who search for satisfaction in life.
People: We turn to God, knowing that divine thoughts are not our thoughts and Holy ways are not our ways. We ask God for mercy and direction.
Leader: Together, we sing and pray; together we expect the Holy One to move among us.
People: Together and individually, we ask God to be present in our world through our thinking and our doing!
(The candles can be lighted, including the Christ candle.)

Prayer Of Thanksgiving (Leader or Unison)

Living God — we are grateful that you make your home with humankind. Body, mind, and soul, we are glad you are here loving us and inspiring us to make your kingdom visible. We feel your presence and we listen for your guidance. Share our joy in this hour and satisfy our hearts. Amen.

Call To Confession (Leader)

There are times when it is not easy to know what is good and what is evil. There are times when we lose our way. In these moments of silence, welcome the Spirit to soothe and guide.

Community Confession (Unison)

Holy One — our minds are open before you.
When temptations come, give us clarity about your will for our lives.
When idols sneak into our thoughts and activities, remind us not to tamper with your grace and power.
Nurture our souls with words and silences, with relationships and fresh opportunities.
We walk the human path Jesus walked; grant us insight to be faithful. Amen.

Sermon Idea

Using Psalm 63, the sermon might explore contemporary yearnings for spiritual satisfaction, touching on the various religions, and concluding with the Christian plan. Consider aspects of our culture that "dry us out," coming back to the psalmist's feeling that we are in the "shadow of God's wings."

The psalm may indicate one way to deal with depression, sadness, and loneliness: verbalize the distress, imagine that God is present in a variety of ways — mother hen, protector, friend, stabilizing rock — and respond with music that touches all the emotions, ending with songs of joy. The psalm reminds us again and again that we are not able to travel this human way alone; we must seek sanctuary and companions.

Contemporary Affirmation (Unison)

The Holy comes to us in many different ways. God continues to create in and around us, leading us to food for our souls and our bodies.

We find courage in Jesus of Nazareth who resisted the temptations that come to humankind: power over others, material wealth that obscures divine goodness, and arrogance that resists attention to divine presence.

With Holy Spirit enthusing us, we choose to live in ways that are hospitable and gracious, insightful and generous in kind deeds.

Together, we have a significant voice in our culture to demand justice for all.

In our living and in our dying, we are not alone. God is with us. Amen.

Offertory Statement (Leader)

Making the world a better place and brightening this corner of town happen because we are blessed. Ministry in this place continues because you faithfully give money to pay the electricity, the water, and repair the walls. Ministry continues here because you give yourself to God.

Doxology

O Love, How Deep, How Broad, How High (v. 5, modified)
tune: DEO GRACIAS

All glory to the living God for love so deep, so high, so broad;
The Trinity whom we adore forever and forever more.

Prayer Of Thanksgiving (Leader)

With mind and body, we praise you, Holy One. We have received inspiration and we are satisfied.

For your constant love and for resources enough to share we give you thanks. Amen.

Intercessory Prayers (Leader or Readers)

Fathering God — life demands that we make choices, that we make decisions about how to buy and sell, how to help and halt, how to serve and be served. We turn to you for clarity. Work through us to halt the terror we feel. With your "right hand," stop the greed for power and material goods that grip our global village.

Mothering God — with your "left hand" compassion, feed the children of this planet; save the water and air so people and land can be healthy. Minister to life plagued with poverty in every nation. Come to leaders in each country and reveal the nasty reality of humanity without shelter, food, compassion, and mercy. Transform the human heart and mind throughout the planet. Move among us with healing for our physical aliments and for our emotional angst.

God of All Life — give us strength and wisdom to carry us along our human journey. Amen.

Benediction (Leader)

    May the road continue smooth before you;

    May there be enough light along the way;

    May peace greet you at every cross road

    And joy accompany you to the end.

    Through whatever pain and suffering is yours to endure

    Know that God is in it with you.

    Amid every temptation that comes to you

    Be aware that wisdom is yours for the asking.

Music

Come, All Of You
    Words: Laotian hymn; trans. Cher Lue Vang, 1987
    Music: Thai folksong
    SOI SON TUD

God, Who Touches Earth With Beauty
    Words: Mary S. Edgar, 1925, alt.
    Music: C. Harold Lowden (20th century)
    GENEVA

Healer Of Our Every Ill
    Words and Music: Marty Haugen, 1987
    HEALER

Holy And Good Is The Gift Of Desire
    Words: Thomas H. Troeger, 1988
    Music: Floyd Knight Jr., 1980
    ANGELIQUE

Out Of The Depths
    Words: Ruth Duck, 1988
    Music: Ann MacKenzie, 1988
    DEPTHS

Lent 4

Joshua 5:9-12   2 Corinthians 5:16-21
Psalm 32   Luke 15:1-3, 11b-32

You shall pass judgment on yourself. That is the hardest thing of all ...
If you succeed in judging yourself, it's because you are truly wise.

(The king on a planet to the prince)
— Saint Exupery, *The Little Prince*

Call To Worship

Leader: It's Sunday again! We're here in this sanctuary together! God, the Great Mystery is here, in and around us.

People: We revel in the signs of spring, knowing that God is still creating! We delight in this place of beauty and in the company of friends.

Leader: This day, like all days, is holy.

People: We praise God for freedoms, for pardon, and for hope that tomorrow is in God's hands and that we are being guided through time to eternity with Divinity.

Leader: The scriptures say that God will teach us the way to go, and we are warned not to be stubborn or cynical.

People: We receive Divine guidance and blessings with acute awareness and with gratitude.

Leader: Together, we enjoy God, now and forever!

(Candles can be lighted.)

Prayer Of Thanksgiving (Leader or Unison)

Living God — we are aware that we stand on holy ground and that here we are in the company of friends who explore ways to be faithful to your voice. Here we experience being new creatures in Christ. We are grateful for the enthusiasm that comes when our debilitating ways are gone and we have no need to judge others. We are aware that you befriend humankind, and we rejoice that you work through us to establish goodness throughout the global village. Amen.

Call To Confession (Leader)

The psalmist speaks of the relief that comes when we feel freed from deceit and wrongdoing. In these moments, we take time to see within ourselves what needs transforming.

Community Confession (Unison)

Holy One — our minds are open before you.
When temptations come — for they surely will — give us clarity about your hopes for our lives.
When idols sneak into our thoughts and activities, remind us not to play games with your grace and power.
Nurture our souls with words and silences, with relationships and fresh opportunities.
We walk the human path Jesus walked; grant us insight to be faithful. Amen.

110

Sermon Idea

Using Philippians and Luke, the sermon could explore who are heroes for Christians today and why. Preachers could also consider how Christians today could use their energies to confront government policies, which do not reach out to families living in poverty. The prophetic message might be that we are seduced by what seems to be truth from our government about justice and care for those in need. Preachers could check how the state of Georgia is doing with elective Bible courses for high school students (legislation in March 2006). Are the students beginning to understand underlying symbols in Western culture as well as literary and religious heroes? Is there understanding about the relationship between Israel, Palestine, and America?

Contemporary Affirmation (Unison)

The Holy comes to us in many different ways. God continues to create in and around us, leading us to food for our souls and our bodies.

We find courage in Jesus of Nazareth who resisted the temptations that come to humankind: power over others, material wealth that obscures divine goodness, and arrogance that resists attention to divine presence.

With the Holy Spirit enthusing us, we choose to live in ways that are hospitable and gracious, insightful and generous in kind deeds.

Together, we have a significant voice in our culture to demand justice for all.

In our living and in our dying, we are not alone. God is with us. Amen.

Offertory Statement (Leader)

When we are "joined to Christ" our attitudes are revised and our goals are transformed to be in sync with the ethics of the Sermon on the Mount. Sharing our resources is one way we participate in making the kingdom of God visible and tangible on this street corner and in various places around the world.

Doxology

O Love, How Deep, How Broad, How High (v. 5, modified)
tune: DEO GRACIAS

All glory to the living God for love so deep, so high, so broad;
The Trinity whom we adore forever and forever more.

Prayer Of Thanksgiving (Leader)

Thanks to you from all of us — for dawn and dusk, for stillness and liveliness. Thanks to you, Holy One, for resources of money and of creation. Our hands, feet, and voices are available to collaborate with you for justice and abundant living. Amen.

Intercessory Prayers (Leader or Readers)

Fathering God — as we search the scriptures, we are aware that you want humankind to be friends — neighbors — in Christ. How far we seem from that goal! So like your people before us, we pray for peaceful and neighborly living. Halt the fanaticism that spews violent judgment and destroys land and life. Help us as individuals and as a country behave in ways that bring about Christ-friendly societies around this globe no matter what the religious preferences.

Mothering God — look with compassion upon the pains we bear: debts, disappointments, multi-generational addictions, disabilities, and despair. Lift us beyond our cynicism to personal responsibility, self-discipline, and real hope. Set us on a path of satisfying relationship with your Spirit; empower us to live as friends of Jesus of Nazareth.

Majestic God — we do love the mountains and oceans, the sand and rocks, the water and sky! We marvel at the whole expanding universe! A part of us wants to think that we human creatures are the pinnacle of creation. Yet we are learning that all creatures and earth systems are interdependent. We are learning that within us is a tenacious connection between psyche and body. Open our eyes to wholesome development from life in the uterus until we take our last breath. Motivate us to cooperate with your healing Spirit.

God of All Life — throughout history, we see you providing resources for daily living. Like people before us, we make space and time, day and night to be aware of your sustaining grace. Thank you for bread and wine, for fruit and vegetables for our journey. Amen.

Benediction (Leader)
(The candles counting the Sundays in Lent can be extinguished.)
    May the road continue smooth before you;
    May there be enough light along the way;
    May peace greet you at every crossroad
    And joy accompany you to the end.
    Through whatever pain and suffering is yours to endure
    Know that God is in it with you.
    Amid every temptation that comes to you
    Be aware that wisdom is yours for the asking.

Music
How Blest Are Those
    Words: Fred R. Anderson, 1986
    Music: Memminger ms., 17th century; harm. George Ratcliffe Woodward, 1904
    ES FLOG EIN KLEINS WALDVÖGELEIN

The Spirit Of The Living God
    Words and Music: Daniel Iverson, 1926
    LIVING GOD

There Is A Balm In Gilead
    Words: African-American spiritual
    Music: African-American spiritual; arr. Harold Moyer
    BALM IN GILEAD

Lent 5

Isaiah 43:16-21   Philippians 3:4b-14
Psalm 126   John 12:1-8

You shall pass judgment on yourself. That is the hardest thing of all ...
If you succeed in judging yourself, it is because you are truly wise.

(The king on a planet to the prince)
— Saint Exupery, *The Little Prince*

Call To Worship

Leader: You're here! Winter seems displaced by the new growth of spring. This is the fifth
            Sunday in Lent — with one more to come: Palm Sunday.

(Candles counting the Sundays in Lent can be lighted.)

People: **We are glad for the longer days and enjoy later sunsets and the brightness of
            the rising moon.**

Leader: This very moment is ours to appreciate. Scriptures tell us not to dwell on the past but
            to watch for the new things that God is doing.

People: **In the spring light, we let go of old guilt and as Easter comes, we relish new
            energies in nature and in our own souls.**

Leader: Thank God for resurrecting us and all creation!

People: **Thank God for Jesus, his teaching, his dying, and his rising again!**

Prayer Of Thanksgiving (Leader)

Living God — how happy we are when beauty and goodness surround us! How pleased we
are when things seem to be going our way! What pleasure we feel when we realize that your
Spirit is sustaining us moment by moment. This hour, our full attention turns to you and we
listen for your voice. Amen.

Call To Confession (Leader)

These moments are for you to reflect on your inner activities. Pray with me and then continue your reverie in silence.

Community Confession (Unison)

Holy One — our minds are open before you.
**When temptations come — for they surely will — give us clarity about your hopes for our
lives.**
**When idols sneak into our thoughts and activities, remind us not to play games with your
grace and power.**
Nurture our souls with words and silences, with relationships and fresh opportunities.
We walk the human path Jesus walked; grant us insight to be faithful. Amen.

Sermon Idea

John's text is known by most Christians, but this sermon might consider the ways we gather
to care for one another and the rituals we use to indicate our appreciation and encouragement.

The Philippians section reminds us that rites and rituals do not necessarily satisfy our longings to be close to God. What aspects of the church's life together might be enriched with new language in liturgy, with reframed baptismal vows, or with time in the context of worship to articulate honest response to the sermon? Is it possible that we really could befriend one another in the faith family with financial support as well as emotional support? What would it look like within the faith family to make resources available as well as a beautiful building? According to John, might the church's goals to feed the hungry and promote justice outside the faith family be secondary to caring for those within the membership? The poor are always with us, Jesus reminds his first-century friends.

Contemporary Affirmation (Unison)

The Holy comes to us in many different ways. God continues to create in and around us, leading us to food for our souls and our bodies.

We find courage in Jesus of Nazareth who resisted the temptations that come to humankind: power over others, material wealth that obscures divine goodness, and arrogance that resists attention to divine presence.

With the Holy Spirit enthusing us, we choose to live in ways that are hospitable and gracious, insightful and generous in kind deeds.

Together, we have a significant voice in our culture to demand justice for all.

In our living and in our dying, we are not alone. God is with us. Amen.

Offertory Statement (Leader or Unison)

Brightening this corner of town is part of our work. Money allows us to help refugees settle into their new homes; money and skills keep our building functioning well; money, skills, and time enable us to mentor the next generation. Give as you are led.

Doxology
O Love, How Deep, How Broad, How High (v. 5, modified)
tune: DEO GRACIAS

All glory to the living God for love so deep, so high, so broad;
The Trinity whom we adore forever and forever more.

Prayer Of Thanksgiving (Leader or Unison)

Great Mystery — we know that your affirmation and guidance empower us for daily living. Thank you for your love that flows through us to make your kingdom palpable in our city. Amen.

Intercessory Prayers (Leader or Readers)

Fathering God — Jesus of Nazareth envisioned humankind being helpful to one another. He spoke of a new reign — a kinship that banished oppression, starvation, war, and destruction of the land. How good that sounds to us 2,000 years later! We pray for that kingdom to come to this planet. We pray for collaboration among all nations and tribes. As the global economy shifts, let us not destroy the earth. As *profit* becomes a vociferously demanding idol, let us not sacrifice children's education and health anywhere in the global village. Bring renewed self-control out of climate changes and out of America's imposition of Western democracy in eastern lands.

Mothering God — Jesus of Nazareth trusted that you and he would establish a neighborly way for humankind to be in the world. We as human creatures have failed to facilitate justice and hospitality. We have feared those different from ourselves. We have accumulated our material goods without recognizing the affect on the earth and other residents. We are frightened that water, food, and health care will exceed the budgets of many people we say are your children. So our prayer is that you enable all humankind to share the available water, oil, and grain. Let it begin with us.

Majestic God — like the psalmist, we admire the oceans, the sand, and the rocks, and we imagine romantic things about the ocean and sky! We crave vacations from our work days to relax in the beauty of creation. Thank you for holding it all together. We admire the bodies we have, too. We're glad when they function well and we retreat to physicians when they are off balance. We pray for health — as much as our bodies and psyches can handle; give us courage when disease invades; give us peace when our days are numbered.

Loving God — thank you for this place we call our church home, for the companions who sit with us week after week. Thank you for the history and for tomorrow's dreams. Make joyful noises among us, dance with us, and paint with vibrant colors and illicit rich music as we are filled with your Presence. Amen.

Benediction (Leader)

May the road continue smooth before you;
May there be enough light along the way;
May peace greet you at every crossroad
And joy accompany you to the end.
Through whatever pain and suffering is yours to endure
Know that God is in it with you.
Amid every temptation that comes to you
Be aware that wisdom is yours for the asking.

Music
Be Still My Soul
    Words: Katharina von Schlegel, 1752; tr. Jane Borthwick, 1855, alt.
    Music: Jean Sibelius, 1899; arr. The Hymnal, 1933
    FINLANDIA

Breathe On Me, Breath Of God
    Words: Edwin Hatch, 1878, alt.
    Music: Robert Jackson, 1888
    TRENTHAM

Come And Find The Quiet Center
    Words: Shirley Erena Murray, 1989
    Music: Traditional American melody; arr. Jack Schrader
    BEACH SPRING

Come Down, O Love Divine
      Words: Bianco of Siena (15th century); tr. Richard F. Littledale, 1867, alt.
      Music: Ralph Vaughan Williams, 1906
      DOWN AMPNEY

Where Restless Crowds Are Thronging
      Words: Thomas Curtis Clark, 1953
      Music: William Lloyd, 1840
      MEIRIONYDD

Palm Sunday
Sunday Of The Passion

Liturgy Of The Palms
Psalm 118:1-2, 19-29   Luke 19:28-40

Liturgy Of The Passion
Isaiah 50:4-9a   Philippians 2:5-11
Psalm 31:9-16   Luke 22:14—23:56 or Luke 23:1-49

Call To Worship

Leader: Six weeks of Lent are almost finished. Our smudges of Ash Wednesday — signs of discipleship on our heads and hands — are invisible. Today we mix the excitement of the parade of palms with the dread of passion.

(The candles can be lighted.)

People: We are glad to be here to consider the stories of Jesus and how they impact our living.

Leader: Our days are longer and we have "anticipatory anxiety" as we watch spring burst out. For the past weeks, we have read the biblical accounts of Jesus teaching along the east end of the Mediterranean. Now we move to Passover week and the murder of Jesus. As we have explored his life and teachings, we have accentuated the goodness that lies within us. We have become aware of the Holy Presence modifying our goals and values.

People: In the spring light, we will let go of old guilt and as Easter comes, we will relish new energies in nature and in our own psyches.

Leader: A Divine Message comes to us in the ancient story of Jesus of Nazareth: God is One who blesses everyone who seeks.

People: We are seeking to live in ways that satisfy, in ways that illustrate neighborliness and justice. Here we receive encouragement and strength to embody the goodness of Jesus.

Prayer Of Thanksgiving (Leader)

Holy One — "Find a donkey," Jesus said. "Book a room; set the table...." We have seen what can happen when Jesus speaks. We also feel anxious as we think about what happened after the palm parade and after the dinner with his friends. We are glad we know the whole story! Thank you for your presence inspiring and caressing us. We open our minds so that new ideas can lead us to fresh experiences with you. We are ready to praise and wait. Amen.

Call To Confession (Leader)

It's fun to be part of a parade. It's so nice to sit down to a meal with friends. It's not so nice when we notice that our attitudes are exclusive and that we have internal conflicts. It's not comfortable when we recognize that our soul values are not in sync with our external behaviors. In these moments of silence, welcome the Spirit to harmonize your inner- and outer-self.

Community Confession (Unison)
Holy One — our minds are open before you.
When temptations come — for they surely will — give us clarity about your hopes for our
    lives.
When idols sneak into our thoughts and activities, remind us not to play games with your
    grace and power.
Nurture our souls with words and silences, with relationships and fresh opportunities.
We walk the human path Jesus walked; grant us insight to be faithful. Amen.

Sermon Idea

The comparison between a spouse sent away and God's distance from the people is power-ful (Isaiah), yet, for us, God does seem "mostly absent," hidden; and it's difficult to identify what constitutes "crimes" (Isaiah) in terms of the inner self/soul/psyche. Our emotions change with events and environments so it is not strange to think that at one moment we say, "Ho-sanna" and the next, "Away with him!" Our souls exist within a continuum: "Thanks be to God" at one end and "to hell with it" at the other, "God's love is eternal" (Psalm 118) to "there is no God" at the other.

Contemporary Affirmation (Unison)

The Holy comes to us in many different ways. God continues to create in and around us, leading us to food for our souls and our bodies.

We find courage in Jesus of Nazareth who resisted the temptations that come to hu-mankind: power over others, material wealth that obscures divine goodness, and arro-gance that resists attention to divine presence.

With the Holy Spirit enthusing us, we choose to live in ways that are hospitable and gracious, insightful and generous in kind deeds.

Together, we have a significant voice in our culture to demand justice for all.

In our living and in our dying, we are not alone. God is with us. Amen.

Offertory Statement (Leader)

We parade our resources in the clothes we wear;
We parade our compassion with the money we share.

Doxology   O Love, How Deep, How Broad, How High (v. 5, modified)
                                                tune: DEO GRACIAS

All glory to the living God for love so deep, so high, so broad;
The Trinity whom we adore forever and forever more.

Prayer Of Thanksgiving (Leader or Responsive)

Creating Presence — thank you for living through us to love the earth;
Thank you for beauty and hospitality that inspires us who are rich and us who are poor.
We are grateful for time and resources enough to share,
Glad we can pay our bills, care for our bodies, and minister to people in need. Amen.

Intercessory Prayers (Leader or Readers)

God of Palms — we get excited when a crowd gathers. Even here, we feel elated when the seats are full and the space is filled with music! We pray for keen awareness of your closeness on Sundays and in our attitudes and decisions the rest of the week. Help us move with the crowd that consistently honors you. We know the whole story of Jesus the Christ and pray that our twenty-first-century understanding of discipleship be continually expanding. In the ways we decorate ourselves, in our conversations, and in our entertainment, we want to enjoy you.

God of Passion — we know Jesus walked on this earth feeding and healing, teaching and learning. So many people need food for their bodies; so many people need soul food; so many people need shelter and health care. Prisons are full, bombs explode, and drugs destroy. Walk on this earth again and bring hope to all creation. As we remember Jesus' last days on earth, we pray for courage to take sides against injustice and grandiosity, against a wealthy few for the common good of the global village.

God of Possibilities — we pray for peace and honest compromises in families and among nations. Let peace rain on all peoples. Jesus died a violent death, and we see that sort of violence throughout this world. Transform the human heart, we pray.

God of Today and Tomorrow — as we reflect on the last week of Jesus' life, we are conscious of our own sufferings. Sometimes like Jesus, we say, "Why do you forsake me?" Sustain us and let us be content with your love — your intangible love. Blow among us like the wind and let us feel divine refreshment. Amen.

Benediction (Leader)
(The candles can be extinguished, except the Christ candle, if one has been used.)
> May the road continue smooth before you;
> May there be enough light along the way;
> May peace greet you at every crossroad
> And joy accompany you to the end.
> Through whatever pain and suffering is yours to endure
> Know that God is in it with you.
> Amid every temptation that comes to you
> Be aware that wisdom is yours for t

Music
All Glory, Laud, And Honor
> Words: Theodulph of Orleans, c. 821; tr. John Mason Neale, 1854, alt.
> Music: Melchior Teschner, 1615; harm. William Henry Monk, 1861
> ST. THEODULPH

Hosanna, Loud Hosanna
> Words: Jeannette Threlfall, 1873
> Music: Gesangbuch der Herzogl Wirtembergischen Katholischen Hofkapelle, 1784, alt.
>   1868
> ELLACOMBE

Mantos Y Palmas (Filled With Excitement)
    Words: Rubén Ruiz Avila, 1972; trans. Gertrude C. Suppe, 1979, 1987
    Music: Rubén Ruiz Avila, 1972; arr. Alvin Schutmaat
    HOSANNA

Ride On! Ride On In Majesty!
    Words: Henry Hart Milman, 1827
    Music: Graham George
    THE KING'S MAJESTY
    or
    ST. DROSTANE

Maundy Thursday

Exodus 12:1-4 (5-10) 11-14   1 Corinthians 11:23-26
Psalm 116:1-2, 12-19   John 13:1-17, 31b-35

A Maundy Meal For The Whole Family

Goals

To acknowledge the downsides of life, the injustices, the evil
To tell the Christian story
To tell the Jewish story
To provide opportunity to prepare foods as small groups ahead of the event
To provide time and space to enjoy healthy, simple foods with friends
To determine to be loyal to the truths of Jesus of Nazareth

This event, one and one half hours in length, with food can be in the sanctuary, though unmovable seating makes sharing difficult as well as clean-up. If the event is in the fellowship hall, encourage people to place foods on at least two serving tables so children and adults can serve themselves — breads all placed together, cheese all in one spot, and beverages all on a separate table (facilitates movement of people). Families could bring blankets to sit together on the floor — like a picnic, though older people may have difficulty sitting down and getting up.

Light candles on the serving table if people are seated on blankets. If people are seated at tables, light a candle on each table.

Shared Simple Communal Meal

Includes traditional Passover ingredients: bread, cheese, wine, lettuce, and herbs.
Have several families make bread earlier in the week.
Have people sign up ahead of time to bring
- cheeses,
- easy casseroles with parsley,
- hard-boiled eggs,
- celery strips, and
- matzos.

Have people sign up to bring beverages
- iced tea,
- wines, and
- vegetable juices.

Provide some romaine and leaf lettuce.
Make *haroset* (a mixture of apples, almonds, and cinnamon).

Greeting

(After people are settled for the meal)
Leader: We're celebrating the life of Jesus and the story of the Passover — freedom from oppression.

Let's enjoy good food and good conversation. After eating, we will tell the stories of this famous Thursday.

Let's thank God for all the ideas and nurturing foods that give us body and soul health.

> God of yesterday and tomorrow —
> Thank you for being available to humankind throughout history.
> Thank you for the Hebrews who trusted that you would see them through years of desert wandering.
> Thank you for Jesus who trusted that you would see him through the suffering of betrayal and physical dying.
> Thank you for being with us, teaching us to love ourselves and one another.
> We appreciate the foods set before us.
> Amen.

(People sit in small groups to enjoy the assembled foods. As people finish eating, call for their attention.)

Judaism Story
(Background "Music From Judiasm" — any clesmer instrumental CD)

Long ago, 4,000 years ago, Hebrew were slaves in the land along the Nile River. One man with his brother and sister mobilized the people with a dream of freedom. Moses, Aaron, and Miriam led the Hebrews out of plagues and Egypt into the Sinai desert where they experienced freedom to be as difficult as slavery! One night, they tiptoed out of Pharaoh's land, grateful for divine help and for all their belongings. The Egyptians woke to find their eldest children dead and the brickyards with out any workers. The Hebrews explained their freedom by saying, "God's messenger passed over our homes and set us free." Each year, the Jews tell this Passover story with words, music, and foods — bitter and sweet!

Christian Story
(A scene from Jesus of Montreal, Jesus Christ Superstar, *or* Godspell *might suffice for this part of the evening. Also, a precocious teen might enjoy making comparisons of Harry Potter images with Christian images of good and evil, friendship and betrayal, and messiah-like people.)*

Jesus was a Jew who lived at the eastern end of the Mediterranean Sea in the first century of this common era. So this story is very old, too. Jesus gathered his friends for Passover celebration in Jerusalem — in a special room with special foods. That evening, one friend — Judas — left early. He went to government and religious authorities and accused Jesus of inappropriate actions. So Jesus was arrested and the assembled mob murdered him. His friends laid his body in a cave and put a big stone in front of the opening. Three days later, the body was gone! The friends were frantic. But they experienced Jesus in the garden and on the road to Emmaus. They believed he had risen from death!

Today, 2,000 years later, we believe that Jesus is the Christ and lives in you and me! We believe that Jesus gives us three directives or mandates: love God, love self, love neighbor!

Congregational Song   Seek Ye First The Kingdom Of God

Contemporary Story   A Guided Meditation
(Tavener's Ikos *would be nice background music.)*

> Be still; breathe gently.
> Imagine receiving these two stories — Jewish and Christian — as a gift.

Recall the Jewish story. What part do you play in that story? Notice how you relate to other people. What would you ask God for?

Recall the Christian story. What would be your part in the story? Notice how you relate to Jesus.

What do you say to God? What does God say to you? Hold God's words in your memory. Enjoy the Holy Presence with you. When you're ready, come to this place.

Congregational Song   This Is The Day The Lord Has Made

Benediction   Sing *Canto de Experanza*: Song of Hope (in English and in Spanish)
(Make a circle, each person placing her/his right hand palm down in the neighbor's left hand palm-up — makes a complete energy circuit.)

May the God of hope go with us every day
Filling all our lives with love and joy and peace.
May the God of justice speed us on our way
Bringing light and hope to every land and race.
Praying, let us work for peace
Singing, share our joy with all,
Working for a world that's new
Faithful when we hear Christ's call!

Music

For The Bread Which You Have Broken
    Words: Louis F. Benson, 1924, alt.
    Music: Charles J. Dickenson, 1861
    AGAPE

Let Us Break Bread Together On Our Knees
    Words: African-American spiritual
    Music: African-American spiritual; arr. Carlton R. Young, 1964, alt.
    LET US BREAK BREAD

Good Friday

Isaiah 52:13–53:12   John 18:1–19:42
Psalm 22   Hebrews 10:16-25

Consider opening the sanctuary from noon until 7:00 p.m. so people can stop by on their way home from work, with fifteen- to thirty-minute "services" at noon, 3:00, and 6:00. Another option is to read one scripture and sing one hymn at the top of each hour. Deacons, Stephen Ministers, Elders, and other leaders may wish to schedule themselves to "cover" a block of time so attendees are not alone with the *Good Friday experience*.

Have available copies of the Celtic knot from the book cover and the hands found on the divider pages.

Record instrumental versions of nineteenth-century cross hymns to play during the hours the sanctuary is open. These hours are for persons who wish to "feel" the pain of injustice, guilt, shame, and betrayal surrounding Jesus' death.

People enter space/sanctuary, dimly lighted, with instrumental music playing quietly, live or recorded — the classical passions, sections from *Jesus Christ Superstar*, jazz masses, Tavener's *Ikos*, and the nineteenth-century cross hymns.

The cross may be draped in black; a single red or white rose might be placed on the communion table along with the chalice, paten (with a loaf of bread), and a single large white burning candle.

In a corner of the sanctuary, between "services," people could fill Easter baskets for a Hospice/AIDS center or for the staff of an emergency room. Individually wrapped candies could be donated several weeks prior to Good Friday. Baskets must be small, wrapped in clear cellophane, and labeled with the church's name. Deacons, Stephen Ministers, or other church leaders can deliver the baskets later in the evening or the next morning.

At prescribed times the leader gathers people for "group" meditation.

Leader: It's Good Friday. Welcome to this time and space. Here you can be saturated with Divine Actions of the past; Palm Sunday slid through Maundy Thursday into "God's Friday." Here you can steep yourself in the present with all your senses and your mind alert for Holy Conversation. Here you can consider the future and how you will honor the time and experience of today.

Hear the story of Jesus of Nazareth, how his culture — the Roman Occupation and religious people — murdered him. In Jesus dying, we see the violent mindset of humanity. His death calls us to be aware of our own sins — prejudice, miserliness, cynicism, arrogance....

Leader gives a brief synopsis of Holy Week

Jesus entered Jerusalem last Sunday with fanfare and a cheerful crowd. However, the high hopes for freedom from oppression vanished by Thursday evening when Judas left Jesus and the other disciples to celebrate the Passover meal without him while he negotiated Jesus' arrest. After a trial and a mob's accusations, Jesus was sentenced to death. Here's the next part of the story.

Leader reads Luke 23:26-56
(Include the burial scene since many people will not read it before Sunday's Resurrection Story.)

Leader/musician plays (live or recorded) "When I Survey The Wondrous Cross"
(Invite people to hum the melody while reading the words in the hymnal silently.)

Leader invites people to look at the Celtic knot
(Read aloud the interpretation found at the front of this book. Lead the people in a brief meditation):

Leader: Look at the undulations in the knot; notice the cross-overs and turns. Each person meanders this cross/star pathway. We each carry within us the characters who walked with Jesus.
Look at the knot. What of you is Peter? How are you like Judas? When are you Mother Mary? When are you Mary Magdalene? What of you participates unwittingly in maligning the Holy? Where are you when God is speaking?
Look at the hands. How do your hands betray God? How do your hands receive God's gift? How do your hands treasure and share God's gift?
Look at the knot and the hands. How does your experience today take you into the world as a vital twenty-first-century disciple of Jesus the Christ?

Leader Prays
Living God — we know that Jesus, your Child, died long ago. Somehow, his death continues to touch us. We regret that his life ended too soon. Somehow, your love impels us to find ways to make you visible in this world. Thank you for Jesus, for his teachings, and for the vitality of his living, then and now. Amen.

Leader concludes the meditation time with a live or recorded solo
(If the people are to stay with the pain — "Were You There When They Crucified My Lord?" or if present time is to be emphasized, a benediction like "May You Run And Not Be Weary," by Hanson and Murakami, found in Sing the Faith *#2281)*

(After concluding the last service, the leader blows out the one candle and turns out the lights except for hallways and stairs and says, "Good night.")

Music
Go To Dark Gethsemane
 Words: James Montgomery, 1820, 1825, alt.
 Music: Richard Redhead, 1853
 REDHEAD 76

Were You There?
    Words: African-American spiritual
    Music: African-American spiritual; arr. Melva Wilson Costen, 1987
    WERE YOU THERE

Season 5
Easter

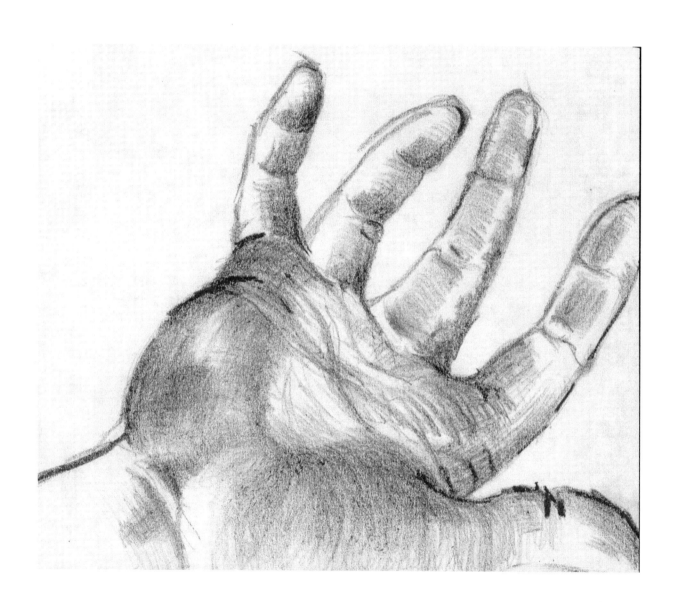

Emotion

Easter Day

Acts 10:34-43 or Isaiah 65:17-25
Psalm 118:1-2, 14-24

1 Corinthians 15:19-26 or Acts 10:34-43
John 20:1-18 or Luke 24:1-12

The Easter story is about the triumph of creativity.
We are all entombed with large boulders blocking our escape
And liberation to the extent our creativity is blocked or stifled.
— Matthew Fox, *Creativity*

Call To Worship

Leader: Christ is risen! Christ lives!
People: Indeed! Christ is alive!
Leader: Hallelujah!

Prayer Of Thanksgiving (Leader)

Christ is alive! How grateful we are that the tomb is empty! That we, too, can be fully alive! We eagerly sing and pray our delight. We express our joy with the news that Jesus lives! This resurrection morning, we welcome new life, new opportunities for creativity, new ways to be your people in this place. We feel your power and your grace. Thank you. Amen.

Sermon Idea

The biblical story will have been read so it will be fresh in people's minds. The question is: How does this story influence our view of the world? What keeps us dried up, stifled, blocked? How can we be opened up? Will we maintain entombed places within our souls? What might open us and let in the light of Christ?

Contemporary Affirmation (Unison)

We experience the love of God
in the words and kindnesses of one another.
We know that life-abundant is offered
by the Creating God, the Risen Christ.
We live as people of God when we work for justice,
feed the hungry, and heal the sick.
The earth is God's dwelling place and
we are to be responsible landscapers.
Christ moves among humankind loving,
teaching, and making whole.
In our living, in our dying, and in our rising again,
Holy Spirit is with us! Hallelujah!

Offertory Statement (Leader)

The earth is God's! We are God's! We illustrate God's Presence as we care for this place and minister to people in need here and throughout the global village.

Doxology   Praise God From Whom All Blessings Flow, tune: OLD HUNDREDTH

Praise God from whom all blessings flow.
Praise God, all creatures here below.
Praise God, above you heavenly hosts.
Creator, Christ, and Holy Ghost.

Prayer Of Thanksgiving (Unison)

Living God —
We are yours, body, mind, and soul.
Use our talents and skills to enrich all the world.
Amen.

Intercessory Prayers (Leader)

God of high and low places, our joy runs wild this morning. The days are longer and the moon rises more leisurely. Our delight comes from the playful, childlike part of ourselves and we anticipate heaven coming to earth with much vibrancy. How fully your grace is in the world!

While we are here, there are people without shelter and food, without friends and companions, without a zest for living. Play with them in the light until they see options and feel energy.

Terror and death still move about despite this morning's glory. Bring an end to war and violence. Halt the rape of the earth. Set all creation free from disease and sorrow. With great hope, our hearts open to your lively Spirit. Amen.

Benediction/Charge (Leader)

Life is not a dead end; it is a surprising journey to God. Say "yes" to life; laugh each day and unwind the threads of the world. Notice new life around each corner. Make new dreams and cultivate a glad heart! Christ lives! Happy Easter!

Music

Alleluia, Alleluia! Give Thanks
    Words: Donald Fishel, 1973
    Music: Donald Fishel, 1973; arr. Betty Pulkingham and Donald Fishel, 1979
    ALLELUIA NO. 1

Come, Ye Faithful, Raise The Strain
    Words: John of Damascus (c. 675-749); trans. John Mason Neale, 1859, alt.
    Music: Bohemian Brethren's Gesangbuch, 1544
    AVE VIRGO VIRGINUM (or ST. KEVIN; music: Arthur Seymour Sullivan (1842-
        1900), alt.

Easter People, Raise Your Voices
    Words: William M. James, 1979
    Music: Henry T. Smart, 1867
    REGENT SQUARE

Now The Green Blade Riseth
    Words: John M. C. Crum, 1928
    Music: French carol
    NOËL NOUVELET

Sing My Song Backwards
    Words: Brian Wren, 1974, rev. 1994
    Music: Ann Loomes, 1974
    HILARY

The Day Of Resurrection!
    Words: John of Damascus (c. 675-749); trans. John Mason Neale, 1862
    Music: Henry Thomas Smart, c. 1835
    LANCASHIRE

Easter 2

Acts 5:27-32   Revelation 1:4-8
Psalm 118:14-29 or Psalm 150   John 20:19-31

The Easter story is about the triumph of creativity.
We are all entombed with large boulders blocking our escape
And liberation to the extent our creativity is blocked or stifled.
— Matthew Fox, *Creativity*

Call To Worship

Leader: Ah, Sunday again, the week after Resurrection Day. Colorful egg hunts are over; chocolate rabbits are almost all consumed.

People: Yes, but Easter season and spring celebrations are not over! Christ is alive!

Leader: Christ is alive and we are the embodiment of that truth.

People: Let it be said that we are friends of Jesus of Nazareth. Let our reputation include this information: We are peace-makers and we are not afraid of living to please the Holy One.

Prayer Of Thanksgiving (Leader or Unison)

Living God — thank you for renewed zest for living and for surrounding us with opportunities to be creative. We sing and beat our drums; we play our pianos and dance because new life is rising all around us! Thank you for freeing us from winter and the boulders that have blocked light. We are glad Jesus of Nazareth is known to us as "risen from the dead." Reveal yourself to us in words, in dreams, and in time, which we share in this place. Amen.

Call To Confession (Leader)

Our words and our behaviors announce the beliefs that motivate us. Check in with yourself and with the Holy. Is your living a consistent, integrated whole? Now is time for that conversation. Pray the printed prayer with me and then make your private prayers.

Community Confession (Unison)

Renewing God — how grateful we are for the life and teachings of Jesus, grateful that he was willing to live beyond boundaries of society and the death-cave!
We know the friends of Jesus kept on telling his story despite the orders of the city council.
We, too, want to be on the side of right and justice, fairness and life-abundant.
Reveal to us the shadows in our souls; help us make changes till we walk in your light. Amen.

Sermon Idea

Given the violence of twenty-first-century young people, willing to sacrifice their lives in order to hurt and kill others, it is difficult to read the lectionary texts and notice the personal pronouns and the condemnations projected onto others. The hope of resurrection is that amid death wishes and murder, we have the courage to find ways to be godly without wreaking havoc on others. The hope includes self-knowledge that expands with each season of the calendar year, each season of church activities, and each stage of human development — self-knowledge that acknowledges inner darkness and welcomes light coming from within and from the Holy. The "Easter Bunny" is an image of prolific life. Though it is not a Christian image, it has been adopted by our culture as a symbol of sweetness, youthful/spring, and generosity. What in our daily living and in our celebrations carries such satiation and contented anticipation? How can we be disciples of Jesus and not unwittingly accelerate terrorism? If the Easter story is about creativity, as Matthew Fox suggests, how can people in the pews get "unstifled"?

Contemporary Affirmation (Unison)

Jesus of Nazareth had the courage to challenge the institutions of his day.

> **He had the strength and wisdom to make heaven a viable option.**

> **In spite of suffering and death, he was faithful to his vision;**

> > **His teachings have influenced all the world.**

> **He imaged God as divine parent, as divine and benevolent ruler, and as creator of all the world.**

> **We believe that God is still creating and welcomes us to participate to make heaven available on earth.**

Through life and death, God is with us.

Offertory Statement (Leader)

Jesus came and went about blessing and healing. We are a bit more limited! We can share our talents and our moneys to spread around goodness. Share as you can.

Doxology   Praise God From Whom All Blessings Flow, tune: OLD HUNDREDTH

Praise God from whom all blessings flow.
Praise God, all creatures here below.
Praise God, above ye heavenly hosts.
Creator, Christ, and Holy Ghost.

Prayer Of Thanksgiving (Leader)

Energy of the Universe — thank you for what we have and for the opportunity to make goodness happen in this building and on this street. We are your faithful people right here. We love you. Amen.

Intercessory Prayers (Leader or Readers)

God of Rabbits and People — thank you for the breath of life, for spring and its beauty, for children and adults, for pets and wild animals. Thank you for the showers that refresh the land. We are aware that some nations are set in desert places and food is nonexistent. People and animals are dying and we don't know what to do. Give us wisdom, compassion, and generous hearts so we might share what is available in our neighborhoods.

God of Eggs and People — we marvel at the way life keeps popping out. Thank you for our children. Help us to mentor them in charity and justice. And we are sorrowful as we become aware that evil invades human psyches and urges self-destruction. We grieve that some of our freedoms are diminished because our spaces and our lives are being threatened. We are afraid. Germinate compassion and justice in the human mind, we pray. Halt war and devastation on every continent. Move among tribes and gangs until genocide turns into appreciation for humanity and its awesome variety. We pray for peace.

Healing God — while we enjoy you this hour, we are aware that some of us hurt, some of us have pain that is penetrating and distracting, some of us find our eyes dim and our ears fogged, some of us are grouchy and have trouble getting up in the morning. Grant us your unmistakable presence and soothe our discomforts. Help us find physicians and caregivers who can aid us along this human journey. Reach to all in need of companionship and comfort. Bless your creatures with inspiring music, colorful arts, and satisfying relationships. Amen.

Benediction/Charge (Leader)
Life is not a dead end;
It is a surprising journey to God.
Say "Yes" to life;
Laugh each day and unwind the threads of the world.
Notice new life around each corner.
Make new dreams and cultivate a glad heart!
Christ lives!

Music
Camina, Pueblo De Dios
    Words and Music: Cesário Gabaráin; trans. George Lockwood
    NUEVA CREACIÓN

Christ Is Alive!
    Words: Brian Wren, 1968, rev.
    Music: Thomas Williams, 1789; harm. Lowell Mason (1792-1872)
    TRURO

Easter People, Raise Your Voices
    Words: William M. James, 1979
    Music: Henry T. Smart, 1867
    REGENT SQUARE

The First Day Of Creation
    Words: Thomas H. Troeger, 1985
    Music: Carol Doran, 1985
    NEW CREATION

Sing Hallelujah
    Words and Music: Linda Stassen-Benjamin, 1974
    SING HALLELUIA

Easter 3
Earth Day

Acts 9:1-6 (7-20)   Revelation 5:11-14
Psalm 30   John 21:1-19

> *The Easter story is about the triumph of creativity.*
> *We are all entombed with large boulders blocking our escape*
> *and liberation to the extent our creativity is blocked or stifled.*
> — Matthew Fox, *Creativity*

Call To Worship

Leader: Ah. Sunday again. The earth is announcing the coming of spring and summer! We can depend upon nature's cycles, though there are always some surprises along the way.

People: **We thank God for the productivity of the land, for the beauty of flowers, and for the coming crops which nurture animals and humans.**

Leader: We sing to the Holy One, expressing our gratitude for divine presence which strengthens us for daily tasks.

People: **We have called to God; God knows our needs. We are not silent; God sustains us in times of sorrow and brings us to a place of joy. We sing to the Holy One.**

Leader: We are not silent for God restores our sense of well-being. We give thanks and we tell others of Holy imagination, apparent in the ecosphere.

People: **We actively care for our planet home!**

Prayer Of Thanksgiving (Leader or Unison)

Living God — we are alive! We praise you for the breath of life! We recognize your goodness each day as we enjoy our family and friends. We appreciate work to do that has meaning and allows us to be consistent in our thoughts and our behavior. Thank you for this earth home and for the miracles of water, land, and air. For this hour, we are alert for your voice. Amen.

Call To Confession (Leader)

Today is *Earth Day*. Ever imagine what the mistletoe thinks about the ozone layer? Ever consider what an earthworm thinks when it runs into a plastic bag? Ever wonder what goes through a homeless person's mind when she sees television commercials for SUVs while she's in the laundromat? Alone, we cannot change our culture. But alone, we can be careful with the land that is ours, with the waste we generate, with the poisons we choose, with the animals we eat. Our words and our behaviors announce the beliefs that motivate us. Check in with yourself and with the Holy. Is your living a consistent, integrated whole? Now is time for that conversation. Pray the printed prayer with me and then make your private prayers.

Community Confession (Unison)

Renewing God — how grateful we are for the life and teachings of Jesus, grateful that he was willing to live beyond boundaries of society and the death-cave!

We know the friends of Jesus kept on telling his story despite the orders of the city council.
We, too, want to be on the side of right and justice, fairness and life-abundant.
Reveal to us the shadows in our souls; help us make changes till we walk in your light.
   Amen.

Sermon Idea

The Revelation passage raises the question of how we imagine the universe. How do twenty-first-century people of faith articulate their awe and loyalty to the Mystery we call God? The gospel of John is that delightful story of Jesus telling his friends to try fishing on the "right side." Thinking about Earth Day, the sermon might explore "the right side" of the food chain, "the right side" of the wet lands, "the right side" of global trade practices, "the right side" of poverty, and so on. The question none of the friends of Jesus dared ask was "Who are you?" Are we also avoiding that question because we fear the consequences of acknowledging that God is Creator of *all* and that much of the *all* is very slow to be replenished? Are we afraid to ask because we suspect we know some of the answers about "the right side" of many issues?

Contemporary Affirmation (Unison)

Jesus of Nazareth had the courage to challenge the institutions of his day.
   He had the strength and wisdom to make heaven a viable option.
   In spite of suffering and death, he was faithful to his vision;
      His teachings have influenced all the world.
   He imaged God as divine parent, as divine and benevolent ruler, and as creator of
      all the world.
We believe that God is still creating and welcomes us to participate to make heaven
   available on earth.
Through life and death, God is with us, even when we are afraid.

Offertory Statement (Leader)

The planet is God's. We are God's. Let us be generous with our material possessions, with our money, and with our time.

Doxology   Praise God From Whom All Blessings Flow, tune: OLD HUNDREDTH
Praise God from whom all blessings flow.
Praise God, all creatures here below.
Praise God, above you heavenly hosts.
Creator, Christ, and Holy Ghost.

Prayer Of Thanksgiving (Leader or Unison)

Energy of the Universe — thank you for adequate moneys and time to be caretakers of this building and the earth. As your faithful people, we use what we have to serve you. Love the earth and all creatures through us. Amen.

Intercessory Prayers (Leader or Readers)

God of Blue Birds and Chicken Hawks — thank you for the breath of life. Thank you for the April showers that prepare the soil for seeds. Let desert places, too, produce sufficient food for the inhabitants. We grieve for the animals that are losing their homes. Help us humans not to be so greedy for space. Give us compassion and generous hearts so we might share the planet and wisely use its resources.

God of Polar Bears and People — we marvel at the way life adapts to changes in nature. But we humans on this continent seem to be resisting the necessary changes so animals can share the earth with us. We realize that each species must produce its next generation. We are glad for our children. May they learn a simple lifestyle "so others may simply live." Help us to mentor them with love and thoughtful guidance.

Creator of Magma and Thunderbolts — what a universe that grabs our imaginations! We humans tend to think we own the cosmos and we have manipulated it to make some people rich. Forgive our religious arrogance that has contributed to pollution and poverty. Open our eyes to the incredible balance of the ecosphere. Halt human greed and competition that maim the earth. Open our minds to the cruelty we perpetuate with chemicals, with animal industries, and with continual light and noise. Give us courage not to participate with the destruction of your world.

Healing God — no one of us wants to suffer with disease; no one of us wants to wear Job's shoes; no one of us wants sleepless nights. We dread facing our mortality and the pain that often precedes our dying. Sustain us as we live fully day and night until we join you in eternity. Be undeniably present with us and heal our discomforts. Soothe us with inspiring images, stimulating music, and graceful friends. Amen.

Benediction/Charge (Leader)
Life is not a dead end;
It is a surprising journey to God.
Say "Yes" to life.
Laugh each day and unwind the threads of the world.
Notice new life around each corner.
Make new dreams and cultivate a glad heart!
Embrace the earth as a gift from God and
Save the wrappings!

Music
All Things Bright And Beautiful
Words: Cecil Frances Alexander, 1848
Music: English melody (17th century); adapt. Martin Shaw, 1915
ROYAL OAK

O God Of Earth And Space
Words: Jane Parker Huber, 1980
Music: Hebrew melody; adapt. Thomas Olivers and Meyer Lyon
LEONI

Sing With Hearts
   Words: Jonathan Malicsi, 1983
   Music: Kalinga melody
   INTAKO

Thank You, God, For Water, Soil, And Air
   Words: Brian Wren, 1973
   Music: John Weaver, 1988
   AMSTEIN

Easter 4

Acts 9:36-43   Revelation 7:9-17
Psalm 23   John 10:22-30

The Easter story is about the triumph of creativity.
We are all entombed with large boulders blocking our escape
A liberation to the extent our creativity is blocked or stifled.
— Matthew Fox, *Creativity*

Call To Worship

Leader: Ah, Sunday again. In some parts of the world this is lambing season. Of course, as
            we read today's scriptures, it's lambing season for us, too, for we recognize Jesus as
            the Good Shepherd, whose voice we know, and whom we choose to follow.

People: **God, Jesus, is our shepherd, we shall not want for anything! Our souls will be
            nourished with living water and good foods. When times are difficult, we have
            faith that God goes with us, giving us strength for each task.**

Prayer Of Thanksgiving (Leader)

Living God — how wonderful life is in this moment. Thank you for the tranquility of
generations gathered here. Together we have so many opportunities to show our love for you
and your creatures! Your presence enlivens us and gives us courage for tomorrow. Sing and
dance with us, we pray. Amen.

Call To Confession (Leader)

Our words and our behaviors reveal our ethical and moral values. Look within yourself. Is
your living a consistent whole? Pray the printed prayer with me and then make your private
prayers.

Community Confession (Unison)

**Renewing God — how grateful we are for the life and teachings of Jesus, grateful that he
challenged the first-century disciples and continues to challenge us to live beyond boundaries that society sets in our way.**

**Reveal to us the shadows in our souls; help us make changes until we walk in your light.
Amen.**

Sermon Idea

John 10:33 raises twenty-first-century questions: While we explore "spirituality" with elements from several world religions, do we risk stoning Jesus? Do we thwart God's goodness in
the world by not recognizing the difference between "social spirituality" and the "journey of
the heart to God"? Once someone has experienced being in the "Heart of God," that is always
the goal of meditation, prayer, and service. Jesus told his audience in John 10 that once someone has been close to him, no one could be convinced that he might not be of God. Notice that
when threatened, Jesus returned to the place of his baptism and initiation.

Contemporary Affirmation (Unison)

Jesus of Nazareth had the courage to challenge the institutions of his day.

He had the strength and wisdom to make heaven a viable option.

In spite of suffering and death, he was faithful to his vision;

His teachings have influenced all the world.

He imaged God as divine parent, as divine and benevolent ruler, and as creator of all the world.

We believe that God is still creating and welcomes us to participate to make heaven available on earth.

Through life and death, God is with us.

Offertory Statement (Leader)

We have opportunity to bless and heal as we care for each other and maintain this house of prayer.

Doxology   Praise God From Whom All Blessings Flow, tune: OLD HUNDREDTH

Praise God from whom all blessings flow.

Praise God, all creatures here below.

Praise God, above you heavenly hosts.

Creator, Christ, and Holy Ghost.

Prayer Of Thanksgiving (Leader)

Energy of the Universe — thank you for what we have and for the opportunity to make goodness happen in this building and on this street. We are your faithful people right here. We love you. Amen.

Intercessory Prayers (Leader or Readers)

God Inside and Outside — when we are still we notice your characteristics everywhere: blue sky lit with the sun by day and the stars by night; soil sprouting grasses and vegetables; people helping people; pets and people companioning one another! Within we recognize your creative activities in our souls and minds. We pray that everyone who is drawn toward you will find your energizing affirmation.

God for Every Continent — we remember that we have prayed for peace between nations for a very long time. We see ancient hatreds acted out now with automatic and long-distance weapons. We hear of children being killed before they can even read and write. We hear of them starving because food can't get to them. We can only imagine the suffering that mothers and fathers must endure as they watch their dreams die. What do you feel, God? Are there no wise leaders on this planet like there were no faithful people in Sodom? Are there so few people who recognize your voice that we are ineffective in peacemaking? We pray for collaboration and compromise between individuals who imprison the common good. We pray for the leaders of our country. Grant them political savvy and personal grace so that peace can be experienced in every land.

Healing God — as we go about our daily chores, we are aware that our bodies are wondrously made. We're also aware that they can be diseased and suffer strokes, cancers grow, bones break, and brains atrophy. Whatever our bodies do, keep us safe in your love. However our bodies deal with each stage of life, give us courage and strength to look up and around; give us ears to hear and minds to patiently be available for your still small voice. Amen.

Benediction (Leader)

Life is not a dead end;
It is a surprising journey to God.
Say "Yes" to life;
Laugh each day and unwind the threads of the world.
Notice new life around each corner.
Make new dreams and cultivate a glad heart!
Christ lives!

Music

Canto De Esperanza
Words: Alvin Schutmaat, 1984
Music: Argentine folk melody
ARGENTINA

Celebrate With Joy And Singing
Words: Mary Jackson Cathey, 1986
Music: R. Bedford Watkins, 1984
EVELYN CHAPEL

Down To Earth, As A Dove
Words: Fred Kaan, 1968
Music: *Piae Cantiones*, 1582; arr. Gustav Theodore von Holst, 1924
PERSONENT HODIE

Here I Am, Lord
Words: Daniel L. Schutte, 1981
Music: Daniel L. Schutte, 1981; harm. James Snyder, 1994
HERE I AM, LORD

Hope Of The World
Words: Georgia Harkness, 1954
Music: Genevan Psalter, 1551
DONNE SECOURS

Immortal, Invisible, God Only Wise
Words: Walter Chalmers Smith, 1867, alt.
Music: Welsh folk melody
ST. DENIO

O God Of Every Shining Constellation
    Words: Albert F. Bayly, 1950
    Music: V. Earle Copes, 1963
    VICAR

We Meet You, O Christ
    Words: Fred Kaan, 1966
    Music: Basque carol; harm. George Mims, 1979
    NORMANDY

When In Our Music God Is Glorified
    Words: Fred Pratt Green, 1971
    Music: Charles V. Stanford, 1904
    ENGLEBERG

Womb Of Life, And Source Of Being
    Words: Ruth Duck, 1986, 1990
    Music: Traditional Dutch melody; arr. Julius Roentgen, 1906
    IN BABILONE

The World Abounds With God's Free Grace
    Words: David G. Mehrtens, 1980
    Music: George F. Handel, 1748; harm. C. Winfred Douglas, 1941
    HALIFAX

Easter 5

Acts 11:1-18   Revelation 21:1-6
Psalm 148   John 13:31-35

The Easter story is about the triumph of creativity.
We are all entombed with large boulders blocking our escape
And liberation to the extent our creativity is blocked or stifled.
                                        — Matthew Fox, *Creativity*

Call To Worship
Leader: Welcome! It's good to be together again. We celebrate the sun and moon, the skies and the earth! We can sing and pray, listen and plan. Together, we can enjoy companionship and Divine Presence.

People: **We are glad to be here and to thank God for life.**

Prayer Of Thanksgiving (Unison)
Living God — thank you for renewed zest for living and for surrounding us with opportunities to be creative. Our minds are eager to receive your Word; our hearts are ready to experience your expansive love. We honor you with careful attention during this hour. Amen.

Call To Confession (Leader)
Consider the week behind us. We cannot return to those hours. Their patterns for decision-making are over. Consider this day. It is fresh with options. Erase what nibbles at your conscience; let go of residual shame and receive inner peace and vitality. Pray the printed prayer with me and then make your private prayers.

Community Confession (Unison)
Renewing God — How grateful we are for life!
There are so many changes happening around us; our minds and souls are lagging behind current information.
Free us from attachment to past perceptions of Godliness; free us from habits that wound us; free us from relationships that are harmful.
Alert us to healthy practices for ourselves and for this earth.
Expand our perceptions of how we can be peacemakers and how we can welcome strangers.
Give us generous clean hearts. Amen.

Sermon Idea
One purpose in the perpetual reading of scriptures in public was to facilitate the memory of the people seeking God and divine blessing. Translating, printing, and copying for a readership that includes young children and individuals who are blind makes the Bible available every day all year long, at home and in public places. The commandments and guidelines for the common good have become "old hat" and are easily set aside as marketing for cars and

toothpaste appeals to the human senses as well as to the practical aspect. Bottles are beautiful; aromas tantalize; motorcycles have style. Television and games dull the senses to real violence and real joy. Given these facts, how do children and adults hear "a new commandment: Love one another" and "I saw a new heaven and a new earth"? How do adults let go of last century's ways to express faith in God? It is vital to note that the book of Revelation is a dream of a first-century man exiled from his friends and livelihood. His dream "makes up" his reality. Yet the promises are ones twenty-first-century faithful Christians want to hear, too: God's home is with humankind; I am the first and the last; for the thirsty there is free cool spring water.... How do we let God live in and through us in a culture that overfills time so that companionship and community are hard to come by? Do we honor God by what we eat or by how much of the Bible we have memorized? Do we honor God by how we dream or by how we love one another? One bit of Easter good news is that we can be creative, imaging differently the energy of the Holy.

Contemporary Affirmation (Unison)

Jesus of Nazareth had the courage to challenge the institutions of his day.
He had the strength and wisdom to make heaven a viable option.
In spite of suffering and death, he was faithful to his vision;
His teachings have influenced all the world.
He imaged God as divine parent, as divine and benevolent ruler, and as creator of all the world.
We believe that God is still creating and welcomes us to participate to make heaven available on earth.
Through life and death, God is with us.

Offertory Statement (Leader)

God is among us. These walls need our care and so does the neighborhood beyond these walls. Let us share the cost by pooling our money and our expertise.

Doxology   Praise God From Whom All Blessings Flow, tune: OLD HUNDREDTH

Praise God from whom all blessings flow.
Praise God, all creatures here below.
Praise God, above you heavenly hosts.
Creator, Christ, and Holy Ghost.

Prayer Of Thanksgiving (Leader or Unison)

Energy of the Universe — thank you for what we have. Together we feel responsible for making visible something of your kingdom so everyone has food, shelter, and jobs. Stretch our money and our ideas to make peace possible. Amen.

Intercessory Prayers (Leader or Readers)

God of Writers — thank you for the scriptures that have survived time and editing. Empower us to explore multiple ways to articulate your "home among humankind" and to express our devotion to "heaven-living." Expand our perceptions of how you are with us and how you energize us to journey from the cradle to the grave. Inspire us with music, with words, with relationships, and with beauty both internal and external.

God of Readers — thank you for the dreams of men and women through the ages, which give us hope; thank you for words that encourage us to live hospitably. Help us be wise in appropriating ancient beliefs for our twenty-first-century living. Help us practice "no difference among individuals" and "love one another."

God of Artisans — you've made us like yourself. Thank you for the abilities to think, to be friends, to make beautiful and practical things, to feel all the feelings that arise in us. Where we are ailing, touch us with wholeness. When we are full of anger, guide us to express it in helpful ways. Where we are grieving, fill the pain of loss with new awareness of how to be lively again. Where we are scarred, soften us so we can trust life in new ways.

God of Wanderers — look at this world and see your creatures wandering in deserts without sufficient food for body and soul. Speak to individuals who are serving evil and terror. Reveal the goodness of this world and the rewards that come when humans care for one another. We pray for peace through the world, in people's psyches, in national capitals, among tribal leaders. Halt the wars and the greed that support them. Comfort the mothers and fathers, partners and children whose lives have been altered by war's catastrophes. Be in this global village in palpable ways.

Creating God — we pray for the Body of Christ in this place and through all nations. Help us update how we "spread the good news" and how we appeal to all the senses. Guard our children from the wounding that shouts to them from "entertainment" shows. Give us words and images that encourage them to walk with holy intentions. Amen.

Benediction (Leader)
Life is not a dead end;
It is a surprising journey to God.
Say "Yes" to life;
Laugh each day and unwind the threads of the world.
Notice new life around each corner.
Make new dreams and cultivate a glad heart!
Christ lives!

Music
Canto De Esperanza
   Words: Alvin Schutmaat, 1984
   Music: Argentine folk melody
   ARGENTINA

Celebrate With Joy And Singing
   Words: Mary Jackson Cathey, 1986
   Music: R. Bedford Watkins, 1984
   EVELYN CHAPEL

Down To Earth, As A Dove
    Words: Fred Kaan, 1968
    Music: *Piae Cantiones*, 1582; arr. Gustav Theodore von Holst, 1924
    PERSONENT HODIE

Here I Am, Lord
    Words: Daniel L. Schutte, 1981
    Music: Daniel L. Schutte, 1981; harm. James Snyder, 1994
    HERE I AM, LORD

Hope Of The World
    Words: Georgia Harkness, 1954
    Music: Genevan Psalter, 1551
    DONNE SECOURS

Immortal, Invisible, God Only Wise
    Words: Walter Chalmers Smith, 1867, alt.
    Music: Welsh folk melody
    ST. DENIO

O God Of Every Shining Constellation
    Words: Albert F. Bayly, 1950
    Music: V. Earle Copes, 1963
    VICAR

We Meet You, O Christ
    Words: Fred Kaan, 1966
    Music: Basque carol; harm. George Mims, 1979
    NORMANDY

When In Our Music God Is Glorified
    Words: Fred Pratt Green, 1971
    Music: Charles V. Stanford, 1904
    ENGLEBERG

Womb Of Life, And Source Of Being
    Words: Ruth Duck, 1986, 1990
    Music: Traditional Dutch melody; arr. Julius Roentgen, 1906
    IN BABILONE

The World Abounds With God's Free Grace
    Words: David G. Mehrtens, 1980
    Music: George F. Handel, 1748; harm. C. Winfred Douglas, 1941
    HALIFAX

Easter 6

Acts 16:9-15   Revelation 21:10, 22—22:5
Psalm 67   John 14:23-29 or John 5:1-9

> *The Easter story is about the triumph of creativity.*
> *We are all entombed with large boulders blocking our escape*
> *And liberation to the extent our creativity is blocked or stifled.*
> — Matthew Fox, *Creativity*

Call To Worship

Leader: God is here! The Holy One looks on us with kindness.

People: **People look at us from city hall, in the grocery store, and at the university and they recognize that we are intentional about our spiritual journeys; they acknowledge that God is leading us in twenty-first century adventures for the soul.**

Leader: Our behaviors must indicate that we are aligned with the Holy One for justice for those who do not have a voice in our society.

People: **Our relationships and our care for the earth, too, must show our appreciation for this planet and its systems.**

Leader: God is here! We feel the mysterious Divine Presence.

Thanksgiving Prayer (Unison)

Ever-Living God — you bless us with strength and beauty, with truthfulness and satisfying relationships. We appreciate who you are and who you are making us to be. In this hour, stretch our minds and expand our souls so that we may dream ways to make your love palpable in this neighborhood, this church, and this nation. We eagerly listen for your voice. Amen.

Call To Confession (Leader)

Our words and our behaviors indicate the beliefs that motivate us. Sometimes our soul's hopes are betrayed by what comes out of our mouths and by where we go. These silent moments can reveal changes that your mind and body need to make. Pray the printed prayer with me and then make your private prayers.

Community Confession (Unison)

Renewing God — thank you for being at home with us.
We want our daily living to honor your presence.
Free us from past expectations about what is enough and what is due us.
Open our minds to people different from ourselves.
Let us participate with the Spirit's movement. Amen.

Sermon Idea

How often can people hear a story and find new inspiration? The Acts story of Lydia is a favorite of women throughout the church. Prior to Paul's arrival at the riverside to talk to the women (I wonder why he chose not to go to the city gates and speak with the men?), he had some difficulty being welcomed to tell his message. A dream finally guided him to Macedonia. Would we trust a dream to guide us to a new place and a new people? How do we "read" the Spirit's guidance? Are we willing to articulate our faith story when we are with strangers? Would we dare invite an unexpected visiting teacher to our homes for the night? How times have changed since Paul prayed with Lydia!

Contemporary Affirmation (Unison)

Jesus of Nazareth had the courage to challenge the institutions of his day.
> **He had the strength and wisdom to make heaven a viable option.**
> **In spite of suffering and death, he was faithful to his vision;**
>> **His teachings have influenced all the world.**
> **He imaged God as divine parent, divine and benevolent ruler, and as Creator of all the world.**
We believe that God is still creating and welcomes us to participate to make heaven available on earth.
Through life and death, God is with us.

Offertory Statement (Leader)

Lydia decided to participate with the Spirit and with Paul. We participate with each other by sharing the burdens of building care, by feeding homeless neighbors, and by investing in social action for the good of humankind. The baskets are large enough to hold the money you can give.

Doxology   Angels We Have Heard On High (refrain)

Gloria in excelsis Deo! Gloria in excelsis Deo!

Prayer Of Thanksgiving (Leader)

Energy of the Universe — thank you for what we have and for the ability to make goodness happen in many places on this planet. We are your faithful people right here. We love you. Amen.

Intercessory Prayers (Leader or Readers)

God of Many Names — we are glad the story of Lydia working with Paul has survived time and editing. We think of them as bold and adventuresome. We'd like to have these traits, too, so we can participate with your kingdom making. Live in us so justice comes to our city; live through us so people have food; live around us as collaboration and peacefulness.

God of New Life — thank you for the good things about our country. Use our minds and mouths to build community. Use our creative energies to include refugees and help them make a home in this foreign environment. Be real to our children so they may love you and themselves. Stir our church family to be yeast for good education, for a wholesome food supply, and for non-violent entertainment.

God of the Continents — the planet seems so small sometimes! We pray for peace in every nation. Remove destructive leaders and refresh countries whose infrastructures are decimated. Rain awareness and skill on United States leaders so Americans do not contribute to the cyclones of terror that hit other continents.

God of Health and Illness — we are glad when our bodies function well; we are discomforted when they ache and when they are struggling with disease. Show us how to eat for health; keep us alert to environments that give us headaches. Show us how to cooperate with you for wholeness in body and mind. Heal us from head to toe. Amen.

Benediction (Leader)

Life is not a dead end;
It is a surprising journey to God.
Say "Yes" to life;
Laugh each day and unwind the threads of the world.
Notice new life around each corner.
Make new dreams and cultivate a glad heart!
Christ lives!

Music

Canto De Esperanza
Words: Alvin Schutmaat, 1984
Music: Argentine folk melody
ARGENTINA

Celebrate With Joy And Singing
Words: Mary Jackson Cathey, 1986
Music: R. Bedford Watkins, 1984
EVELYN CHAPEL

Down To Earth, As A Dove
Words: Fred Kaan, 1968
Music: *Piae Cantiones*, 1582; arr. Gustav Theodore von Holst, 1924
PERSONENT HODIE

Here I Am, Lord
Words: Daniel L. Schutte, 1981
Music: Daniel L. Schutte, 1981; harm. James Snyder, 1994
HERE I AM, LORD

Hope Of The World
Words: Georgia Harkness, 1954
Music: Genevan Psalter, 1551
DONNE SECOURS

Immortal, Invisible, God Only Wise
  Words: Walter Chalmers Smith, 1867, alt.
  Music: Welsh folk melody
  ST. DENIO

O God Of Every Shining Constellation
  Words: Albert F. Bayly, 1950
  Music: V. Earle Copes, 1963
  VICAR

We Meet You, O Christ
  Words: Fred Kaan, 1966
  Music: Basque carol; harm. George Mims, 1979
  NORMANDY

When In Our Music God Is Glorified
  Words: Fred Pratt Green, 1971
  Music: Charles V. Stanford, 1904
  ENGLEBERG

Womb Of Life, And Source Of Being
  Words: Ruth Duck, 1986, 1990
  Music: Traditional Dutch melody; arr. Julius Roentgen, 1906
  IN BABILONE

The World Abounds With God's Free Grace
  Words: David G. Mehrtens, 1980
  Music: George F. Handel, 1748; harm. C. Winfred Douglas, 1941
  HALIFAX

The Ascension Of Our Lord

Acts 1:1-11   Ephesians 1:15-23
Psalm 47 or Psalm 93   Luke 24:44-53

Our lives end in the middle of the story. We leave the stage before discovering how our story will turn out ... Religion is our human response to the dual reality of being alive and having to die ... I do not disbelieve in an afterlife; I simply have no experience of an afterlife ... Nothing could be weirder or more amazing than life before death.

— Forrest Church, *Love and Death*

Call To Worship

Leader: It's Ascension Day, the day we celebrate Jesus' return to God, forty days after Easter. The scriptures say that the disciples were filled with joy when Jesus was taken up into heaven. After that, they spent all their time in the temple giving thanks to God.

People: They must not have had to work for a corporation! Or punch a time clock!

Leader: In fact, times are very different but the image of Jesus returning to God is essential for our faith.

People: He didn't stay dead and buried! He returned to life and to God!

Leader: In all of our texts for today, there is reference to Jesus' return to the divine home.

People: With Jesus absent, people looked forward to the coming of the Holy Spirit. We are thankful for the stories of Jesus' ascension to heaven, and we anticipate a fresh presence of the Holy Spirit.

Prayer Of Thanksgiving (Leader)

God of Heaven and Earth — we are glad you are our God. We find ourselves turning to you like disciples through the ages; we experience you as loving and dependable. We celebrate Jesus' ascension to heavenly places. In his absence, we expect a fresh outpouring of the Holy Spirit. Speak through us so that the kingdom of God Jesus spoke of comes to our town. Amen.

Call To Confession (Leader)

The writer of Luke and Acts thought repentance and forgiveness were vital for friends of Jesus. Pray with me the printed prayer and then continue your own conversation with God.

Community Confession (Unison)

God of Jesus, Mary, and Paul — our burdens sometimes are very heavy.

Sometimes our shame and our guilt depress our hopes.

Whatever road we've taken to get where we are, let your Spirit move through us freeing us from the ties to earthly greed and jealousy; set us on a new path — straight for the kingdom of God. Amen.

Word Of Grace (Leader)

God is present with us — Christ Spirit, Holy Spirit, Divine Spirit! Look around; notice the Spirit supporting and challenging us in our attitudes and our actions. It is good news that Jesus reigns on high and we are forgiven, free from guilt.

Sermon Idea

What is the meaning of ascension for twenty-first-century friends of Jesus? We do not have monarchs; our cosmology doesn't allow us to envision a tiered universe with God and Jesus at the top; our understanding of God and nations is more inclusive than the writer of the psalms would allow. The meaning for now might include going beyond the boundaries of the temple, beyond the Jews, to other peoples and nations, beyond geography and physics. Ascension might draw us to practice walking with mystery, without understanding; it might focus us on the absent Jesus and the invisible present Spirit. Ascension might encourage us to let go of what preceded our story and look forward to the next one. The story of Jesus' life on earth is concluded but his influence continues. Another theme might be: Standing still, looking up, and participating with the Spirit's creative endeavors! And there is that statement that Jesus will return in a similar way. How does Jesus come to us? Does Jesus "come again" now?

Contemporary Affirmation (Unison)

We believe Jesus lived, died, and rose to new life.

From heaven he came; to heaven he returned.

In his absence, he sent the Holy Spirit to comfort us and to empower us to care for the earth, for the oppressed, for the hungry, and for justice.

We celebrate his life and his teachings with words and with our lifestyles.

We proclaim that the "kingdom of God" is coming now and we are cocreators with the Holy One! Amen. Let it be so!

Offertory Statement (Leader)

Up and down, side to side — everywhere divinity is present! Everywhere there is blessing and need. Let's combine our resources so bills can be paid and justice has a chance to win over violence.

Doxology   Alleluia! Sing to Jesus! (v. 2), tune: HYFRYDOL stanza 2

Alleluia! Not as orphans Are we left in sorrow now.
Alleluia! He is near us; faith believes nor questions how.
Though the cloud from sight received him when the forty days were o'er.
Shall our hearts forget his promise, "I am with you ever more"?

Prayer Of Thanksgiving (Leader)

For the stories of Jesus and for the wonders of life, we are grateful. For the places of God — up and down, in and out — we rejoice! For money, talents, and jobs we are thankful. Amen.

Intercessory Prayers (Leaders or Readers)

God of Up — we have been taught that "up" is positive and that "down" is negative. Yet at the same time we declare that all the world has been declared "good." As we walk the way of Jesus, let us be awake enough to notice the value in all creatures and in all creation. When our paths take us "down" into the shadows, let us feel your presence and sustaining wisdom. When our paths take us "up" to ecstasy, let us celebrate the breath of life and the mysteries inherent in our human journey.

God of Yesterday and Tomorrow — our stories parallel Jesus' in many ways. He is our Savior as we learn to translate his compassion into twenty-first-century issues. He is our Messiah as we explore peace-making. He is the Christ as we practice loving God, self, and neighbor. Let yesteryear's stories give us a sense of direction for tomorrow.

God of Stillness and Motion — our hands and our hearts are often so busy that we miss your subtle grace. Throughout the world we see people who are frantic with physical pain, emotional wounds, and financial requirements. Whatever the suffering, let healing move in close; let inner peace swell; let there be enough nurture and money for each day.

God of Teachers and Students — humankind is learning so much about how the universe functions. We are learning how the human body works, what it will tolerate, and what causes it to die. We eagerly pass all this knowledge on to the next generation. Let us also mentor them in compassion, honesty, gentleness, and kindness. Amen.

Benediction (Leader)

As you leave here, greet one another.
As you leave here, look up for signs of Divine creativity.
As you leave here, look around for the invisible Christ.
As you leave here, look down for the darkness and shadows that are yours to walk through.
As you leave here, rejoice in the mysteries of resurrection and ascension.
Amen. Let it be so!

Music

Colorful Creator
    Words: Ruth Duck, 1992
    Music: Carlton R. Young, 1992
    HOUGHTON

God, Who Stretched The Spangled Heavens
    Words: Catherine Cameron, 1967
    Music: William Moore, Columbian Harmony, 1825
    HOLY MANNA

Ours The Journey
    Words and Music: Julian B. Rush, 1979
    OURS THE JOURNEY

We Are Not Our Own
    Words: Brian Wren, 1987
    Music: Brian Wren, 1987; arr. Fred Graham
    YARNTON

When, In Awe Of God's Creation
    Words: Jane Parker Huber, 1991
    Music: Rowland H. Prichard, 1844; harm. *The English Hymnal*, 1906
    HYFRYDOL

Easter 7

Acts 16:16-34   Revelation 22:12-14, 16-17, 20-21
Psalm 97   John 17:20-26

The Easter story is about the triumph of creativity.
  We are all entombed with large boulders blocking our escape
  And liberation to the extent our creativity is blocked or stifled.
                        — Matthew Fox, *Creativity*

Call To Worship

Leader: Be glad! Today has come. God is here! The whole planet is alive with the elements that sustain our lives.

People: **We breathe air; we are kept warm with fire; we are cooled with cloudy skies; we drink spring waters. All creatures need these elements of nature to continue living.**

Leader: The universe has many systems created by God and called "good." God calls us to care for nature and to resist evil and injustice.

People: **Our relationships and our care for the earth, too, must show our appreciation for this planet and its systems. We are glad for all God has made.**

Leader: Our gratitude shows up in our choices and in our use of time!

Prayer Of Thanksgiving (Unison)

Creating God — thank you for giving us minds to think and hands to work and feet to play! Thank you for this planet home and the beauty you have created to show up at different seasons. We are glad for Sundays, glad for this place, and these companions. Our minds are wide open, expecting you to challenge us, to affirm us, and to give us peace. Amen.

Call To Confession (Leader)

Our words and our behaviors declare the beliefs that motivate us. What do you believe about God's claim on your life? How do you perceive the Holy empowering you? Here are a few minutes to consider the baggage that weighs you down and impedes your inner peace as well as your participation in society. Pray the printed prayer with me and then make your private prayers.

Community Confession (Unison)

Renewing God — how grateful we are for the life and teachings of Jesus.
In him we see the way to be in the world and in you.
Free us from thoughts and behaviors that do not bring your kingdom to earth.
Give us audacity to change.
Expand our curiosity so we explore what is possible.
Reveal to us the shadows in our souls; help us to walk in your light. Amen.

Sermon Idea

The Acts story of Paul healing the "fortune teller" shows the consequences of our actions; there's usually a down-side as well as an up-side. In this case, the woman lost her means of making a living; Paul and Silas were jailed. In the global village, most of our national decisions have a down-side for someone, usually the powerless. Consider the many crafts organizations that teach third-world citizens to make items to sell elsewhere. Which ones actually put food on the table and a roof overhead? Which ones do not add to city garbage dumps? How does Paul's concern for "salvation" translate to a global economy and to global warming? It's fascinating that Paul is vocal about his citizenship and refuses to allow the violence perpetrated against him to go away silently!

Contemporary Affirmation (Unison)

Jesus of Nazareth had the courage to challenge the institutions of his day.

> **He had the strength and wisdom to make heaven a viable option.**
> **In spite of suffering and death, he was faithful to his vision;**
> > **His teachings have influenced all the world.**
> **He imaged God as divine parent, as divine and benevolent ruler, and as creator of all the world.**

We believe that God is still creating and welcomes us to participate to make heaven available on earth

Through life and death, God is with us.

Offertory Statement (Leader)

Jesus came and went about blessing and healing. We can share our talents and our moneys to spread goodness. Share as you can.

Doxology   Angels We Have Heard On High (refrain)

Gloria in excelsis Deo! Gloria in excelsis Deo!

Prayer Of Thanksgiving (Leader)

Energy of the Universe — we are grateful for food, money, and time to share. Work through us to establish a reputation for generosity and kindness. Amen.

Intercessory Prayers (Leader or Readers)

God of Jailers and Fortune Tellers — we are aware that sometimes we play these roles. Help us to be wise enough to know when and where each might be appropriate. Inspire us with words, paintings, music, and movement. Live through us so your kingdom is a reality in some way.

God of Jesus and Mary — thank you for the stories that remind us how to be in relationship with you and one another. Guide us to live the teachings of Jesus so we are at peace with ourselves and with our neighbors. Like men and women before us, we pray for peace in our neighborhoods and among nations. We pray for a powerful rush of Easter Life and Pentecostal Spirit so peace can come to every tribe.

God of Chaos and Order — we pray for the church, the organization that tries to be helpful to us who seek to be at one with you. We pray for the church, the institution that tries to practice the compassion of Christ and the inclusiveness of Jesus. Help us not to put old duties and responsibilities before our twenty-first-century loyalty to you.

God of Body and Soul — we pray for ourselves. We need courage to endure being consciously human. Our bodies ache, our minds slow down, society is not kind, violence is everywhere, and our souls long for your satisfying Spirit. Soothe our bodies. Shape our attitudes and our hopes so that our children and grandchildren honor you in caring for the earth and all its creatures. Amen.

Benediction (Leader)
Life is not a dead end;
It is a surprising journey to God.
Say "Yes" to life;
Laugh each day and unwind the threads of the world.
Notice new life around each corner.
Make new dreams and cultivate a glad heart!
Christ lives!

Music
Canto De Esperanza
    Words: Alvin Schutmaat, 1984
    Music: Argentine folk melody
    ARGENTINA

Celebrate With Joy And Singing
    Words: Mary Jackson Cathey, 1986
    Music: R. Bedford Watkins, 1984
    EVELYN CHAPEL

Down To Earth, As A Dove
    Words: Fred Kaan, 1968
    Music: *Piae Cantiones*, 1582; arr. Gustav Theodore von Holst, 1924
    PERSONENT HODIE

Here I Am, Lord
    Words: Daniel L. Schutte, 1981
    Music: Daniel L. Schutte, 1981; harm. James Snyder, 1994
    HERE I AM, LORD

Hope Of The World
    Words: Georgia Harkness, 1954
    Music: Genevan Psalter, 1551
    DONNE SECOURS

Immortal, Invisible, God Only Wise
    Words: Walter Chalmers Smith, 1867, alt.
    Music: Welsh folk melody
    ST. DENIO

O God Of Every Shining Constellation
    Words: Albert F. Bayly, 1950
    Music: V. Earle Copes, 1963
    VICAR

We Meet You, O Christ
    Words: Fred Kaan, 1966
    Music: Basque carol; harm. George Mims, 1979
    NORMANDY

When In Our Music God Is Glorified
    Words: Fred Pratt Green, 1971
    Music: Charles V. Stanford, 1904
    ENGLEBERG

Womb Of Life, And Source Of Being
    Words: Ruth Duck, 1986, 1990
    Music: Traditional Dutch melody; arr. Julius Roentgen, 1906
    IN BABILONE

The World Abounds With God's Free Grace
    Words: David G. Mehrtens, 1980
    Music: George F. Handel, 1748; harm. C. Winfred Douglas, 1941
    HALIFAX

Season 6
Early Pentecost

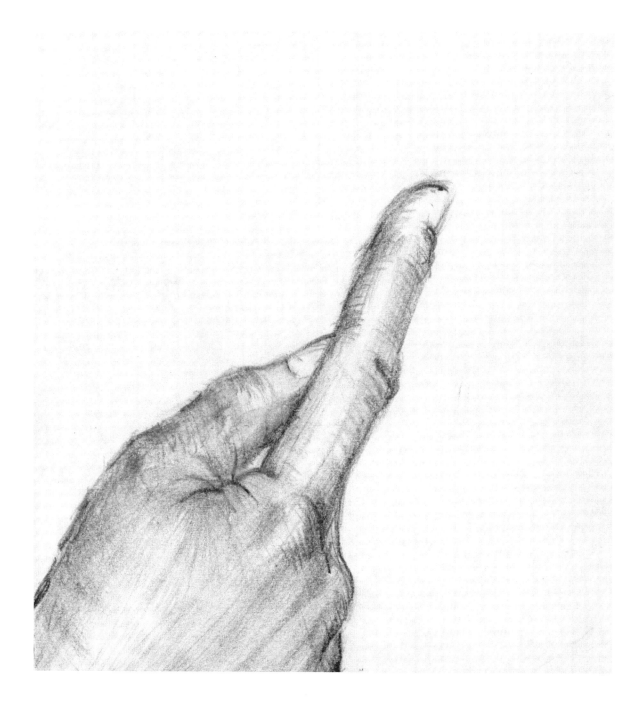

Promotion

The Day Of Pentecost

Acts 2:1-21 or Genesis 11:1-9   Romans 8:14-17
Psalm 104:24-34, 35b   John 14:8-17 (25-27)

Zoos are no longer in people's good graces.
Religion faces the same problem.
Certain illusions about freedom plague them both.

— Yann Martel, *Life of Pi*

(The week before this day, invite people to wear colors of fire to acknowledge the vitality and passion of the Spirit.)

Call To Worship

Leader: It's a good morning! We're awake, breathing, and conversing!

People: We thank God for the breath of life, for mystery and majesty and light!

Leader: We are surrounded with beauty and we thank God, creator of all, for the varied manifestations of divine imagination!

People: In songs, in conversation, and in silence we celebrate the Holy among us!

Prayer Of Thanksgiving (Leader or Unison)

Energy of the Universe — your emanations amaze us. The ocean and the mountains, the birds and the whales, the moon and the sun, ice and fire, blue eyes and brown — all around us we see your work. We recognize your liveliness in the seasons that come and go. Thank you for your dependable care of us and of all creation. Thank you for inviting us to be cocreators with you. In this hour, we await your revelation and we explore ways to spell and say, "God." We are eager to be engaged with your Spirit. Amen.

Call To Confession (Leader)

Throughout the global village this morning, people are pronouncing "God" in their own languages, spelling "God" with their own alphabets. Everywhere, people are asking questions about the meaning of their lives. We have our own questions and now there is time to reflect on the Holy Presence with us, noticing the attitudes and ideas that separate us from our sisters and brothers with different alphabets. Pray with me the printed prayer and then have your personal conversation with the Holy One.

Community Confession (Unison)

Designer of Alphabets — there is so much we do not understand.

Why do some people spell you "Allah" and "Adonai" and "God"?

Why do some say you call for peace and then do violence to their neighbors?

Why do some say you call for justice and then are not fair or honest in their practices?

There is so much we do not understand.

We do know that deep within us is an urge to be connected to what is eternal. So, in this very moment, we want to be free from anything that retards our journey to Holy Mystery and psyche peace.

Transform our priorities and our goals; reshape our relationships and our professions. Amen.

Sermon Idea

Behind the scenes at Babel and Pentecost is the human desire to be close to the Holy, to be intimate with Mystery. The Sacred does not need a tower or a building of any kind to communicate with the human mind and psyche. The Divine does not need a labeled birthday cake or a singular alphabet to describe the Eternal Energy. But humans need words to talk about their experiences with that Energy. Humans need words to describe the "Help in Ages Past." Adjectives and verbs, nouns and adverbs help us explain how the Deity is with humankind and how we relate to Deity. Muslims say there are 99 names for God — like Wise One, the Good, the Merciful, the Compassionate, the Real Close, the First, the Last. Judaism and Christianity share these attributes of God. In the Pentecost story, one alphabet, one word, one experience of the Holy is expanded to be available in all languages among all people! As Yann Martel suggests in *The Life of Pi*, the Holy is too mysterious to be fit into any one name, any one word, any one animal; so there are many ways to spell God and we need them all if our psyches are to be free. The task/goal is to help ourselves remember that God loves us; another is to practice loving the way Jesus loved.

Whether it was fifty days after the ascension or fifty days after the crucifixion, Pentecost was a time of celebration, of jubilee. The Pentecost story is the first opportunity the disciples have at marketing their understanding of the Holy Spirit. Peter is a most articulate promoter. Pentecost promotion goes on until Advent. During this time (also called "proper" and "ordinary"), the church is serious about mission and about increasing the numbers of believers.

Contemporary Affirmation (Unison)

We know God, the Creator, by many names;
we believe that God, the Holy One, loves us and all creation.
We know Jesus of Nazareth taught people to love friends and enemies;
we believe Jesus' teachings lead us to satisfaction in living.
We believe the Holy Spirit is moving throughout the global village,
inviting all peoples to live peaceably together;
we experience the Holy Spirit to be motivating us to journey toward
internal contentment and external service for justice.
In community, we are stimulated intellectually to ask questions
about the meaning of life and Mystery.
We are challenged to know ourselves and to relate to God.
We are soothed during the painful parts of life and in good times,
we share our rejoicings! Hurrah! Yippee! Hallelujah!

Offertory Statement (Leader)

With your own language, your own talents, and your own moneys, this is the moment when you can respond with generosity to Holy Generosity so that tangible goodness continues in this place.

Doxology   The Lone, Wild Bird (v. 2, modified), tune: PROSPECT

The ends of earth are in God's hand, The sea's dark deep and far-off land.
And I am yours! I rest in you. Great Spirit, come, and rest in me.

Prayer Of Thanksgiving (Leader)

God of Babel and Pentecost — we are grateful for the ways you are among us, blessing us with multiple gifts. Thank you for this money and for the talents gathered here. Amen.

Intercessory Prayers (Leader or Readers)

God of Words — in poetry and prose, in sound waves and visual images, we experience your life-changing activity. For those of us in pain, speak encouragement; for those of us struggling with disease, speak healing; for those of us who are depressed and disillusioned, speak hope. For those of us whose burdens seem unbearable, lift us with options; for those of us whose baggage hampers wholeness, touch us with surprising possibilities. Whatever our need, meet us in our own languages, in our own images, on our own paths.

God of Thoughts — some of us think literally, some of us think symbolically. Some of us imagine how things might be; some imagine how you think and speak and plan. Some of us ask questions and answer them with stories to explain what is important to us. Some define how you work with humankind. Some of us feel you in silence; some are inspired with thoughts amid clutter. Some of us build spires and some build crosses. However you come to us, thank you. Thank you for your everywhere-present Spirit. Help us not be arrogant or stubborn about our own experiences with freedom and grace.

God of Religions — we've tried since human beginnings to understand how the cosmos came into being, what holds the earth in place, why the sun is golden and the moon silvery. We've wondered if you have a beard, if you have hair, and if your ears hug your head; we wonder what makes some people kind and some cruel. These questions are not answered in ways that satisfy our curiosity, but we do understand that people of today are in a long line of humans who seek to know you and one another. With bricks and mortar, with prayers and names, with rules and ceremonies, we have tried to make sure you love us and that we please you. Each of us has a nickname for you to express our loyalty and love. Guide us in our questing; open us to the possibilities of your ways throughout this planet.

God of Bread and Grapes — rain and drought cycle through days and nights on every continent. Insects and diseases ravage crops in every nation. We pray for peace and food for the children and adults in every tribe. Come to politicians, raining on them wisdom and compassion, compelling them to share their wealth with people whose blessings are minimal, whose skills do not support their will to live. Banish corruption and evil intent; stop hatred and ugliness. Let us and this planet experience again real truth, real neighborliness, and real godliness. Let there be no more war; instead, inspire all humankind to wage peace. Amen.

Benediction (Leader)

Life is a surprising journey to God.
Experiment with multiple names for God;
Explore different ways to respond to the Holy Spirit.
Laugh each day and unbuild the overwhelming towers of the world.
Notice possibilities around each corner;
Make dreams and cultivate a glad heart!
Holy Spirit empowers you and me to live *real life* —
Peace be yours, deep peace. Amen.

Music

Every Time I Feel The Spirit
    Words: African-American spiritual
    Music: African-American spiritual; arr. Joseph T. Jones (1902-1983); adapt. Melva W.
        Costen
    PENTECOST

The Lone, Wild Bird *(note: the second verse of this hymn is also suggested for use as the*
        Doxology for the entire Pentecost season)
    Words: Henry Richard McFadyen, 1925, alt.
    Music: as in *Twelve Folksongs and Spirituals*, 1968; harm. David N. Johnson, 1968
    PROSPECT

Spirit
    Words and Music: James K. Manley, 1975
    SPIRIT

Spirit Of The Living God
    Words: Daniel Iverson, 1935; adapt.
    Music: Daniel Iverson, 1935
    LIVING GOD

Wind Upon The Waters
    Words and Music: Marty Haugen, 1986
    WIND UPON THE WATERS

The Holy Trinity

Proverbs 8:1-4, 22-31   Romans 5:1-5
Psalm 8   John 16:12-15

Zoos are no longer in people's good graces.
Religion faces the same problem.
Certain illusions about freedom plague them both.

— Yann Martel, *Life of Pi*

Call To Worship

Leader: Welcome. Last week was a fiery Sunday. Today is a white one. Today we mark the description of God as three parts — Father, Son, and Holy Spirit. Another way to describe God as three parts is: mind, body, and psyche. We're here to sing and pray to God, the Holy One.

People: **We are here to "keep the sabbath." We are glad for one day to rest and to do different things from the rest of the week. We want to listen for God, to gain wisdom, and to receive strength.**

Leader: We are surrounded with beauty and we read poetry from Proverbs about God having a child at the divine knees while sinking the foundations for the world! We'll read about children adoring God in songs. We'll hear the psalmist marveling at the universe and at God's goodness to humankind. We will hear scriptures invite us to be wise.

People: **In songs, in conversation, and in silence we celebrate the written word, the spoken word, and the creating word among us!**

Prayer Of Thanksgiving (Leader)

Creator of the Universe — your emanations amaze us. The horizon and the clouds, the owls and the porpoises, the balanced earth, and the expanding cosmos all speak of your creative imagination. We recognize your liveliness in the seasons that come and go. Thank you for the poets who have described how you are with us; we are glad for the pleasure each time we read their imaginative descriptions. This hour, we anticipate guidance to help us mature and bring us to wisdom. Amen.

Call To Confession (Leader)

In old and new cities, people have tried to make the best use of a little bit of space. In Babylon, in New York City, and in our town, buildings seem to touch the sky and even pierce the heavens. We can be glad that God makes a home with us so that we can be cocreators with the Holy. In these few minutes, consider the language you use to talk about your work, your leisure, and your faith. Pray with me the printed prayer and then have your personal conversation with the One God.

Community Confession (Unison)
Sun Stopper — how easy it is to dream a building and make it real!
How amazing it is to see the moon and go there!

We long to be close to you, to be at home with you, yet our lifestyles often leave little time to listen to you and little energy to talk with you.

Shift our priorities so we feel your affirmation and feel contented with living.

We long to be close to you, body, soul, and mind. Amen.

Sermon Idea

The biblical scenes at Babel and Pentecost remind us of the human desire to be close, to be intimate with Mystery. The Holy One does not need mathematics and numerology to be present in the human heart. The Trinity concept emerged several centuries after the death of Jesus as a way to explain the relationship of *nous*, *soma*, and *spiritus/pneuma*, God Father, God Son, God Spirit: mind, body, and soul. Converts to *The Way* were attempting to articulate the connection between Jesus of Nazareth and the God in heaven, Yahweh/Adonai. They tried their best to articulate the wisdom and vision they experienced when walking with Jesus. The Proverbs and Psalm readings present images different from the Hellenistic images of "sameness/essence." One translation of Proverbs 8:22f suggests that a part of God functioned as a nursling/child/architect beside the Holy One while creation was happening. An interesting image, that a part of God inspired play and creativity, which resulted in the world! Psychologists have told us for more than half a century about the child-within. We are made in the Divine mold and we have various creative parts of ourselves that help us along our human paths. It might be interesting to compare the pre-scientific view of the world with the contemporary one. The preacher could also consider human perceptions of how and why God intervenes in history.

Contemporary Affirmation (Unison)

We know God, the Creator, by many names;
   we believe that God, the Holy One, loves us and all creation.

We know Jesus of Nazareth taught people to love friends and enemies;
   we believe Jesus' teachings lead us to satisfaction in living.

We believe the Holy Spirit is moving throughout the global village,
   inviting all peoples to live peaceably together;
   we experience the Holy Spirit to be motivating us to journey toward
      internal contentment and external service for justice.

In community, we are stimulated intellectually to ask questions
   about the meaning of life and Mystery.

We are challenged to know ourselves and to relate to God.

We are soothed during the painful parts of life and in good times,
   we share our rejoicings! Hurrah! Yippee! Hallelujah!

Offertory Statement (Leader)

We have many opportunities to serve God and the church. This is one of them. The money you put in the basket and the time you use to teach, fix things, and listen to someone enhance our life together and make reaching out to others a bit easier. Give as you can.

Doxology   The Lone, Wild Bird (v. 2, modified), tune: PROSPECT

The ends of earth are in God's hand, The sea's dark deep and far-off land.

And I am yours! I rest in you. Great Spirit, come, and rest in me.

Prayer Of Thanksgiving (Leader)

God of Languages and Buildings — we are glad for the ways you are among us especially for being like a parent, a child, and a gracious Spirit. Thank you for this money and for the talents gathered here. Amen.

Intercessory Prayers (Leader or Readers)

God of Words and Numbers — we venture into mathematics and physics to get of glimpse of what you might be like. We wonder with rhyme and paragraphs, with decibels and colors, and with dramatic architectural designs how you answer prayers. We can only imagine how you heal us and how you protect us. With gratitude we acknowledge that you work in us until we are whole. Comfort us who grieve; soothe our distressed psyches; mend our bodies.

God of Thoughts — some of us think symbolically in ones and threes, in unities and trinities. Some of us think that you whisper and write down words in our own language. What we know is that the scriptures enrich our thinking and help us see humanity with all its foibles and graces seeking to be with you. Guide us along the way.

Builder of the Cosmos — with bricks and mortar, with prayers and names, with rules and ceremonies we have tried to be sure you love us and we try to please you. Guide us in our questing; open us to perceiving you in ways beyond those of today. Make us whole as you are whole.

God of Deserts and Rain Forests — as in Bible times, lands are dry and food crops are insufficient to feed the hungry, especially in Africa. We know that human behaviors cause detrimental changes to the earth's ecosystems. Give us courage to do things differently so food and energy resources serve more people for a very long time. May peace between leaders trickle down to make peace between neighbors. Amen.

Benediction (Leader)

Go from this place with ideas that will build bridges between peoples.

Go with a song in your heart and a lilt in your step.

Go, aware that Divinity resides in you.

Go, as a peacemaker, friend of the living Christ.

Music

Holy, Holy, Holy! Lord God Almighty!
 Words: Reginald Heber, 1826, alt.
 Music: John B. Dykes, 1861; descant O. I. Cricket Harrison, 1994
 NICAEA

Womb Of Life, And Source Of Being
 Words: Ruth Duck, 1986, 1990
 Music: Traditional Dutch melody; arr. Julius Roentgen, 1906
 IN BABYLONE

Creating God, Your Fingers Trace
    Words: Jeffery Rowthorn, 1974
    Music: Thomas Tallis, 1561
    TALLIS' CANON

Come, Great God Of All The Ages
    Words: Mary Jackson Cathey, 1987
    Music: Cyril V. Taylor, 1941
    ABBOT'S LEIGH

God Is Here
    Words: Fred Pratt Green, 1978
    Music: Cyril V. Taylor, 1941
    ABBOT'S LEIGH

Proper 4
Ordinary Time 9
Pentecost 2

1 Kings 18:20-21 (22-29) 30-39   Galatians 1:1-12
   or 1 Kings 8:22-23, 41-43
Psalm 96 or Psalm 96:1-9   Luke 7:1-10

> *Atonement, [sometimes called at-one-ment] takes place where men and women, races, classes, and nations are made one, where reconciliation, release, renewal, the reunion of life with life are experienced.*
> — J. A. T. Robinson, *The Human Face of God*

Call To Worship

Leader: We're here again! It must be Sunday! The Old Testament poet invites us to sing to God — a new song! With the sky overhead and the earth suspended mysteriously in its place among the planets, it is easy for us to be awed and to sing and dance our praise.

People: We certainly do not want to bore God with repetitious songs or old dances.

Leader: Let's try some new songs, some new words, and some new rituals.

People: Hmm, we're not sure we are comfortable enough to do that.

Leader: How are you willing to stretch your faith and to honor God?

People: Let's sing a new song — maybe the *doxology* toward the end of the service — and speak different words. But let's not dance or try new rituals today.

Leader: Perhaps the earth and sky, the trees and animals will shout their joy!

People: We trust God to establish justice and fairness no matter what words we say and what rituals we do. For another day, we will practice new songs and new dances as our faith expands and as all our senses experience the living God!

Prayer Of Thanksgiving (Unison)

Living God — we open our hearts and minds to you with words we think and with feelings that arise. We do not want to bore you with worn out arts nor with habits that are done without awareness. We do love you and want to proclaim your mystery wherever we are. In this hour, stretch our faith, enlarge our repertoire of praise, and expand our courage. Amen.

Call To Confession (Leader)

Perhaps this is the day to notice what we believe and how we integrate it with our view of the world and with our decisions. Pray with me and then continue your own prayer in silence.

Community Confession (Antiphonal)

Left side: **Awesome God, we believe what we've been told without figuring out what is mythical truth and what is functional reality.**

Right side:	**Gracious God, sometimes we are ignorant as to the effect of violent stories on our psyches and we continue to abuse our souls with obsolete views of blood and healing.**
Left side:	**Creating God, open our eyes to your present activity in this world and in our minds.**
Right side:	**Mysterious God, open our ears to your voice speaking in events, in conversations, and in beauty.**
All:	**Merciful God, thank you for the myriad of ways you reveal yourself. We don't want to miss a single sound or sight; we don't want to ignore a single bit of radiance or shadow. Save us from our doting on our preferred ways of being. Do something new with us! Amen.**

Word Of Grace (Leader)

Our experience with God the Creator is that of a healing and affirming Deity. In turn, God invites us to be in relationship with the Holy and with one another. In our attitudes and our actions, let us cocreate beauty and fairness. Jesus asks us to be good neighbors and to align ourselves with his teachings. We can do this and be at peace with God and with ourselves. Let it be so!

Sermon Idea

The 1 Kings passage is a success story for the prophet Elijah of ancient times with ancient rituals. It is a gory story, a story of animal sacrifice and human sacrifice. It is a story we see on the news of the mideast week after week: twenty-first-century people trying to appease Divinity as they understand him and in the process destroy land and humankind.

The gospel story is different; Jesus heals a person of another ethnic group. Both Jesus and the centurion are people of faith and they get their hopes met. As in some other biblical texts, the stranger is respected. This story is wholesome for adults and children and is consistent with other stories we have of Jesus. This story promotes peace rather than a hard-nosed deity demanding a particular kind of loyalty. If stretched a bit, the preacher might include the topic of immigration as well as ethnic differences as this text is exegeted.

In the Galatians passage, there is contention between Paul and some church folk. The question seems to be whether he is a legitimate apostle of Jesus. This is another story we hear again and again in the Christian church: Who shall have power and what is the *real* dogma.

This particular week, the title/theme might be: Mending Fences and Healing the Planet. The Paul and Elijah stories are not helpful to adults and youth trying to figure out their relationship with the Holy One and how to make the loving God tangible in this decade. These stories *are* helpful in understanding something of what is happening in Israel and Palestine — the biblical feuds go on with lethal tools/weapons that maim the next generation psychologically, spiritually, and physically, not only in the mideast but throughout the global village. Do Christians want to perpetuate this violence?

As Christians, we are called to heal the sick, free the oppressed, and provide for those without life's basic necessities. "Let the children come" needs to be a lively and healthy encounter with the Holy. How else can there be peace across boundaries? How else can the land be cleared of mines (weapons and coal) so children have natural playgrounds? The preacher has the challenge of telling the Bible stories without allowing violence to be acceptable. Or perhaps the challenge is to acknowledge the evolution of human culture, human psyche, and Spirit from antiquity to now.

Contemporary Affirmation (Unison)

The Creating God is a great mystery, inviting us to be cocreators in this world.

The Christ is the teacher, calling us to live wholesome lifestyles that satisfy our souls.

The Holy Spirit is the live-in presence of the Creating God, urging us to welcome personal growth and to reach out to others.

The Body of Christ is the gathered friends of Jesus, sustaining one another through times of hardship, grief, and joy.

Life together allows us to worship God, walk with Christ, and respond to the Spirit.

Together, we sing, pray, listen, speak, and enjoy wine and bread.

Together, we make it from the cradle to the grave. We are not alone!

Offertory Statement (Leader)

If we share what we have, there is enough for everyone — enough food, clothing, and money. Sharing our money means we can maintain this building *and* fill the shelves at the Community Pantry with good foods. Sharing our skills means we can keep this space beautiful and functional as well as construct a Habitat House downtown. Let's pass the baskets!

Doxology   Sovereign God Of All Creation (v. 1, modified), tune: GENEVA

Sovereign God of all creation, Ground of being, life and love;
Height and depth beyond description Only life in you can prove:
You are mortal life's dependence; Thought, speech, sight are ours by grace;
Yours is every hour's existence, Sovereign God of time and space.

Prayer Of Thanksgiving (Leader)

Generous God — thank you for more-than-adequate resources to help make this place and our neighborhoods safe and lovely. Amen.

Intercessory Prayer (Leader or Readers)

Creating Spirit — listening to the news disturbs our souls. Is there peace anywhere? Is there a collaborative attitude somewhere in our nation? Let wisdom spring up in Israel and in Palestine, in Iraq and in Iran, in Afghanistan and Pakistan, and in America so that peace can escape from ancient feuds and a benevolent global village can be a reality.

Healing Spirit — our mortality shows! Sustain us through life's stages and let us learn to grow and to learn something about ourselves and about you each day. When we feel down, let us look within to find the goodness in the shadows. When we feel up, let us share our delight with living. When we ache, let us experiment with massage and conversation, with heat and cool until we have relief. In our coming and going, we rejoice that we are held in your energy.

Designing Spirit — we think we are created to be in relationship with Divinity and with humanity. Yet we often feel lonely and fearful. Let us learn to trust one another and to value our differences. Let us celebrate our similarities and revel in the good times we share. Thank you for the women and men who maintain this building and our programs so we may have a satisfying *life together*. Thank you for the prayers and tenderness that hold us together.

Singing Spirit — even silence has a sound as the stars and planets move about space. Our silence is full of sighs and *hmmms* as we consider how our time is spent. Sing to us of new ways to think; sing of sustainable lifestyles so we can banish poverty, hunger, and homelessness. Let us listen carefully and understand.

Loving Spirit — we know so many people who need care, so we pray for them. We name them in the quiet places of our minds: *(pause for silent prayers)* Thank you for being present with us. Amen.

Benediction (Leader)

We've considered the scriptures we've received.
We've sung our praise and prayed our angst.
We've honored God with our thoughts and our attitudes.
Go from here with a glad heart, a lively step, and hope for tomorrow.
Be peacemakers everywhere! God is your strength!

Music

Bring Many Names
    Words: Brian Wren, 1987
    Music: Carlton R. Young, 1987
    WESTCHASE

Creating God, Your Fingers Trace
    Words: Jeffery Rowthorn, 1974
    Music: Thomas Tallis, 1561
    TALLIS' CANON

Mothering God, You Gave Me Birth
    Words: Jean Janzen, 1991, based on the writings of Julian of Norwich (14th century)
    Music: Brent Stratten, 1994
    JULIAN

Source And Sovereign, Rock And Cloud
    Words: Thomas H. Troeger, 1987
    Music: Joseph Parry, 1879
    ABERYSTWYTH

Proper 5
Ordinary Time 10
Pentecost 3

1 Kings 17:8-24   Galatians 1:11-24
Psalm 30 or Psalm 146   Luke 7:11-17

Zoos are no longer in people's good graces.
Religion faces the same problem.
Certain illusions about freedom plague them both.

— Yann Martel, *Life of Pi*

Call To Worship

Leader: A good summer morning to you! Are you alert, centered, and talkative? Are you joyfilled? Are you ready to sing?

People: Ah, yes. We are thankful for life and we are seeking security and happiness.

Leader: We have called to God many times and the Holy One has sustained us and restored us to hopefulness.

People: With music and dance, with words and silence, we thank God for divine goodness among us!

Prayer Of Thanksgiving (Leader)

God of Words and Silence — we are glad for the many ways we can express our love for you, and we are grateful for the myriad of ways you make your presence known to us. We are glad for scripture stories that encourage us to care for one another. We offer you our undivided attention so that we might know and feel your grace. Amen.

Call To Confession (Leader)

Elijah moved among the Hebrews with words of judgment and words of healing. Like the widow in the 1 Kings story today, we have many concerns. Do we have enough food? Will our resources last as long as we live? Will our bodies and minds stay strong? At some point each of us will die but until that moment, let us live fully, doing what is pleasing to the Holy One and caring for one another. Pray the printed prayer with me.

Community Confession (Unison)

Story Keeper — we are like the widows in the Bible stories.
We lose so much day by day, year by year.
We get numb to the pain and advertising.
We forget to wait for you to heal us and to show us a new way.
We entertain ourselves and neglect making time for conversation with you.
We want the healing touch of Jesus to strengthen us and wipe away our tears. Amen.

Sermon Idea

Galatians 1:23 raises our eyebrows! What happens internally that transforms us today? What changes our perceptions of truth? And then, how do we articulate psyche/soul metamorphosis? How do we break previous habits and behave in new (wholesome) ways? Another issue in this text is that of public and institutional validation of our inner experience. It is an awesome experience to have "walked with the Spirit" and then have no one believe "your truth." Ask any schizophrenic who has not taken his/her medication. What about the fundamentalist in every religion who perceives God speaking, often claiming personal advantage/reward at the expense of others? Reputation is as important to the apostle as it is to any congregation/individual today; it is part of our identities and must be guarded from theft and defilement. In a culture where it is important to know the "right" people in order to get a job or accepted into an educational program, reputation sometimes carries more weight than actual accomplishments and qualifications.

The Luke story asks, "What makes us afraid spiritually and what do we do when we have had an awesome experience?" Some theologies say that when life is going well, people tend to forget God. Others suggest that joy and awe, curiosity and imagination are perpetual avenues to Mystery. From the texts in Luke and 1 Kings, what is dying in us that needs rejuvenated?

Contemporary Affirmation (Unison)

    We know God, the Creator, by many names;
        we believe that God, the Holy One, loves us and all creation.
    We know Jesus of Nazareth taught people to love friends and enemies;
        we believe Jesus' teachings lead us to satisfaction in living.
    We believe the Holy Spirit is moving throughout the global village,
        inviting all peoples to live peaceably together;
        we experience the Holy Spirit to be motivating us to journey toward
            internal contentment and external service for justice.
    In community, we are stimulated intellectually to ask questions
        about the meaning of life and Mystery.
    We are challenged to know ourselves and to relate to God.
    We are soothed during the painful parts of life and in good times,
        we share our rejoicings! Hurrah! Yippee! Hallelujah!

Offertory Statement (Leader)

With your own language, your own talents, and your own moneys, you can respond with generosity so that tangible goodness continues in this place.

Doxology   The Lone, Wild Bird (v. 2, modified), tune: PROSPECT

The ends of earth are in God's hand, The sea's dark deep and far-off land.
And I am yours! I rest in you. Great Spirit, come, and rest in me.

Prayer Of Thanksgiving (Leader)

Giver of Hope — we are grateful for the ways you are among us, blessing us in multiple ways. Thank you for this money; multiply it to pay our bills and feed the hungry. Amen.

Intercessory Prayers (Leader or Readers)

Life-Giving Spirit — how quickly the beauty of spring turns into the heat of summer! Global warmth is in our backyards! Fresh water is beyond our grasp! We pray for gentle rains to refresh the land and our own souls. We also recognize the pain and loss of people whose homes and crops have been destroyed by the violence of storms. Awaken in all of us the wisdom to cooperate with the earth's systems and with your resuscitation for our spirits day by day.

God of Thinkers — we read the stories of return to life and wish that death only came to all creatures when it was "appropriate." Like men and women before us, we long for security, health, and peace. We want wars to cease and sons and daughters in every nation to live wholesome and neighborly lives. Guide our thoughts so that peace is deep in our behaviors and decisions.

Integrator of Mind and Body — we are grateful for the knowledge science has accumulated. We pray for the next generation. May technology and economics enrich their understanding and may their hearts turn toward the teachings of Jesus. Like the widows' sons in scripture, may our sons and daughters receive soul life that enables them to carry good news and civil habits everywhere they go. Rejuvenate cultures so that people establish gentleness and honesty as every-day-ways to do business and make peace.

Community Builder — we are grateful for the women and men who enrich our lives. We are glad for resources to pay our bills and sustain ministry in this place. Satisfy our longings and let our decisions manifest your vitality here at church home and in our city. Amen.

Benediction (Leader or Readers)

Life is a journey to Mystery.
Experiment with multiple names for God;
Explore different ways to respond to the Holy Spirit.
Laugh each day and unbuild the overwhelming towers of the world.
Notice possibilities around each corner;
Make dreams and cultivate a glad heart!
Holy Spirit empowers you and me to live *real life* —
Peace be yours, deep peace. Amen.

Music

God, You Spin The Whirling Planets
    Words: Jane Parker Huber, 1978
    Music: Franz Joseph Haydn, 1797
    AUSTRIAN HYMN

Help Us Accept Each Other
    Words: Fred Kaan, 1974
    Music: John Ness Beck, 1977
    ACCEPTANCE

O God Of Vision
    Words: Jane Parker Huber, 1981
    Music: *Erneuerten Gesangbuch*, 1665
    LOBE DEN HERREN

Sing Of A God In Majestic Divinity
    Words: Herbert O'Driscoll, 1980
    Music: Johann H. Reinhardt's Choralbuch, Üttingen, 1754
    ÜTTINGEN

Proper 6
Ordinary Time 11
Pentecost 4

1 Kings 21:1-10 (11-14) 15-21a   Galatians 2:15-21
     or 2 Samuel 11:26—12:10, 13-15
Psalm 5:1-8 or Psalm 32   Luke 7:36—8:3

Zoos are no longer in people's good graces.
Religion faces the same problem.
Certain illusions about freedom plague them both.

— Yann Martel, *Life of Pi*

Call To Worship

Leader: Let me guess: You've come here to enjoy one another?
People: **Yes. But more importantly, we've come to be still in Divine Presence and respond with words, music, and silent thoughtfulness.**
Leader: Together, then, let us sing joyfully and listen reverently.
People: **God invites us to be cheerful and expects us to be honest.**
Leader: In Holy Presence, we learn to be do-ers of goodness, to be compassionate, and to be thankful for what life brings to us.
All: **Together, we will listen for God's voice and be thankful for divine love.**

Prayer Of Thanksgiving (Leader)

Gracious God — thank you for this place and your presence among us. Thank you for bringing us to this point in our living and learning. We want to be happy and so we seek to be continually aware of your affirmation. We are loyal companions on this trek to eternity and we watch for your guiding light. Amen.

Call To Confession (Leader)

Throughout the global village this morning, violence and hatred maim bodies and minds. Here in our own city people go hungry and homeless. Yet the teachings of Jesus challenge us to end poverty and establish justice. The cruel and gruesome lurk on our streets. Yet Jesus challenges us to be peace-makers and to love even our enemies. These teachings are difficult to carry out. We each have our own prejudices, our own disappointments, and our own guilt. Pray with me the printed prayer and then have your personal conversation with the Holy One.

Community Confession (Unison)

Designer of Humankind — as we look into our own motives, we see attitudes that are not consistent with the teachings of Jesus.
Some of us pray for peace but are resentful of our neighbors.
Some of us are tangled by attitudes, which deny others healthcare and clean water; some of us are enmeshed with friends who indulge in unwholesome habits.
Some of us are blinded by our own desires.

Some of us have murderous jealousies.
Set us free from all deceit and help us learn how to be your hands and mind in this world.
   Amen.

Sermon Idea

The 1 Kings story is about Ahab pouting, not getting his way and allowing, maybe expecting, his spouse to fix things by having someone else to do the dirty work of assassination of character and then murder.

Second Samuel 11 is the story of envy and murder of a person while 1 Kings is about land and murder. These "texts of terror" (Phyllis Trible's phrase) reveal human jealousy about things and intimacy; such darkness seems to be inherent in every generation.

Luke 7:36 ff suggests that the judging of others is arrogant. To individuals and to small communities, The Law shows what wrongdoing is (Colossians 2:15-21). Yet, The Law does not give us satisfying relationships and happiness. Struggling with our human relationships and with spiritual contentment makes us feel alive and willing to manifest our experience with Christ.

Contemporary Affirmation (Unison)

   We know God, the Creator, by many names;
      we believe that God, the Holy One, loves us and all creation.
   We know Jesus of Nazareth taught people to love friends and enemies;
      we believe Jesus' teachings lead us to satisfaction in living.
   We believe the Holy Spirit is moving throughout the global village,
      inviting all peoples to live peaceably together;
      we experience the Holy Spirit to be motivating us to journey toward
         internal contentment and external service for justice.
   In community, we are stimulated intellectually to ask questions
         about the meaning of life and Mystery.
   We are challenged to know ourselves and to relate to God.
   We are soothed during the painful parts of life and in good times,
         we share our rejoicings! Hurrah! Yippee! Hallelujah!

Offertory Statement (Leader)

We are blessed with the responsibility of sharing God's love and the teachings of Jesus on this street. We reach in and we reach out. This takes skill, knowledge, time, and money. As the basket comes to you, give what you can to keep our lights on, our air conditioner working, and our contributions to missions mailed on time.

Doxology   The Lone, Wild Bird (v. 2, modified), tune: PROSPECT
   The ends of earth are in God's hand, The sea's dark deep and far-off land.
   And I am yours! I rest in you. Great Spirit, come, and rest in me.

Prayer Of Thanksgiving (Leader)

Giver of Meaning — we are grateful for work to do that provides for our way in the world. We are glad to be known as people who are generous with encouragement, food, and money.
   Thank you for this money and for the beauty of this place. Amen.

Intercessory Prayers (Leader or Readers)

Energy of the Universe — touch this world again with gardens and relationships, which bring you close to humankind. Create on this planet in every creature the desire to walk with you; disarm the human greed that erupts with owning land and oil. Change our human habits that make us gluttonous for travel and gadgets, for information and technology. Slide into every country and negotiate collaboration; sit at every table and provide determination for peace; let there be light in every home, more than enough food, and nurture for every child. Help us not to be weary with the challenges you give us.

Inspiration for Living — we see humanity on the pages of the Bible and we are alarmed that malice and warfulness wreak havoc in our own times as in ages before us. Come to this world again so that peace has a chance. Let compassion be greater than greed, neighborliness greater than envy, benevolence greater than vengeance. Empower us with the central themes of Jesus until this world can experiment again with your reign throughout the global village.

Guardian of Life — thank you for being like a parent to us. We are grateful for the men who have provided the DNA for our lives. Though some of them have abandoned us and mistreated us, we believe they did the best they could. So free us from feelings of being unwanted and unloved. Free us from hurtful memories. Free us to love ourselves and to be glad for the adults who are kind and fair with us. Thank you for our wise internal parents.

Galaxy Thrower — how can we know you? How can we respond to your invitation to co-creativity? How can we articulate our experience with the Mystery of your voice? We think we are learning; day by day we are experimenting with words and paints, with clay and seeds, with silence and dance. See our endeavors toward performing our faith in your love; see our expressions of awareness of Holy Mystery. See our aches and pains that make us morose and short-tempered; see our disappointments and betrayals that shorten our memories and minimize our hope. Soothe us body and soul, mind and psyche until we overflow with gentleness and joy. Be palpable to those whose bodies struggle against disease; lift them above the pain and give them peaceful healing. Amen.

Benediction (Leader)

Life is a journey to Mystery.
Experiment with multiple names for God;
Explore different ways to respond to the Holy Spirit.
Laugh each day and unbuild the overwhelming towers of the world.
Notice possibilities around each corner;
Make dreams and cultivate a glad heart!
Holy Spirit empowers you and me to live *real life* —
Peace be yours, deep peace. Amen.

179

Music

Kum Ba Yah
    Words and Music: Marvin Frey, 1938
    DESMOND

O Holy Spirit, Root Of Life
    Words: Jean Janzen, 1991, based on the writings of Hildegard of Bingen (12th century)
    Music: Trier manuscript (15th century); adapt. Michael Praetorius, 1609; harm. George
        R. Woodward, 1904
    PUER NOBIS NASCITUR

Out Of Need And Out Of Custom
    Words and Music: Ken Medema, 1972
    GATHERING

Wellspring Of Wisdom
    Words: Miriam Therese Winter, 1987
    Music: Miriam Therese Winter, 1987; harm. Don McKeever, 1987
    WELLSPRING

Proper 7
Ordinary Time 12
Pentecost 5

1 Kings 19:1-4 (5-7) 8-15a or Isaiah 65:1-9   Galatians 3:23-29
Psalms 42 and 43 or Psalm 22:19-28   Luke 8:26-39

Zoos are no longer in people's good graces.
Religion faces the same problem.
Certain illusions about freedom plague them both.

— Yann Martel, *Life of Pi*

Call To Worship

Leader: I'm so glad you're here! There are seats for everyone; there's slight air movement; the windows engender tranquility and imagination and words will stimulate fresh thoughts.

People: It's good to be here, in sanctuary. We're glad for opportunities to gather and to express our gratitude to God and our appreciation for one another.

Leader: Set aside the remnants of last week; close the calendar for the week ahead. Be emotionally present for this hour, expecting Holy refreshment.

Prayer Of Thanksgiving (Leader)

Holy One — as wild creatures search for water, so we search for you. We thirst for the living God! Thank you for being among us, for preparing refreshment for our bodies and souls. In the midst of the hassles of the world, we are eager to receive your grace and to respond with gratitude. Amen.

Call To Confession (Leader)

We each have demons that haunt us. In these next moments, we have opportunity to pay attention to internal chaos and to allow the Holy Spirit to give us peace and a plan to be free. Pray with me the printed prayer and then have your personal conversation with the Holy One.

Community Confession (Unison)

God of Jesus and Us — there is insistent clamoring inside our heads and outside our ears: calls to be loyal to this and that, claims for energy from drugs and herbs, promises of satisfaction with certain merchandise.

But what we really need and want is freedom from external goods so that we have room for your Spirit.

Send away the rogues and set before us, again, the path toward home with your love. Amen.

Sermon Idea

First Kings 19:1-15 is great as a dramatic reading! Then for the sermon, pull in themes from the gospel and the psalms. Several ideas can be fun to explore:

- twenty-first-century exile — from puritan roots, from early American values, from civility
- demons — (negative energy) such as cynicism, criticism, judgmentalism, prejudices
- freedom to explore the realm of Spirit, psyche, and soul and be an activist for justice and resources enough for everyone, yet not welcomed by the world; Jesus was asked to leave the village (Luke 8:26-39)
- wilderness — (see T. S. Eliot, *The Wasteland*) inner space/attitude, life view
- wish to die — consider slang expressions like "It kills me" or "It'll be the death of me"; Elijah was so weary, so tired and hungry that death seemed a viable option; what fatigues us so much that death seems appealing? Psalms speak of wishing to be dead and of feeling abandoned, alone, fearful. When do we get to that point? What do we do when we are wishing to be dead? What role does *community* play in our experience of aloneness and weariness?
- rest and nutritious food as responses to a depressed affect
- telling our story as the freed man in Luke did as a means of wholeness

A Dramatic Rendering Of 1 Kings 19:1-15
7 Readers
King Ahab, Jezebel, messenger/servant, Elijah, servant/friend, angel, God's voice (offstage whisper)

Props
lapel microphones or cordless mics are helpful, paper and pen for Jezebel's letter to Elijah, facsimile of tree, food tray with loaf of bread, carafe of water and glass, cave entrance

Costumes
Jezebel in seductive contemporary outfit; Ahab in handsome suit and tie; Elijah in khaki slacks and long-sleeve white turtleneck shirt carrying a jacket; servants in blue jeans and black T-shirts

(Jezebel is seated at stage/chancel right doing some hand work. A messenger/servant stands nearby. Ahab hurries in from the far left.)

Ahab: Jezebel, darling. I'm glad you're here. I need someone to talk to! I am so mad! So upset! Elijah has done it again. He's brought fire from the skies and devoured a sacrifice meant for Baal! Then he killed all those prophets — men we liked. Then he told me *(mockingly)* to get in my chariot and hurry home to you before it began to rain. We haven't had rain for more than three years! But he was right! Rain's in the air!

Jezebel: *(stands, in a tizzy)* How dare he! Mock my husband and kill my prophets! I'll give him a piece of my mind! *(takes pen and paper and ostentatiously, hastily, jots a note)* "May the gods strike me dead if by this time tomorrow I don't do the same thing to you that you did to Baal's prophets." *(to the messenger)* Here, take this to Elijah the Prophet, now!

(Ahab, Jezebel, and messenger/servant exit the sanctuary stage right. Elijah and his friend/servant begin walking from the back of the sanctuary toward stage left.)

Elijah: *(to his servant/friend)* Darn. I'm tired of running. I'm tired of Jezebel. Tired of Ahab. Tired of living like this. I'm glad you are willing to travel with me. But you know what? I think I want to be alone for a while. Will you wait here for me?

(At the front pew, so the congregation can see him, the servant/friend sits down to wait. Elijah meanders to chancel/stage left and sits down under the tree.)

Elijah: God, I'm tired. So tired, even here in the shade of this tree. I'm tired of Jezebel's threats. I wish I could die right now. Take my life. I'd rather be dead than keep on struggling with Ahab and running from Jezebel. God, she's awful.

(Elijah slumps into sleep. An angel appears from the back of the sanctuary carrying a tray of food, touches Elijah, speaks, and moves some distance behind Elijah.)

Angel: Wake up, Elijah. Wake up and enjoy this bread and water.

(Elijah sits up, looks around, and examines the food. He nibbles a bite or two and lays back down.)

Angel: *(touches Elijah, shakes him awake)* Get up, Elijah. You must eat before you set out on the journey ahead of you.

(Elijah stands, stretches, eats, drinks, then begins to weave a walk toward the cave — in center aisle or back of chancel if there is room — nibbling a piece of bread.)

Elijah: *(looks around)* How quickly it got dark. I'm tired — ready for bed. Hope I can sleep.

(Elijah relaxes in front of the cave.)

God's Voice: Elijah, what are you doing?

Elijah: *(sleepily)* Hmmm, you know I'm doing what you asked me to do. I'm very loyal to you, you know. But I'm tired. The people haven't kept their promises; they have destroyed altars built to honor you; they have killed all my faithful classmates — I'm the only prophet left! And they're trying to kill me!

God's Voice: Well now, you're rather morose. Get up and look around you.

Elijah: *(stands, looks around)* Oh, my! Where did that furious wind come from? My! Trees are shattering! Oh! The ground is shaking! Fire is lighting all around! God, where are you? *(very frightened)* God!?

God's Voice: I'm here, Elijah, but not in the wind or the earthquake or the fire. I'm here with you as a soft whisper.

(Elijah puts on his jacket and pulls it close, looks around, and listens.)

God's Voice: What are you doing now, Elijah?

Elijah: I'm trying to do what you asked. I'm loyal to you. But the people are not. I'm the only prophet they haven't killed. I'm afraid they'll kill me.

God's Voice: Elijah, I am with you. When morning comes, return to the desert area near the city. I will be with you.

(Elijah packs up the props and exits by the aisle where the servant/friend is waiting. Together they exit the sanctuary. A bell tolls the hour.)

Contemporary Affirmation (Unison)
> We know God, the Creator, by many names;
>> we believe that God, the Holy One, loves us and all creation.
>
> We know Jesus of Nazareth taught people to love friends and enemies;
>> we believe Jesus' teachings lead us to satisfaction in living.
>
> We believe the Holy Spirit is moving throughout the global village,
>> inviting all peoples to live peaceably together;
>> we experience the Holy Spirit to be motivating us to journey toward
>>> internal contentment and external service for justice.
>
> In community, we are stimulated intellectually to ask questions
>> about the meaning of life and Mystery.
>
> We are challenged to know ourselves and to relate to God.
>
> We are soothed during the painful parts of life and in good times,
>> we share our rejoicings! Hurrah! Yippee! Hallelujah!

Offertory Statement (Leader)

With your own creativity as well as your own fears, you may give of your resources to continue ministry in this place.

Doxology   The Lone, Wild Bird (v. 2, modified), tune: PROSPECT

The ends of earth are in God's hand, The sea's dark deep and far-off land.
And I am yours! I rest in you. Great Spirit, come, and rest in me.

Prayer Of Thanksgiving (Leader)

God of Elijah and Us — thank you for being with us as guiding whispers. Thank you for this money and for the talents gathered here. Amen.

Intercessory Prayers (Leader or Readers)

God of Fire and Rock — in sound waves and visual images, in drama and conversation, we experience your life-changing activity. For those of us in pain, speak encouragement; for those of us struggling with disease, speak healing; for those of us who are depressed and disillusioned, speak hope. For those of us whose burdens are too heavy, lift us with options; for those of us whose baggage weighs us down, touch us with surprising possibilities. Whatever our needs, meet us and fill us with shalom.

God of Whispers and Loud Noises — some of us put our imaginations in boxes and forget to get them out on Sunday mornings. Some of us get depressed and can't imagine anything good. Some of us think we know exactly how you think and speak and plan. Some of us don't even bother to ask questions and find guidance in ancient stories. Do come to us as you did to Elijah. Thank you for your Spirit always close by.

God of Storms and Gentle Breezes — we are informed people; we know that storms and breezes are simply a part of the created order. Yet the storms in our minds are not so easily explainable. Sustain us like you did Elijah when he was too tired to think and feel. Guide us in our sleeping and dreaming; open us to the possibilities of your ways in our lives.

God of Activists and Pacifists — political maneuvering has been around for a very long time! Peace escapes us year after year; hungry children and adults go on being hungry; homeless people find bridges to protect them. Come to politicians with visions of how to be honest and how to use their power for all people, especially for those whose blessings are minimal, whose skills do not support their will to live. Banish corruption and evil intent; stop hatred and ugliness. Let us and this planet experience real truth, real neighborliness, and real godliness. Let there be no more war; instead, inspire all humankind to wage peace. Amen.

Benediction (Leader)
Life is a journey to Mystery.
Experiment with multiple names for God;
Explore different ways to respond to Holy Spirit.
Laugh each day and unbuild the overwhelming towers of the world.
Notice possibilities around each corner;
Make dreams and cultivate a glad heart!
Holy Spirit empowers you and me to live *real life* —
Peace be yours, deep peace. Amen.

Music
As Deer Long For The Streams
Words: Christopher L. Webber, 1986
Music: *Second Supplement to Psalmody in Miniature*, 1783; harm. Edward Miller, 1790
ROCKINGHAM

Come, O Spirit
Words: John A. Dalles, 1983
Music: *Union Harmony*, 1837; harm. Hilton Rufty, 1934
BOUNDLESS MERCY

Gather Us In
Words and Music: Marty Haugen, 1981
GATHER US IN

Silence, Frenzied, Unclean Spirit
    Words: Thomas H. Troeger, 1984
    Music: Carol Doran, 1984
    AUTHORITY

Spirit
    Words and Music: James K. Manley, 1975
    SPIRIT

Proper 8
Ordinary Time 13
Pentecost 6

2 Kings 2:1-2, 6-14 or 1 Kings 19:15-16, 19-21   Galatians 5:1, 13-25
Psalm 77:1-2, 11-20 or Psalm 16   Luke 9:51-62

Zoos are no longer in people's good graces.
Religion faces the same problem.
Certain illusions about freedom plague them both.

— Yann Martel, *Life of Pi*

Call To Worship
Leader: Good morning! It's a beautiful summer day in our neighborhoods!
People: **It's morning in the United Stated of America — our home by birth or by choice!**
Leader: With people around the world, we are God's people.
People: **With all the citizens of America, we thank God for our freedoms. We are grateful for the men and women who ventured into the unknown *territory of democracy* hundreds of years ago.**
Leader: Thank God for the vision of "One Nation Under God."
People: **We are glad for laws and rites, which describe religion and state.**
Leader: Thank God for the freedom to pray when and how we feel works for us.
People: **We pray and sing, laugh and cry, dance and meditate to express our thoughts to God.**
Leader: Then let our celebration begin!

Prayer Of Thanksgiving (Leader)
God of all Nations — this land we call "our land" demonstrates your creativity with mountains and rivers, fertile soil and bright skies. This country we call "our country" offers us abundant freedoms and responsibilities. Thank you for the opportunities that have come to us. During this hour, we open our minds and hearts to your refining presence, alert for your guiding voice. Amen.

Call To Confession (Leader)
Distress and disease are part of the human journey. In fear and desperation we often turn to God for comfort — because there is no other place to go! "Help," we plead. Sometimes our minds play tug of war with our hearts: God has no power — God has all power and can help me; God is absent from this world — God lives in me, feeling all my agony and ecstasy. Pray with me the printed prayer and then have your personal conversation with the Holy One.

Community Confession (Unison)
God of Turbulent Winds and Gentle Breezes — we believe we are empowered by the Holy Spirit to embody love, joy, peace, patience, kindness, and self-control.

Continue to live through us to accomplish your reign of justice, your kingdom of peace.
We live in a country that touts personal choice and self development.
Let our decisions and actions never cause harm to others.
Help us to share what we have so that everyone has enough of the necessities for living well.
Remove our nation's need to invade other countries because we covet their resources.
Light us within so we can promote freedom and peace throughout the global village, in our homes, and on our streets. Amen.

Sermon Idea

Holding Onto The Past Is Not Helpful might be a sermon title that could encompass Christian history as well as national history in relation to contemporary issues like language, gender inclusion, age inclusion, race inclusion, expansive images for religious expression, intelligent design, animal slaughter for human pleasure, immigration, profit and meaningful work, USA's place in the world market, and so on. Luke's text might be shaped to ask what our nation does and what we as individuals do when we don't get the reaction we want. Though Psalm 77:10 is not a part of the lectionary reading, it is a real grabber as we consider how to pray, what to believe, and how to live in a culture that has a wide gap between haves and have nots: What hurts me most is this — that God is no longer powerful (TEV). The story of Elijah passing on his power and reputation to Elisha is a way to ask who the leaders in our country are grooming for public service; we can also ask how and who the church is preparing for leadership responsibilities in the next decade.

Contemporary Affirmation (Unison)

We know God, the Creator, by many names;
    we believe that God, the Holy One, loves us and all creation.
We know Jesus of Nazareth taught people to love friends and enemies;
    we believe Jesus' teachings lead us to satisfaction in living.
We believe the Holy Spirit is moving throughout the global village,
    inviting all peoples to live peaceably together;
        we experience the Holy Spirit to be motivating us to journey toward
            internal contentment and external service for justice.
In community, we are stimulated intellectually to ask questions
    about the meaning of life and Mystery.
We are challenged to know ourselves and to relate to God.
We are soothed during the painful parts of life and in good times,
    we share our rejoicings! Hurrah! Yippee! Hallelujah!

Offertory Statement (Leader)

Be aware that you are here either by human or by divine guidance. Be aware that your basic needs, not necessarily your wants, are met. Give as you can to provide resources for this building and for its influence in the neighborhood. Give as you can so that others can be cared for.

Doxology
The Lone, Wild Bird (v. 2, modified), tune: PROSPECT

The ends of earth are in God's hand, The sea's dark deep and far-off land.
And I am yours! I rest in you. Great Spirit, come, and rest in me.

Prayer Of Thanksgiving (Leader)

Holy One — we are grateful for the resources that make ministry possible on this street. Thank you for this money and for the talents gathered here. Amen.

Intercessory Prayers (Leader or Readers)

God of the Stranger — we have all been aliens in one place or another, at one time or another. So while we are thankful for this country, we pray for people who attempt to better their lives by crossing borders illegally. It seems our country cannot any longer absorb the tired and the poor from other nations. Help all humankind to be realistic about the numbers of people this planet can sustain.

God of the Good Samaritan — as we make our human journey, we are sometimes the brutalized character in Jesus' story. Sometimes we are those who looked the other way. Sometimes we are the ones who bandage wounds and pay for care. Knowing that all these roles belong to most of us, we pray for people around the world who are hungry and homeless, wounded and weary, abused and imprisoned. Enlarge our compassion and shrink our desire to bully others.

God of all Nations — every clan wants a "promised land" to call home. We all want to be a shining success story. Raise our awareness to the smallness of this planet village and help humankind to learn peace-making, collaborating, and compromising. We pray for Native Americans who struggle to survive with their ancient stories in a complicated world. Open our eyes to options for entertaining ourselves without war games and gambling and fierce competitions. Open our minds to alternate ways of being neighbors needing resources that are beyond our own boundaries. Equip leaders with wisdom beyond their experience.

God of Individuals — thank you for your sustaining presence day by day. Give us strength sufficient to heal. Give us hope enough to share. Give us joy that runs over to bless each person we meet. Give us peace, contagious peace to spread through every continent. Make real for us the words of the prayer Jesus gave his disciples: Our Father.... Amen.

Benediction (Leader)

Life is a journey to Mystery.
Experiment with multiple names for God;
Explore different ways to respond to the Holy Spirit.
Laugh each day and unbuild the overwhelming towers of the world.
Notice possibilities around each corner; make dreams and cultivate a glad heart!
Holy Spirit empowers you and me to live *real life* —
Contentment be yours, deep tranquility. Amen.

Music

For The Fruit Of All Creation
   Words: Fred Pratt Green, 1970
   Music: Traditional Welsh melody; harm. Luther Orlando Emerson, 1906
   AR HYD Y NOS

Now Thank We All Our God
   Words: Martin Rinkart, 1636; tr. Catherine Winkworth, 1858, alt.
   Music: Johann Crüger, 1647; harm. Felix Mendelssohn, 1840
   NUN DANKET

This Is My Song
   Words: Sts. 1-2 Lloyd Stone, 1934; st. 3, Georgia Harkness, ca. 1939
   Music: Jean Sibelius, 1899; arr. from *The Hymnal*, 1933
   FINLANDIA

We Are Not Our Own
   Words: Brian Wren, 1987
   Music: Brian Wren, 1987; arr. Fred Graham
   YARNTON

Proper 9
Ordinary Time 14
Pentecost 7

2 Kings 5:1-14 or Isaiah 66:10-14   Galatians 6:(1-6) 7-16
Psalm 30 or Psalm 66:1-9   Luke 10:1-11, 16-20

A sacred teaching must be examined from at least three points of view:
the intellectual, the metaphorical and the universal (or mystical).
— Neil Douglas-Klotz, *Prayers of the Cosmos*

Call To Worship

Leader: It is summer time! Week after week we come here. The space is beautiful, the seating is comfortable, and the company is good.

People: We come here to be with each other as we thank God for creation and for divine love.

Leader: Together we see the wonderful things God does and we can rejoice.

People: Together we also recognize the not-so-good things in our lives. Together we know that we are not alone on this journey through time.

Leader: We need one another.

People: We can see what God is doing but we rarely understand so we need to talk about our perceptions and our feelings. We want to hear the stories of scripture and consider how they speak to us. We want our relationships here to nurture us Monday through Saturday.

Leader: Those are high expectations!

People: We are not solitary creatures; we want to be with others who appreciate what God is doing; we want to enjoy human companionship.

Leader: Then let our music and our prayers begin!

Prayer Of Thanksgiving (Leader)

Great God — we honor you with songs and prayers, with deep thoughts and with honest conversations. Thank you for being among us, enthusing us with Spirit, promoting gentleness and blessing. We sing our thanks and our hopes; we lay before you and one another the concerns of our hearts. We eagerly receive your strength. Amen.

Call To Confession (Leader)

Jesus gathered friends and taught them what a new social order could be like. He sent them to other places to give people the same dream. He valued hospitality and loyalty. He encouraged no one to hold grudges, which are like dust impeding shiny beauty. He taught that the Reign of God is near. Pray with me the printed prayer and then have your personal conversation with the Holy One.

Community Confession (Unison)

Loving God — we long for your kingdom to be present in our time!

When we look around, we see a society that markets things to fill our homes and to decorate our bodies and to keep up with our neighbors.

But our souls are not satisfied.

We are easily seduced by lithe youthfulness and savvy technology.

We give up companionship and community for solitary tasks and before we know it we feel alone in the world.

Free us from these temptations and help us promote the community of the Holy Spirit.

Coax us from our private journeys into aspirations for the common good — of this faith community and the global village. Amen.

Sermon Idea

The Naaman story easily develops into a dramatic reading/skit.

Isaiah 66:1-14, 22-24 — God's home, the heavens/skies comprise the central place while earth/lands form the footstool/sturdy foundation. One challenge is to care for the planet so that prosperity is available for all peoples; another challenge is to find ways to quiet violence. Matthew Fox has spoken of the earth as God's body. Have on hand a clear plastic inflatable globe. Throw it to someone close by. It is often a jolt to realize that we have the world — God's home — in our hands! Consider how we promote responsibility for caring for God's home, how we promote faith groups that spend a lot of time talking about the Bible and children and cups of water while behaviors undercut the central teachings of Jesus. Consider Jesus (Matthew 10) pairing his friends to promote peace; one need not be a solitary representative of a different sort of social structure (kingdom of God).

Given this generation's technology and dependence upon multiple nations for supplies, we may want to think about non-literal meanings for "shake off the dust" of a place that is not accepting of a particular promotion style of Jesus' teachings. The scriptures hold out hope for wholeness — spiritual, physical, governmental — for people and the earth. The element of God's justice/judgment must be handled gently, without arrogance. Some of the ideas used for Earth Day in April might be repeated this day.

A Dramatic Rendering Of 2 Kings 5
9 Readers

Narrator, Mrs. Naaman (nonspeaking), King of Israel, Housekeeper, Elisha, Naaman, Butler, King of Syria, Companion of Naaman

Props

The Housekeeper needs a dustcloth and a broom. Mrs. Naaman needs a chair to sit in and something to keep her hands busy, like an embroidery hoop. The King of Syria needs a scroll. Naaman needs a "horse." The baptismal bowl can be filled with water to serve as a wet Jordan. Naaman needs a "bag of gold" to give to Elisha at the end of the story.

Costumes

Street dress for all characters plus crowns for the two kings (clearly distinguishing them from each other), a cloak/cape for Elisha, a breastplate armor and cloak/cape for Naaman, an apron for the Housekeeper, a black bowtie and white towel for the Butler, and a colorful scarf for Naaman's Companion.

(On chancel/stage, the Housekeeper is dusting and sweeping. Mrs. Naaman is embroidering something.)

Narrator: Naaman was commander of Syria's army. He had won many battles and captured many people. He took one young woman home to be his wife's housekeeper. The King of Syria valued Naaman as a brave and successful man. One day, Naaman noticed some strange spots on his arm. Then the housekeeper noticed them. Soon she spoke with Mrs. Naaman about a prophet in her home country who could heal Naaman.

Housekeeper: *(to Mrs. Naaman)* I wish Mr. Naaman would be in Israel! I know a man who could heal him, even of leprosy!

(housekeeper and Mrs. Naaman exit)

Narrator: Of course, Mrs. Naaman promptly told her husband. And Naaman promptly went to the king to get his permission to seek foreign medical care.

(enter Naaman and King of Syria)

Naaman: *(addressing the king)* Sir, a young woman from Israel says that if I am willing to go to her country, there is a prophet who can heal me.

King of Syria: *(to Naaman)* Well, pack your bags. What are you waiting for, Naaman? I'll send a letter to the King of Israel introducing you as an important dignitary. You can take it with you.

Naaman: *(first to the king and then to the congregation)* Well. Let's see. Let's see. What will I take? What does a stranger need to get into the good graces of a prophet and a king? I'll take some gold. I'll take some beautifully woven fabric. Let's see. What shall I wear? Oh. The letter of introduction.

(King of Syria hands Naaman a scroll and they exit.)

Narrator: So Naaman and a companion set off for Israel. They went directly to the King of Israel and gave him the letter of introduction from Syria's monarch. Israel's King opened the letter.

(Enter the King of Israel, clearly different from Syria's monarch. He is holding the scroll.)

King of Israel: *(reads the letter)* "When you have this letter in your hands, you will know that I have sent Naaman, my loyal commander to you so he will be cured of leprosy." *(looks confused)* I don't get it. What is going on? What does Syria really want? *(re-reads the letter silently)* Oh, no! He thinks I can cure leprosy! Come on! *(somewhat angry)* Am I God to kill and to heal? What is his real, devious motive? Is he trying to push me into quarreling with him?

(Elisha enters.)

Narrator: Fortunately, Israel's King had a prophet-friend with good ears!

Elisha: *(to King of Israel)* My king and friend, why do you agonize over this letter? I can handle this situation. Simply send the commander Naaman to me. He'll soon learn that there is a true prophet in this land of Israel.

(Naaman, on a "horse," and Companion enter)

Narrator: So when Naaman arrived, Israel's King sent Naaman to Elisha's home. Naaman, with his strong horses, stopped at the prophet's door. He knocked. Then his companion knocked and knocked.

Butler: *(ceremoniously opening the door)* You must be the famous visitor from Syria. Welcome. I already know your name and I know what you want. So, Naaman, I have a message for you from Prophet Elisha. "Go down to the Jordan River and dunk yourself seven times. Then you will be whole; your skin will be baby smooth and soft."

Naaman: *(feels slighted, becomes angry)* What do you mean? How dare you! Where is the prophet? I want to speak directly with him. Surely he will come to me and call God to cure me! Really! The rivers in Damascus are better than all the rivers in Israel! I could wash in one of them and be clean, couldn't I?

(Butler shakes his head "no.")

Narrator: Naaman, in a rage, turned his horse toward home! His companion spoke gently to him.

Companion: My friend, if the prophet had asked you to do some great and daring thing, you would have been proud to do it. Right? But he only asked you to go to a little, old river and get wet.

Naaman: Yeah. Some funky river, the River Jordan.

Companion: All he wants you to do is take a bath in Israel's water.

Naaman: *(grumpily)* Hmmm.

Companion: I bet you can do it easily in a few minutes and we can be on our way. And maybe you'll be leprosy-free.

Naaman: *(grumpily)* Oh, all right, I guess you have a point. All right, I will wash in the Jordan. I'll dip seven times as that butler told me to do. You count.

(They are at the baptismal bowl. Naaman splashes himself and Companion counts.)

Companion: One, two, three, four, five, six; one more time, Naaman! Seven!

Naaman: Ugh. *(dries himself with his cloak)* Yuck. Ooh. Look! Wow! Look at this skin! How smooth my arm is!

(Companion oohs and ahs with Naaman.)

Naaman: Quick! Let's go back to the prophet's house. I want to give him a thank-you gift!

(They return to Elisha's house.)

Narrator: Naaman was delighted with the result of his seven dips in the Jordan River. And he hurried back to the prophet to register his awe and his gratitude.

(Naaman knocks and the door is opened this time by Elisha.)

Elisha: So ... you've come back.

(Companion gives Naaman a bag of gold that he holds out as a gift to Elisha.)

Elisha: *(refuses the gift)* Thanks, but no thanks.

Naaman: But look! I am healed! Surely you are a prophet of the living God.

Elisha: Yes. I am a prophet of the Holy One, God of Israel. God healed you.

Naaman: Now I know. I know who God is! I will serve and honor this healing God. Thank you.

(Naaman and Companion "ride" away, stroking the healed arm, saying, "Thank you, hallelujah, praise God." Elisha watches them a moment before he closes his door behind him and exits into the congregation.)

Narrator: Naaman, the Syrian Commander, was healed of leprosy. You can read more stories of Elisha's adventures before 722 BCE in the Old Testament book of 2 Kings.

Contemporary Affirmation (Unison)
>We know God, the Creator, by many names;
>>we believe that God, the Holy One, loves us and all creation.
>
>We know Jesus of Nazareth taught people to love friends and enemies;
>>we believe Jesus' teachings lead us to satisfaction in living.
>
>We believe the Holy Spirit is moving throughout the global village,
>>inviting all peoples to live peaceably together;
>>we experience the Holy Spirit to be motivating us to journey toward
>>>internal contentment and external service for justice.
>
>In community, we are stimulated intellectually to ask questions
>>about the meaning of life and Mystery.
>
>We are challenged to know ourselves and to relate to God.
>
>We are soothed during the painful parts of life and in good times,
>>we share our rejoicings! Hurrah! Yippee! Hallelujah!

Offertory Statement (Leader)

We gather to promote the reign of God on this earth;
We assemble to share the expenses of promoting the kingdom of heaven.
With money and talent and skills, we manifest Divine hospitality.
With a gentle manner and kind demeanor, we make Holy love conspicuous.
As the plates/baskets come to you, give what you can to expand the health of the planet.

Doxology   The Lone, Wild Bird (v. 2, modified), tune: PROSPECT

The ends of earth are in God's hand, The sea's dark deep and far-off land.
And I am yours! I rest in you. Great Spirit, come, and rest in me.

Prayer Of Thanksgiving (Leader)

God of Feet and Hands — we are grateful for the ways you bless us in so many tangible ways. Thank you for the health of this congregation, for all our resources, and for all the talents gathered here. Amen.

Intercessory Prayers (Leader or Readers)

God of Naaman and Jesus — people around this planet seek wholeness. We are so fearful when we learn that disease has invaded our bodies! We want the best a health care system has to offer and there is a price to be paid. We pray for people who do not have access to health care, to wholesome food, and to dynamic relationships. We pray for ourselves as we hear the stories of Jesus, we know that we want to be on your side, one with you in our living and in our dying. Reach each of us and others with healing and hope. Where there is injury, let there be new skin and bone. Where there is pain and distress, let there be comfort and peace. Where there is fear, soothe the psyche. Where guns and knives and accidents have abused the body, work a miracle of love and grace. Where there are doubts about you, sustain the questions.

God of Travelers and Readers — we go through life learning about ourselves, about the world, and about you. Meet us in information and relationships that guide us to become what you want us for us. Speak through us words that inspire and comfort. Throughout the world, we ask for peacefulness. Banish ignorance and arrogance from negotiating meetings. Replace small lord-doms with benevolent states. Put your reign in place for our times.

God of Galaxies — we yearn to understand, to have intellectual food, which also satisfies our souls. Guide us to ideas that nurture our psyches and stretch our minds. Encourage us to let down our defenses and to be real with one another. Let us see the whole continuum of agony and ecstasy and let us experience your sustaining grace. Walk with us through evil and good; heal us as we become aware of our wounds. Give us strength for the life process that comes to us. Amen.

Benediction (Leader)

Life is a journey to Mystery.
Experiment with multiple names for God;
Explore different ways to respond to the Holy Spirit.
Laugh each day and unbuild the overwhelming towers of the world.
Notice possibilities around each corner;
Make dreams and cultivate a glad heart!
Holy Spirit empowers you and me to live hospitably.
Contentment be yours and deep joy. Amen.

Music

For Beauty Of Meadows
 Words: Walter H. Farquharson, 1969
 Music: Welsh folk melody
 ST. DENIO

Lord, You Give The Great Commission
 Words: Jeffery Rowthorn, 1978
 Music: Cyril V. Taylor, 1941
 ABBOT'S LEIGH

Morning Has Broken
 Words: Eleanor Farjeon, 1931
 Music: Gaelic melody; arr. Dale Grotenhuis, 1985
 BUNESSAN

She Is The Spirit
 Words and Music: John Bell, 1988
 THAINAKY

When, In Awe Of God's Creation
 Words: Jane Parker Huber, 1991
 Music: Rowland H. Prichard, 1844; harm. *The English Hymnal*, 1906
 HYFRYDOL

Proper 10
Ordinary Time 15
Pentecost 8

Amos 7:7-17 or Deuteronomy 30:9-14   Colossians 1:1-14
Psalm 82 or Psalm 25:1-10   Luke 10:25-37

Zoos are no longer in people's good graces.
Religion faces the same problem.
Certain illusions about freedom plague them both.

— Yann Martel, *Life of Pi*

Call To Worship
Leader: It's a good morning! Are you awake? Are you ready to sing?
People: Ah, yes. We are thankful for life and we express our gratitude to the living God!
Leader: We have called to God many times and the Holy One has sustained us and restored us to hopefulness.
People: With music and dance, with words and silence, we thank God for divine goodness among us!

Prayer Of Thanksgiving (Leader)
Holy One — sometimes your presence among us is so subtle, we almost miss you. Stretch our imaginations till we can perceive your amazing grace. Strengthen our voices so we can say what we experience and think. Thank you for the various ways you are among us and for the multiples ways you bless us. We sing to you and we enjoy one another. Amen.

Call To Confession (Leader)
We have many ways of measuring what is important to us. We take a few moments to look within ourselves and notice what is not measuring up to our hopes for our lives. Pray with me the printed prayer and then have your personal conversation with the Holy One.

Community Confession (Unison)
Ceaseless Creator — we do not want to be like walls out of kilter or people with crooked behaviors. Create in us minds that are eager to live into mystery and to be bear-ers not of plumb lines but of hope and nurturing actions. Let our living reflect the teachings of Jesus and the light of your love. Amen.

Sermon Idea
The story of Amos' plumb line is easy to transpose to twenty-first-century politics, international justice, and systemic oppression of the bottom 2/3 of society. With a plumb line, it is easy to make the story graphic. Depending on the congregation, the sermon might explore the good Samaritan story with the people identifying with the wounded person. If generalized, how might American citizens respond to the government's continual blindness to people not earning enough

to eat or to shelter and to provide care for a family? Do Americans think the middle and lower socioeconomic groups are being mistreated? Perhaps the plumb line measuring justice and fairness in the USA is reasonably straight. The sermon also might explore the perception of the president's responding to the moral and ethical challenges in America that affect the whole global environment. Amos says that he does not make his public statements for pay. How does that idea bounce off moneys for preachers and politicians?

Contemporary Affirmation (Unison)
> **We know God, the Creator, by many names;**
>> **we believe that God, the Holy One, loves us and all creation.**
> **We know Jesus of Nazareth taught people to love friends and enemies;**
>> **we believe Jesus' teachings lead us to satisfaction in living.**
> **We believe the Holy Spirit is moving throughout the global village,**
>> **inviting all peoples to live peaceably together;**
>> **we experience the Holy Spirit to be motivating us to journey toward**
>>> **internal contentment and external service for justice.**
> **In community, we are stimulated intellectually to ask questions**
>> **about the meaning of life and Mystery.**
> **We are challenged to know ourselves and to relate to God.**
> **We are soothed during the painful parts of life and in good times,**
>> **we share our rejoicings! Hurrah! Yippee! Hallelujah!**

Offertory Statement (Leader)
With your own sense of what is appropriate and helpful, this is the moment when you can respond with generosity to Holy Generosity so that tangible goodness continues in this place.

Doxology   The Lone, Wild Bird (v. 2, modified), tune: PROSPECT
The ends of earth are in God's hand, The sea's dark deep and far-off land.
And I am yours! I rest in you. Great Spirit, come, and rest in me.

Prayer Of Thanksgiving (Leader)
Creating God — we are glad that we are made in your image and can be creative in many ways. We are grateful for the call to care for people and the earth and for the resources to do what you ask. Amen.

Intercessory Prayers (Leader or Readers)
God of the Ancients and the Contemporaries — we like to think of ourselves as "Good Samaritans," as people who care effectively for others. As we read the scriptures, we examine our motives and our ability to stick to our goals. Give us strength and courage to meet the challenges that come to us.

Fathering God — remember our origin and do not challenge us beyond what our talents are. For those of us in pain, speak encouragement; for those of us struggling with disease, speak healing; for those of us who are depressed and disillusioned, speak hope. For those of us whose burdens seem unbearable, lift us with options; for those of us whose baggage hampers wholeness, touch us with surprising possibilities. Whatever our need, heal us and fill us with shalom.

Mothering God — we want to think you preside over the whole world. When we think literally, we get confused over what we can expect of you. We want to hold you accountable for

199

our problems and for our prosperity. Help us connect the dots between our prayers and our actions, between our thoughts and our words, and between communal values and human wants.

God of Religions — you are Mystery and light for our lives. We try again and again to understand your teachings, your kindness, and your constant love. Violence makes us afraid yet many people live in peril every day. War repels us yet we participate in terrorizing people around the planet in order to get what our nation wants or needs. Hunger and disease plague children and adults. Competition between religious systems stoke murderous actions. We find solace in the psalms: Remember your mercy toward us; relieve us of our worries and save us from our troubles. Feed the hungry and heal the sick. With trust, we turn to you for safety.

God of Reason — we have come to see that thinking about things is not adequate to grow our faith community nor to save the planet. Unite us humans to see ourselves whole and to live caringly in the world so that our children receive the gifts of fresh air, sparkling waters, tall trees, and nourishing foods. Amen.

Benediction (Leader)
Life is a journey to Mystery.
Experiment with multiple names for God;
Explore different ways to respond to the Holy Spirit.
Laugh each day and unbuild the overwhelming towers of the world.
Notice possibilities around each corner;
Make dreams and cultivate a glad heart!
Holy Spirit empowers you and me to live *real life* —
Peace be yours, deep peace. Amen.

Music
Bring Many Names
    Words: Brian Wren, 1987
    Music: Carlton R. Young, 1987
    WESTCHASE

Colorful Creator
    Words: Ruth Duck, 1992
    Music: Carlton R. Young, 1992
    HOUGHTON

Let The Whole Creation Cry
    Words: Stopford A. Brooke, 1881, alt.
    Music: Robert Williams, 1817
    LLANFAIR

Restless Weaver
    Words: O. I. Cricket Harrison, 1988, rev. 1993
    Music: Attr. B. F. White, 1844; harm. Ronald A. Nelson, 1978
    BEACH SPRING

When In Our Music God Is Glorified
    Words: Fred Pratt Green, 1971
    Music: Charles V. Stanford, 1904
    ENGLEBERG

Proper 11
Ordinary Time 16
Pentecost 9

Amos 8:1-12 or Genesis 18:1-10a   Colossians 1:15-28
Psalm 52 or Psalm 15   Luke 10:38-42

> *Zoos are no longer in people's good graces.*
> *Religion faces the same problem.*
> *Certain illusions about freedom plague them both.*
>
> — Yann Martel, *Life of Pi*

Call To Worship

Leader: It's a good morning! A good day to welcome friends and share good food!

People: Ah, yes. We are thankful for the goodness in our lives, glad for homes and wholesome foods.

Leader: We have called to God many times and the Holy One has sustained us and restored us to hopefulness.

People: With music and dance, with words and silence, we thank God for opportunities to feel contented and satisfied!

Prayer Of Thanksgiving (Leader)

Living God — surely, goodness and mercy follow us from sunrise to moonrise. We are grateful for this faith home and for the companions who share our search for intimacy with you. We choose to explore your ways and to practice what is honest and helpful. With our thoughts and our voices, we turn our attention to your presence. Amen.

Call To Confession (Leader)

In Jesus the Christ, we see how to be in relationship with God. In Jesus we see how to be in relationship with one another. In the teachings of Jesus, we find hope for a society that values peace. Pray with me the printed prayer and then have your personal conversation with the Holy One.

Community Confession (Unison)

We do know that deep within us is an urge to be connected to what is eternal.
In this very moment, we want to be free from anything that retards our journey to the Holy Mystery and psyche peace.
Transform our priorities and our goals; reshape our relationships and professions. Amen.

Sermon Ideas

The texts present a continuum with bad things for the people at one end and good things at the other end. Abraham hears that he and Sarah will have a child but Sarah laughs, and there's a hint at retribution for her lack of faith. Amos sees fruit in a basket but hears of famine and war.

202

The psalmist speaks of harmful aspects of politics and the environment and balances them with the bribe that *if you do what is right, you'll not have to worry about security.* Then Jesus on one hand affirms Mary's desire to sit down with him and does not invade her boundaries by suggesting that she help Martha in the kitchen. That's the way life is; it is comprised of satisfying events and of disappointing events. Jesus indicates how we can make it through the thick and the thin: stay in touch with the Holy Spirit, avoid allowing others to bash our boundaries, and spend time with companions who share our desire to be close to God. A title might be: Problems, Poetry, and Pregnancy, articulating how Jesus meets and affirms the heart's longing while not denying the practical; relationships and creativity can help us feel at one with the Divine.

Contemporary Affirmation (Unison)

We know God, the Creator, by many names;
> **we believe that God, the Holy One, loves us and all creation.**

We know Jesus of Nazareth taught people to love friends and enemies;
> **we believe Jesus' teachings lead us to satisfaction in living.**

We believe the Holy Spirit is moving throughout the global village,
> **inviting all peoples to live peaceably together;**
> **we experience the Holy Spirit to be motivating us to journey toward**
> > **internal contentment and external service for justice.**

In community, we are stimulated intellectually to ask questions
> **about the meaning of life and Mystery.**

We are challenged to know ourselves and to relate to God.

We are soothed during the painful parts of life and in good times,
> **we share our rejoicings! Hurrah! Yippee! Hallelujah!**

Offertory Statement (Leader)

Which of the characters in today's Bible stories are you identifying with: the poet-psalmist? Amos? Sarah? Abraham? Paul? Mary? Martha? Jesus? Our faith family needs to pay our bills, to offer help, and to enrich our journeys. You will have a response to the inner voice just as the Bible characters did to the situations they ran into. As you respond, may your psyche be satisfied.

Doxology   The Lone, Wild Bird (v. 2, modified), tune: PROSPECT

The ends of earth are in God's hand, The sea's dark deep and far-off land.

And I am yours! I rest in you. Great Spirit, come, and rest in me.

Prayer Of Thanksgiving (Leader)

God of Mary and Jesus — your voice beckons us to make time to listen for your whispers of love and challenge. We each have our own ways we can respond — with money, with action, and with hope. We are grateful for all of them. Thank you for this money; elasticize it to care for our building, to serve the community, and to offer goodness throughout the global village. Amen.

Intercessory Prayers (Leader or Readers)

God of Amos and Martha — we love beautiful and tasty foods like baskets of juicy fruits and succulent green vegetables. We don't like looking past them to see who produced them or the pesticides that might have touched them or how they were savage to the land. We are fearful of not enough to eat; we dread seeing the pictures of starving children; we look away from the maimed and brutalized. We pray for the kingdom of God to come in our time to all the world!

God of Singers and Speakers — we want to be free from worry like the psalmist 4,000 years ago. We say we'll do and be whatever it takes to feel secure and to have companions who help us along the journey. But when the moment comes, we have difficulty keeping our word. We want to see Christ in others, as the apostle says is true; we want to say that we walk with you and we want to really do it; we want to sing of our love for you and for creation. Heal our broken parts, control our pains, soothe our scars, and give us strength to take the next steps.

God of Work and Play — like Mary, we want to listen for your affirmation; like Martha, help us hospitably welcome guests. Like Jesus, let us not be judgmental or bossy. Like Paul, let our goals honor your claim on our lives.

God of the Free and the Oppressed — we pray for peace and food for children and adults in every tribe. Come to politicians raining on them wisdom and compassion, compelling them to share their wealth with people whose blessings are minimal, whose skills do not support their will to live. Banish corruption and evil intent; stop hatred and ugliness. Let us and this planet experience again real truth, real neighborliness, and real godliness. Let there be no more war; instead, inspire all humankind to wage peace. Amen.

Benediction (Leader)

Life is a journey to Mystery.
Experiment with multiple names for God;
Explore different ways to respond to the Holy Spirit.
Laugh each day and unbuild the overwhelming towers of the world.
Notice possibilities around each corner;
Make dreams and cultivate a glad heart!
Holy Spirit empowers you and me to live *real life* —
Peace be yours, deep peace. Amen.

Music

Come, Holy Spirit, Our Souls Inspire
    Words: Attr. Rabanus Maurus (9th century); trans. John Cosin, 1627, alt.
    Music: Plainsong, Mode VIII; arr. Healey Willan (1880-1968)
    VENI CREATOR SPIRITUS

God Is One, Unique And Holy
    Words: Brian Wren, 1983
    Music: Peter Cutts, 1983
    TRINITY

Holy Wisdom
    Words: Patrick Michaels, 1989
    Music: *Choralemelodien zum heiligen Gesange*, 1808; arr. Hal H. Hopson, 1991
    SALVE REGINA COELITUM

O God, We Bear The Imprint Of Your Face
    Words: Shirley Erena Murray, 1987, alt.
    Music: Dan Damon, 1994
    RAUMATI BEACH

Spirit Of God, Unleashed On Earth
    Words: John W. Arthur, 1972, alt.
    Music: Attr. Elkanah Kelsay Dare, as in Pisbury's *United States Harmony*, 1799
    KEDRON
    LM

Proper 12
Ordinary Time 17
Pentecost 10

Hosea 1:2-10 or Genesis 18:20-32   Colossians 2:6-15 (16-19)
Psalm 85 or Psalm 138   Luke 11:1-13

Zoos are no longer in people's good graces.
Religion faces the same problem.
Certain illusions about freedom plague them both.

— Yann Martel, *Life of Pi*

Call To Worship

Leader: It's a good morning! Are you awake and breathing deeply? Are you thankful, angry, secure, defeated? Are you ready to sing?

People: Ah, yes. We are thankful for life and we are seeking security and happiness.

Leader: We have called to God many times and the Holy One has sustained us and restored us to hopefulness.

People: With music and dance, with words and silence, we thank God for divine goodness among us!

Prayer Of Thanksgiving (Leader)

Energy of the Universe — dawn reminded us that you are still creating! Dawn reminded us that we are surrounded by all sorts of beauty and all sorts of suffering. Thank you for being with us through every day, all day and all night. In this hour, we listen carefully for your voice and we articulate what is going on with us. Be real with us, for we value your intimacy with us. Refresh us with your tenderness. Amen.

Call To Confession (Leader)

We have been praying for divine mercy with the United States and with Israel. We believe that righteousness and peace will embrace both nations. We have been praying for personal abundance and for an end to terrorism around the globe. This morning's scriptures remind us that human beings have always turned to one god or another when they are backed into a corner. Pray with me the printed prayer and then have your personal conversation with the Holy One.

Community Confession (Unison)

Listening God — violence and hunger are apparent in every nation.
Betrayals and dis-ease plague our homes.
Apathy and fear breed in our faith family.
Individually, we are hungry for something that is not satisfied with calories and flavors.
Restore our vision of what is possible when you are among us.
Open our ears to your voice; open our mouths to speak life-affirming words. Amen.

Sermon Idea

The gospel lesson describes what happens when a person decides to make God visible in choices, entertainment, use of resources, in relationships, and decides to participate in the Reign of God. Jesus speaks of an experience with holiness that is both contagious and divisive. When any one of us chooses to live simply, respecting all creatures and the earth, we set ourselves against the dominant culture. In Hosea's story, Gomer by her own decision, apparently, chooses gifts and sex outside of her primary relationship. Her religious practices are not acceptable to her husband, Hosea. They are divided by their preferences and their interpretations of faithfulness. Paul teaches the Colossians to hold on to their understanding of union with Jesus and to have an attitude of gratitude. Such a decision and lifestyle magnified their religious and ethic practices. Is this an essential challenge for today's Christians?

Contemporary Affirmation (Unison)

We know God, the Creator, by many names;
> **we believe that God, the Holy One, loves us and all creation.**

We know Jesus of Nazareth taught people to love friends and enemies;
> **we believe Jesus' teachings lead us to satisfaction in living.**

We believe the Holy Spirit is moving throughout the global village,
> **inviting all peoples to live peaceably together;**
> **we experience the Holy Spirit to be motivating us to journey toward**
>> **internal contentment and external service for justice.**

In community, we are stimulated intellectually to ask questions
> **about the meaning of life and Mystery.**

We are challenged to know ourselves and to relate to God.

We are soothed during the painful parts of life and in good times,
> **we share our rejoicings! Hurrah! Yippee! Hallelujah!**

Offertory Statement (Leader)

Let us "honor the Holy One." When Jesus told his disciples to "Pray," he said, "that we would have the daily food we need." We have other needs, as well. In our culture, it takes money to buy what we need and what we want; it takes money, time, and skills to sustain ministry here. Give what you can.

Doxology   The Lone, Wild Bird (v. 2, modified), tune: PROSPECT

The ends of earth are in God's hand, The sea's dark deep and far-off land.
And I am yours! I rest in you. Great Spirit, come, and rest in me.

Prayer Of Thanksgiving (Leader)

Holy One — we are grateful for the teachings of Jesus and for his encouragement *to ask, seek, and knock.* We expect to receive enough money to keep this building beautiful and to help feed the hungry in our neighborhood and throughout the global village. Thank you for the diligence and generosity of these people. Amen.

Intercessory Prayers (Leader or Readers)

Unifying Spirit — we gather as companions on the journey to the Holy. We are making decisions based on our interpretations of the words of Jesus. We are grateful that you are present in us and among us, giving us contentment and visions for the tomorrows. Let us not be enslaved by the deceitful practices of our culture nor by a bondage to material things. Keep us maturing in spiritual practices.

God of Cities — we are glad Abraham was thoughtful enough to ask if you would destroy good people along with evil people in Sodom. We too ask that as we look at the world and see violent men taking advantage of children. We ask you, "Is there an end in sight to human greed and savagery in Darfur, Israel, and Palestine, in Pakistan, Napal, and India, in China, Columbia, and in the United States?" We long for the good news of peace. We long for young women and men to learn and to work and to travel and to provide love for children. We wait eagerly for the good news of peace.

Enlivening Spirit — when we are surrounded by troubles, we turn to you. When we are in pain and facing disaster, we expect you to help us. When we face uncertain tomorrows, we look for the courage of Jesus. We know your love for us is eternal. Continue to work within us and guide us to safety and tranquility. Heal us from the inside out.

Divine Verb and Noun — your creativity calls to us and we, too, find new and multiple ways to benefit our living on this earth. We live forward into the future and pray for the next generation, for our children and grandchildren. May they learn compassion, truthfulness, generosity, beauty, and self-control. Let them know and feel your creating presence. Amen.

Benediction/Charge (Leader)
Life is a journey to Mystery.
Experiment with multiple names for God;
Explore different ways to respond to the Holy Spirit.
Laugh each day and unbuild the overwhelming towers of the world.
Notice possibilities around each corner;
Make dreams and cultivate a glad heart!
Holy Spirit empowers you and me to live *real life* —
Peace be yours, deep peace. Amen.

Music
Camina, Pueblo De Dios
    Words and Music: Cesário Gabaráin; trans. George Lockwood
    NUEVA CREACIÓN

In Loving Partnership
    Words and Music: Jim Strathdee, 1983
    PARTNERSHIP
    LM

Joyful, Joyful, We Adore Thee
    Words: Henry van Dyke, 1907, alt.
    Music: Ludwig van Beethoven, 1824; arr. Edward Hodges, 1864
    HYMN TO JOY

Wind Upon The Waters
    Words and Music: Marty Haugen, 1986
    WIND UPON THE WATERS

Proper 13
Ordinary Time 18
Pentecost 11

Hosea 11:1-11 or Ecclesiastes 1:2, 12-14; 2:18-23   Colossians 3:1-11
Psalm 107:1-9, 43 or Psalm 49:1-12   Luke 12:13-21

Zoos are no longer in people's good graces.
Religion faces the same problem.
Certain illusions about freedom plague them both.

— Yann Martel, *Life of Pi*

Call To Worship

Leader: This is a good place to be this morning. The world goes on around us while we are in *sanctuary*. Here, together, we know that evil and good exist in our global village yet we choose to rest a while, giving our psyches and bodies a chance to be tranquil.

People: Sometimes we feel like the philosopher in the biblical essay, "Ecclesiastes," thinking that "everything is useless." We work hard and have little to show for it. The sun rises and sets; the wind blows round and round; rivers flow into the sea ... everything seems to lead to weariness! It seems that the more we know and the wiser we get, the more we have to worry about!

Leader: The philosopher, Qohelet, goes on to say that he would enjoy himself and find out what makes him happy.

People: We must find out what makes us happy, too.

Leader: Happiness is a solitary task.

People: We can encourage each other by articulating what we find along the path to happiness.

Leader: Right here, we can be honest about our questions, our doubts, and our findings.

People: In music and words, in silence and in conversation, we thank God and one another for this opportunity to be real.

Prayer Of Thanksgiving (Leader)

Energy of the Universe — however we spell your name, whatever we call you, however we experience your presence, we are grateful that you make your home among humankind. Thank you for the many ways you exhibit your caring for your creatures. We open our minds and bodies to your love, expecting to hear your affirmation and your guiding voice. We are your loyal people, ready to be still in your presence. Amen.

Call To Confession (Leader)

Throughout the global village this morning, people are using various nouns to describe the ceaseless creativity in the natural universe and in the human psyche. Everywhere, people are asking questions about the meaning of their lives. We have our own questions and now we make time to reflect on what is Holy, noticing the attitudes and ideas that separate us from our sisters and brothers with different descriptive words. Pray with me the printed prayer and then have your personal conversation with the Holy One.

Community Confession (Unison)
Center of the Universe — we desperately want you to engage with us in ways we can see
    and understand.
We frantically search for things that satisfy us.
We try words and drugs and relationships hoping to be close to you.
But we are not happy; we are not content; we are not loyal to our friends and commitments.
Whisper hope and satisfaction to us; sing us a love song; touch us with the fiery magma of
    creativity and peace.
So, in this moment, we want to be free from anything that retards our journey to Holy
    Mystery and peaceful psyche.
Transform our priorities and our goals; reshape our relationships and professions. Amen.

Sermon Idea
Ecclesiastes works up nicely as a first person monologue/soliloquy by Philosopher Qohelet with the title something like, Life Isn't Fair. Observations about work, rest, happiness, aging, taxation, and spirituality can be made with some subtle humor. She/he could "rant" and reflect in the center aisle of the sanctuary.

Hosea 11, preceded by reference to 11:12—12:1, could be a poignant reflection on the political situation of Israel and Palestine rooted in the spiritual hopes of the ages.

A red flag for both texts: The writers present what today appear as cynical and masculine/ patriarchal views; the preacher will have to be skillful in not violating the sensitivities of younger women and men in the congregation.

As in the story of Mary and Martha, Jesus resists taking on the role of conflict manager. He tells the parable of the man who didn't recognize "enough" but he refuses to invade the boundaries of the brother-brother discussion. It might be interesting to explore some of the global issues that create national and international conflict like: the USA and immigration, big houses and vanishing food-producing land, water and irrigation, corn production for ethanol, and more. A title for the gospel emphasis might be True Life and Real Things or Real Life and True Things.

Contemporary Affirmation (Unison)
We know God, the Creator, by many names;
    we believe that God, the Holy One, loves us and all creation.
We know Jesus of Nazareth taught people to love friends and enemies;
    we believe Jesus' teachings lead us to satisfaction in living.
We believe the Holy Spirit is moving throughout the global village,
    inviting all peoples to live peaceably together;
    we experience the Holy Spirit to be motivating us to journey toward
        internal contentment and external service for justice.
In community, we are stimulated intellectually to ask questions
        about the meaning of life and Mystery.
We are challenged to know ourselves and to relate to God.

**We are soothed during the painful parts of life and in good times,
we share our rejoicings! Hurrah! Yippee! Hallelujah!**

Offertory Statement (Leader)

We know that Quohelet saw the world as unfulfilling and God as non-helpful, yet he continued to be active in his community. We too may be struggling to remain faithful to Jesus' teachings, but we can stay engaged with each other, articulating our questions and learning to be tolerant of the ambiguities. We need this sanctuary, this place of holy quietness, to ask, listen, and respond to the Spirit. Give what you can to maintain this building, to minister to the neighborhood, and to reach out beyond our city.

Doxology   The Lone, Wild Bird (v. 2, modified), tune: PROSPECT

The ends of earth are in God's hand, The sea's dark deep and far-off land.
And I am yours! I rest in you. Great Spirit, come, and rest in me.

Prayer Of Thanksgiving (Leader)

Holy One — we are grateful for the ways you are among us, blessing us with multiple gifts. Hear our questions and despite our doubts, use our resources and our talents to make this world a more hospitable place. Amen.

Intercessory Prayers (Leader or Readers)

Energy of the Universe — take us into ourselves and let us find you there, giving us satisfaction with life and giving us compassion for people beyond our own skins. Throughout this day, we wish to receive stimulation from your presence in nature and companions rather than from shopping or television or computer games. We want to receive your healing and your radiance. Reveal to us whatever blocks your flow to us; we want to let it go. Let us tune in to your rhythms so we are aware of a myriad ways to enjoy living.

Desert Spirit — brighten our interior landscapes; let us be colorful like the Grand Canyon; let us find images that open us to adventure with Great Mystery. Flow in and out of us to a world choking on obsolete symbols and perceptions of another era. Lift our faith from the ruts of paths well traveled to explore contemporary styles; help us step from the still life of the institutional church and move with vitality to the shapes and colors of new life.

Generous Spirit — warfulness and catastrophe visit so many places and people! Sitting here in the safety of this sanctuary, we abandon the compulsion to make sense of suffering. We perceive that life works better in good and bad times when there is cooperation rather than confrontation; when food, plants, animals, and people are part of the whole planetary process. Yet people are dying in the name of freedom. Visit leaders with compassion and hospitality; work through them to alleviate hunger, disease, homelessness, and violent behaviors.

God of Thoughts — like Qohelet and Hosea, some of us ask questions and answer them with stories to explain what is important to us. Help us not be arrogant or stubborn with our own experiences of love and grace.

Prism of Sacredness — shine through our conversations with new descriptions of everything old; let us reflect the Divine in the ways we live with the earth and our neighbors. Help us to handle gracefully the imperfections and complexities that surround us. Let us greet each new day with insight and hopefulness. Amen.

Benediction (Leader)

Life is a journey to Mystery.
Experiment with multiple names for God;
Explore different ways to respond to the Holy Spirit.
Laugh each day and unbuild the overwhelming towers of the world.
Notice possibilities around each corner;
Make dreams and cultivate a glad heart!
Holy Spirit empowers you and me to live *real life* —
Peace be yours, deep peace. Amen.

Music

Come, O Thou Traveler Unknown
    Words: Charles Wesley, 1742
    Music: Trad. Scottish melody; harm. Carlton R. Young, 1963
    CANDLER

O Lord Of Every Shining Constellation
    Words: Albert F. Bayly, 1950, alt.
    Music: V. Earle Copes, 1963
    VICAR

Open My Eyes, That I May See
    Words and Music: Clara H. Scott, 1895
    OPEN MY EYES

Una Espiga (Sheaves Of Summer)
    Words: Cesareo Gabaraín, 1973; tr. George Lockwood, 1989
    Music: Cesareo Gabaraín, 1973, alt.; harm. Skinner Chávez-Melo, 1973
    UNA ESPIGA

We Meet You, O Christ
    Words: Fred Kaan, 1966
    Music: Carl F. Schalk, 1987
    STANLEY BEACH

Woman In The Night
    Words: Brian Wren, 1982
    Music: Charles H. Webb, 1989
    HAIZ

Proper 14
Ordinary Time 19
Pentecost 12

Isaiah 1:1, 10-20 or Genesis 15:1-6
Psalm 50:1-8, 22-23 or Psalm 33:12-22

Hebrews 11:1-3, 8-16
Luke 12:32-40

Zoos are no longer in people's good graces.
Religion faces the same problem.
Certain illusions about freedom plague them both.

— Yann Martel, *Life of Pi*

Call To Worship
Leader: We've come here from a variety of places; each of us for our own reasons. Each of us has a perception of the Holy and we anticipate having that perception satisfied.
People: **We experience God as judge or as storm or as fire or as gentle voice or as creative friend.**
Leader: One thing we know is that God is Creator of the world and invites us to be responsible caretakers for the earth and its creatures.
People: **The Holy One does not ask us to appease divinity by killing animals and humans; rules and recited dogma are not required by God, either.**
Leader: So what does God want from us?
People: **God wants us to be hospitable, generous, and honest — all intangible qualities that declare our loyalty to "heaven on earth" living.**

Prayer Of Thanksgiving (Leader)
Gracious God — we are ready to live in ways that manifest "heaven on earth." Thank you for your lively presence here among us. We are glad for the many ways we can show our appreciation — and for the many ways you inspire us. We are open and ready to receive your love. Amen.

Call To Confession (Leader)
Our scriptures consider two primary themes: Faith is ... and God wants.... Pray with me the printed prayer and then have your personal conversation with the Holy One.

Community Confession (Unison)
God of the Past, Present, and Future — our concepts of thinking and faith, trust and belief are enmeshed.
We have faith that you are the I AM, our God.
We trust that you love us. We believe that you are the Creator of the universe.
But you are Great Mystery to us and we do not fully know what you expect from us.
We do not think you want blood sacrifices.
We think that our caring for the earth and for strangers pleases you.

We think you want us to love you, be honest, not steal, not invade others' property — the commandments you gave Moses.
So help us pay attention to your whispers.
Help us following your leading. Amen.

Sermon Idea

The Hebrews text could lead to an exploration of the relationship of science and religion — creationism and evolution, the cosmos as a finished entity and as an ever-expanding one. Without going over the ancient rationalizations, the text asks us to consider what our understanding of God compels us to think, believe, do, and become. Since the word "faith" along with "love" and "trust" is over used by various religious groups in our culture, other verbal constructions would challenge the listeners in fresh ways. In the Genesis text, the Psalms, and the gospel, the theme is "Pay attention and be ready for whatever comes." This theme could be explored through developmental stages — what is to be expected for each stage of our lives, physically and psychically/spiritually. It could also be explored through international issues: If Americans had been paying attention, we might not be addicted to oil or we might have figured out that Saudi Arabia could control our economy or we might have been more observant about the effect of international trade agreements. A sermon title might be: I'm Tired of Your Bloody Behavior! — God. An honest question might be: Can we trust God to be on our side? as the psalmist insists.

Contemporary Affirmation

We know God, the Creator, by many names;
    we believe that God, the Holy One, loves us and all creation.
We know Jesus of Nazareth taught people to love friends and enemies;
    we believe Jesus' teachings lead us to satisfaction in living.
We believe the Holy Spirit is moving throughout the global village,
    inviting all peoples to live peaceably together;
    we experience the Holy Spirit to be motivating us to journey toward
        internal contentment and external service for justice.
In community, we are stimulated intellectually to ask questions
        about the meaning of life and Mystery.
We are challenged to know ourselves and to relate to God.
We are soothed during the painful parts of life and in good times,
    we share our rejoicings! Hurrah! Yippee! Hallelujah!

Offertory Statement (Leader)

Jesus tells the rich man that he should be concerned about his investments in heaven. We, too, must pay attention to our spiritual wealth. Some we invest in our building and share the costs of being a household of faith; some we invest in society by helping feed those who are hungry; some we invest in medical mission projects; some we invest in the education of the next generation. We take a few minutes to pass baskets to receive your investment for today.

Doxology   The Lone, Wild Bird (v. 2, modified), tune: PROSPECT
The ends of earth are in God's hand, The sea's dark deep and far-off land.
And I am yours! I rest in you. Great Spirit, come, and rest in me.

Prayer Of Thanksgiving (Leader)

Investing God — we thank you for making your home, your investment in us and in the Universe. We want to be loyal in the use of our riches — money, time, and talent. Multiply what we have to share so that others may have what they need to be well nourished. Amen.

Intercessory Prayers (Leader or Readers)

Creating Spirit — summer is here with its heat and harvests. We're aware of how the seasons cycle by us providing varied foods, weather patterns, and beautiful sights. We pray for this whole planet and its health. Work wisdom in us so that we problem-solve for the earth's harmony and the universe's welfare. Let the seasons come and go to bless all creatures.

Creating Spirit — we think of our ancestors whose understanding of the Bible was quite literal and their faith was not dependent upon logic or scientific data. As we learn more about how the intricate systems of the human body and the universe work, help us integrate what we learn with what we experience as Divine Presence. We imagine that to be made from clay means that sometimes we feel cracked and discarded. Mend our broken places; establish us among companions who are honest with us and who are willing to help carry our burdens. Sustain us when we are afraid.

Energy of the Universe — we used to think that the teachings of Jesus would establish the kingdom of heaven on the earth. But it seems we are a long way from a social order based on honesty, justice, peace, and shared resources. Raise among Americans — and in every nation — leaders whose vision includes goodness for every person and opportunities for physical and mental wholeness. We pray for the end of war everywhere it maims people and destroys the land.

Creating Spirit — we are glad for the adults and children who make this faith family a safe place for exploring the Holy, for asking questions, and for holding the unanswerable in some sort of creative tension. Sustain our fascination and loyalty to the Mystery we name God. Amen.

Benediction (Leader)

Life is a journey to Mystery.
Experiment with multiple names for God;
Explore different ways to respond to the Holy Spirit.
Laugh each day and unbuild the overwhelming towers of the world.
Notice possibilities around each corner;
Make dreams and cultivate a glad heart!
Holy Spirit empowers you and me to live *real life* —
Peace be yours, deep peace. Amen.

Music

Creating God, Your Fingers Trace
    Words: Jeffery Rowthorn, 1974
    Music: Att. to Elkanah Kelsay Dare, 1799
    KEDRON

God Of Many Names
    Words: Brian Wren, 1985
    Music: William P. Rowan, 1985
    MANY NAMES

O God Of Every Shining Constellation
    Words: Albert F. Bayly, 1950
    Music: V. Earle Copes, 1963
    VICAR

O God Who Shaped Creation
    Words: William W. Weid Jr., 1987
    Music: Dale Wood, 1968, 1988
    TUOLUMNE

What Does The Lord Require For Praise?
    Words: Albert F. Bayly, 1949
    Music: Norman L. Warren, 1969
    BISHOP TUCKER

What Gift Can We Bring?
    Words and Music: Jane Marshall, 1980
    ANNIVERSARY SONG

Proper 15
Ordinary Time 20
Pentecost 13

Isaiah 5:1-7 or Jeremiah 23:23-29   Hebrews 11:29—12:2
Psalm 80:1-2, 8-19 or Psalm 82   Luke 12:49-56

Zoos are no longer in people's good graces.
Religion faces the same problem.
Certain illusions about freedom plague them both.

— Yann Martel, *Life of Pi*

Call To Worship

Leader: It's a good summer morning! We are gathered again. We can ask questions, sing,
          pray, listen, and talk!
People: Yes. We are thankful for life and for the opportunities that come to us.
Leader: We have called to God many times and the Holy One has sustained us and restored
          us to hopefulness.
**People: We trust the Holy Spirit to minister to our needs and to guide us along the path
          of joy and service.**

Prayer Of Thanksgiving (Leader)

God of morning and evening — we are grateful for the breath of life, grateful for the option of gathering here to acknowledge our devotion to you. When we gather to sing and pray, we feel your gracious goodness. During this hour, we honor you, giving you our full attention and our best responses as you speak to us. Thank you for your creative presence. Amen.

Call To Confession (Leader)

God is here and everywhere! No one can hide from the One who is Great Mystery. Pray with me the printed prayer and then have your personal conversation with the Holy One.

Community Confession (Unison)

**Holy Spirit — we read in scriptures about judgment and punishment, about love and
    justice.**
They are always issues for us personally and as a nation.
**We know that nations who have ignored the poor and hungry and favored the wealthy
    have not fared well in history books.**
Open our eyes to the evils we foster in the name of "freedom," "capitalism," and "profit."
Open our ears to the harmful words in our relationships and in our conversations.
Set us on a different path that we may live the teachings of Jesus. Amen.

Sermon Idea

If the preacher enjoys wine and vineyard husbandry, s/he might present the necessary care of a vineyard and then show how "grapevine" for the psalmist and Isaiah represent the potential

218

productivity of Israel. But without fruit, there seem to be two options: destroy it or find a way to refurbish it. It would be great if there is a musician in the congregation who could chant the story from Isaiah 5. A person who has good pantomime skills might also give some vitality to the Isaiah story. The story in Luke is one of the hardest of Jesus' sayings. It would be interesting to explore how weather is predicted and link it with Jesus asking how people can have such vital knowledge but not know about spiritual things. "Setting the earth on fire" might refer to the constant upheavals between world religions. If it's a communion Sunday, emphasis might be focused on the gathered people at the table expecting a good wine as a reminder of Jesus. A catchy sermon title might be: Juicy Possibilities.

Contemporary Affirmation (Unison)

We know God, the Creator, by many names;
   we believe that God, the Holy One, loves us and all creation.
We know Jesus of Nazareth taught people to love friends and enemies;
   we believe Jesus' teachings lead us to satisfaction in living.
We believe the Holy Spirit is moving throughout the global village,
   inviting all peoples to live peaceably together;
   we experience the Holy Spirit to be motivating us to journey toward
      internal contentment and external service for justice.
In community, we are stimulated intellectually to ask questions
   about the meaning of life and Mystery.
We are challenged to know ourselves and to relate to God.
We are soothed during the painful parts of life and in good times,
   we share our rejoicings! Hurrah! Yippee! Hallelujah!

Offertory Statement (Leader)

Let our generosity be part of our reputation. The baskets are coming your way.

Doxology   The Lone, Wild Bird (v. 2, modified), tune: PROSPECT

The ends of earth are in God's hand, The sea's dark deep and far-off land.
And I am yours! I rest in you. Great Spirit, come, and rest in me.

Prayer Of Thanksgiving (Leader)

God of Isaiah and Jesus — we are thankful that you refurbished the grapevine of ancient Israel. And we are grateful for the variety of vines we enjoy today. Use this money to make this world a more hospitable place. Amen.

Intercessory Prayers (Leader or Readers)

Farmer God — we are aware that agriculture varies from place to place; we are also aware that you are everywhere, capable of planting and harvesting, cultivating and plowing under. Not only are we grateful for the stories of scripture, we are also glad for grapes to eat and to make juices. We pray for the helpless, the homeless, and the hungry for whom grapes in our culture are too expensive. Visit humankind again with news that there is enough food and water for all creatures.

Fiery God — Jesus said he came to set the earth on fire. One way we look at that image is exciting: Jesus will cleanse the earth of its rubble and nonsense. Another way we see that image is scary: The people of the world will incinerate all that is not consistent with preparation for your kingdom on earth. Instead of a flood story, it threatens a fire story! We pray for religious leaders in every country. Let bigotry and judgment no longer be part of passing on the news of your dynamic presence in human life.

Fearsome God — we see the wars and hear the rumors of wars right in our own living rooms. We see children and soldiers, men and women going about their daily work being killed. Why? Muslims and Christians, Arabs and Americans pray for safety and democracy, whatever that means in countries far away. Why is it that atrocities continue? We pray for an end to hostilities in every nation. We pray for wise leaders whose goal is to govern so people have safety and food. We pray for relief from greedy, power-hungry men — in Africa, in China, in Pakistan, in Iraq, in Iran, in Saudi Arabia, in Afghanistan, and in America. Hear our prayers.

Feeling God — see your children suffer. Don't neglect your creatures on any continent. Work among scientists and physicians, among politicians and scholars to heal deep ethnic wounds. Reach to us whose backs are wearing out, whose circulation systems get clogged, whose minds are confused; heal us all and lift our fears as we prepare to meet you in eternity.

Freeing God — see our children grow and learn. Keep them safe from harm and guide them to be leaders for a fresh dream of possibility for all peoples. Help us mentor them in compassion and hospitality so that they are not overcome with competition and mediocre projects. Amen.

Benediction (Leader)
Life is a journey to Mystery.
Experiment with multiple names for God;
Explore different ways to respond to the Holy Spirit.
Laugh each day and unbuild the overwhelming towers of the world.
Notice possibilities around each corner;
Make dreams and cultivate a glad heart!
Holy Spirit empowers you and me to live *real life* —
Peace be yours, deep contentment. Amen.

Music
Come, O Spirit
Words: John A. Dalles, 1983
Music: *Union Harmony*, 1837; harm. Hilton Rufty, 1934
BOUNDLESS MERCY

God, You Spin The Whirling Planets
Words: Jane Parker Huber, 1978
Music: Franz Joseph Haydn, 1797
AUSTRIAN HYMN

In Loving Partnership
  Words and Music: Jim Strathdee, 1983
  PARTNERSHIP
  LM

Maker, In Whom We Live
  Words: Charles Wesley, 1747
  Music: George J. Elvey, 1868
  DIADEMATA

O Holy Spirit, Root Of Life
  Words: Jean Janzen, 1991, based on the writings of Hildegard of Bingen (12th century)
  Music: Trier manuscript (15th century); adapt. Michael Praetorius, 1609; harm. George
    R. Woodward, 1904
  PUER NOBIS NASCITUR

Proper 16
Ordinary Time 21
Pentecost 14

Jeremiah 1:4-10 or Isaiah 58:9b-14   Hebrews 12:18-29
Psalm 71:1-6 or Psalm 103:1-8   Luke 13:10-17

Zoos are no longer in people's good graces.
Religion faces the same problem.
Certain illusions about freedom plague them both.

— Yann Martel, *Life of Pi*

Call To Worship
Leader: It's a good morning! Welcome to this place where our souls can rest and praise God.
People: We are thankful for life and we are seeking security and happiness.
Leader: We have called to God many times and the Holy One has sustained us and restored us to hopefulness.
People: We are standing straight and tall! With our minds and bodies, we thank God for divine goodness among us!

Prayer Of Thanksgiving (Leader)
God of the Straight-Standers and the Bent-Overs — thank you for your constant presence caring for us no matter what our posture is, no matter what our doubts are, no matter what our certainties are. In this hour, as we listen for your voice, stretch our imaginations so we can be creative with you; expand our perceptions so we can admire your handiwork; enlarge our understanding of how divinity is with humanity. We are eager to sing and pray, to listen and to respond to your voice. Amen.

Call To Confession (Leader)
Throughout the global village this morning, people are praying for relief from the consequences of their behaviors, praying that God would make things okay and easier: "Listen to us and save us," we say. Everywhere, people are asking questions about the meaning of their lives. Now there is time to reflect on Holy Presence and to ask God our questions and to listen for a response. Pray with me the printed prayer and then have your personal conversation with the Holy One.

Community Confession (Unison)
Designer of the Human Psyche — there is so much we do not understand.
Why do we want to do what is right ethically and morally and then don't do it?
Why do we find a way around the commandments and ignore our responsibility?
Why do we seek happiness in relationships and things beyond our own homes?
Reveal our fantasies; give us the courage to be honest and to do what we know to be life-giving. Amen.

Sermon Idea

The gospel lesson provides an opportunity to explore what causes twenty-first-century Christians to bend over. The list probably includes: our food supply, sexism, debate about reproduction and human sexuality, extended work hours, pay that is inadequate to put a roof over head and nutritious food on the table, building a Supreme Court, international terrorism, immigration, torturing enemies, and other social issues. If we are like the woman in Jesus' story, we are to stand ourselves up. Can we praise God, can our lives be a light for others, can we honor God if our soul/psyches are bent over/crippled? The movie *Rain Man* shows a savvy determination to live fully, also the story of Christopher Reeves. If we are to stand straight, we must have wholesome foods for the body and for the mind. What is the role of sports, movies, television, music, visual art, and dance in providing cognitive and affective nutrition for adults and children? Does the church and its interpretation of scriptures enable women as well as men to stand up and walk their journey with the Holy? The book *Eat, Pray, Love* stimulates discussion about ways culture and our personal diversity push us to step outside the experiences of our pasts. Another approach might be to take the Hebrews text and consider what draws us to God and how we respond — such as running for government offices to influence care for the earth, safe foods, education for our children, and a reasonable fair way of articulating our varying understandings of the Holy.

Contemporary Affirmation (Unison)

We know God, the Creator, by many names;
>   **we believe that God, the Holy One, loves us and all creation.**

We know Jesus of Nazareth taught people to love friends and enemies;
>   **we believe Jesus' teachings lead us to satisfaction in living.**

We believe the Holy Spirit is moving throughout the global village,
>   **inviting all peoples to live peaceably together;**
>   **we experience the Holy Spirit to be motivating us to journey toward**
>   **internal contentment and external service for justice.**

In community, we are stimulated intellectually to ask questions
>   **about the meaning of life and Mystery.**

We are challenged to know ourselves and to relate to God.

We are soothed during the painful parts of life and in good times,
>   **we share our rejoicings! Hurrah! Yippee! Hallelujah!**

Offertory Statement (Leader)

Despite our questions and the ambiguities in our lives, we can be thankful for the breath of life and for the resources that help sustain it. We share the expenses of ministry on this street and through out the global village. In our work and play together, we learn to unbend and look each other in the eye and see the Christ. Share as you can.

Doxology   The Lone, Wild Bird (v. 2, modified), tune: PROSPECT

The ends of earth are in God's hand, The sea's dark deep and far-off land.
And I am yours! I rest in you. Great Spirit, come, and rest in me.

Prayer Of Thanksgiving (Leader)

Holy One — we are grateful for money to make our way in the world. We want to use it to make clean water and good foods available to all people. Thank you for the moral and ethical courage to stand straight and to follow the teachings of Jesus. And when we forget, help us to encourage each other. Amen.

Intercessory Prayers (Leader or Readers)

God of Body and Mind — our awareness of you changes as the years go by. Our bodies change; our minds entertain strange ideas. We trust your continuing presence to guide us through the experiences that weigh heavy on our shoulders and through the events that give our days and nights meaning. We know the journey on this earth includes pain and suffering. Sustain us as our bodies ache and our minds forget; encourage us to play fairly and appreciate our opponents. Move among us adults and kids so that peacemaking is a satisfying habit.

God of all Ages — give us clear voices and words to speak appropriate to our age. However old the ancient prophets were, they were never too young to be truthful. We, too, want to learn to be honest about what is happening in our bodies and souls. We want to take into our selves only that which is life-giving; we do not want to be bent over by half-truths, abusive images, and political accusations. Help us.

God of Religions — how we have struggled to understand your hopes for your creatures. We've made rules and rituals, fences and doors, formulas and theories hoping to present ourselves well to you and keep away contaminating influences. But the more we try, the more rumors of war erupt; the more judgments are rendered against people who experience you differently; the more angst we feel in our own bodies. Stretch our imaginations to see you at work in other nations and their attempts to honor you. Visit us and world leaders in dreams that are clearly peaceful and genuinely empowering.

God of People and Polar Bears — we pray for ourselves and our planet. We want to be your mind and hands in our neighborhoods, responding with compassion to creatures in need. Some days we wonder what real compassion is. Help us not to be blinded by irresponsibility, by ethnic identities or by disease. Guide us through our questions and our dilemmas of climate changes, aging, children's activities, relationships, loneliness, and soul health. Increase our self-control so that we do not abuse the earth and its gifts necessary for life. Amen.

Benediction (Leader)

Life is a journey to Mystery.
Experiment with multiple names for God;
Explore different ways to respond to the Holy Spirit.
Laugh each day and unbuild the overwhelming towers of the world.
Notice possibilities around each corner;
Make dreams and cultivate a glad heart!
Holy Spirit empowers you and me to live *real life* —
Peace be yours and strong contentment. Amen.

Music

Every Time I Feel The Spirit
    Words: African-American spiritual
    Music: African-American spiritual; arr. Joseph T. Jones (1902-1983); adapt. Melva W.
        Costen
    PENTECOST

The Lone, Wild Bird *(note: the second verse of this hymn is also suggested for use as the
        Doxology for the entire Pentecost season)*
    Words: Henry Richard McFadyen, 1925, alt.
    Music: as in *Twelve Folksongs and Spirituals*, 1968; harm. David N. Johnson, 1968
    PROSPECT

Spirit
    Words and Music: James K. Manley, 1975
    SPIRIT

Spirit Of The Living God
    Words: Daniel Iverson, 1935, adapt.
    Music: Daniel Iverson, 1935
    LIVING GOD

Wind Upon The Waters
    Words and Music: Marty Haugen, 1986
    WIND UPON THE WATERS

Season 7
Late Pentecost

Slow Motion

Proper 17
Ordinary Time 22
Pentecost 15

Jeremiah 2:4-13 or Sirach 10:12-18   Hebrews 13:1-8, 15-16
Psalm 81:1, 10-16 or Psalm 112   Luke 14:1, 7-14

> *If we love the Lord with all our hearts, minds, and strength,*
> *we are going to have to stretch our hearts, open our minds,*
> *and strengthen our souls ... God cannot lodge in a narrow mind;*
> *God cannot lodge in a small heart. To accommodate God they must be palatial.*
>
> — William Sloan Coffin, *Credo*

Call To Worship

Leader: Some people look forward to Sundays as a time to relax. Some look forward to Mondays when classes begin; some look forward to Fridays when the weekend begins. Some people are always looking ahead; some frequently look to the past. What about you?

People: **We are "some people" who live fully in this moment, aware that the breath of life is a gift that has an ending. We want to enjoy God and one another.**

Leader: Are you preparing for autumn and slowing down till Advent?

People: **This week, we intentionally take stock of how we spend our time — especially examining the work we do with our hands, our minds, our bodies, and our psyches.**

Leader: Look carefully. In the past, people have allowed the culture to extract energy and loyalty, leaving little for God and family.

People: **We know the biblical prophets accused the ancient Hebrews of exchanging their God-concept for the goods and values of other cultures.**

Leader: Even though they were provided water and food through the desert years, Bible stories tell us that the people neglected their relationship with the giver of finest wheat and honey!

People: **This weekend, we determine again to honor the Giver of Life by doing creative, meaningful work, maintaining empowering relationships, and sharing what we have with others.**

Prayer Of Thanksgiving (Leader)

Giver of Life — thank you for days to rest, for opportunities to celebrate the changing of the seasons, to be grateful for jobs that put bread on our tables, and for work that satisfies our minds and souls. Thank you for your dependable presence with us. Bring us close to your heart; let us feel Christ animating us. Amen.

Call To Confession (Leader)

We say we see ourselves in Bible stories. Today's stories point out our tendencies to resist divine guidance and neglect being grateful for what comes to us. In these moments, look within and clarify for yourself and with God the prejudices and narrow thoughts, which diminish your ability to reveal the Great Mystery we call God. Pray with me and then make your own prayers.

Community Confession (Unison)

Great Mystery — we hear you call to us; we recognize that you make our burdens lighter. We acknowledge that our basic needs are met.

Yet we spend our resources on things the culture values, sometimes stubbornly resisting what we think you would have us be and do. We tend to ignore our neighbors and our enemies.

Amplify our minds; expand our hearts; stretch our souls to accommodate your love; encourage us to participate with you in developing a bit of heaven on earth. Amen.

Sermon Idea

A *job* is what we do to earn money necessary to survive in our culture. *Money* is the medium by which we barter for what we want/need. *Work* is how we manifest our creativity and thoughts. For people whose work and job coincide — wow, living can be good! Psalm 112 describes happiness for those whose work honors the Holy One. Luke 14:7-14 suggests that competition and profit cannot be the goals of our jobs or our work. Perhaps the primary focus could be on jobs we are afraid to get out of and the jobs that compromise our perception of Divine grace and the jobs that satisfy us and make the world a better residence. Satisfying jobs and vital work stimulate us to be humble and hospitable. Another issue that might be explored through all the texts is: Capitalism and an economy based on profit cannot be hospitable, democratic, and promote justice.

A more negative approach could be explored with Jeremiah who says the people ruined the fertile land, explored idols, and accused God of being useless. It might be difficult to make a comparison between ancient Israel and America without also comparing ancient Israel with contemporary Israel. This could be "touchy."

Contemporary Affirmation (Unison)

The Divine Imagination continues to be at work in the world;
> **God breathes life and proclaims it good.**

The Divine Worker was revealed in Jesus of Nazareth
> **who moved among people healing, mentoring, feeding, and renewing.**

The Divine Artist continues to create through us,
> **inspiring us to exhibit the Christ in our choices and decisions.**

In community, we encourage one another to explore who we
> **can become as twenty-first-century friends of Jesus.**
> **Together, we can be honest, compassionate, and hopeful.**

Let it be so. Amen!

Offertory Statement (Leader)

Be grateful people; praise the sky and the earth.
Honor the Creator with your resources and your loyalty.

Doxology   Christ, Whose Glory Fills The Skies (v. 1)

Christ, whose glory fills the skies, Christ, the true, the only light,
Sun of Righteousness, arise, triumph o'er the shades of night;
Dayspring from on high, be near; Daystar in my heart appear.

Prayer Of Thanksgiving (Leader)

Great God — we honor you with our work and our jobs, with our gifts and our attitudes. Thank you for abundant life, for the beauty of the world, and for the friends who sit with us today. Use our talents and our money to make this world more hospitable. Amen.

Intercessory Prayers (Leader or Readers)

Busy God — we see you continually creating and re-creating. We see evidence of your expansive imagination. We feel you busy among us, making things different from last year, refocusing our thoughts and compelling us to expand our perceptions of divinity and humanity. We want to love you with our whole selves; revamp our souls to be palatial.

Midwifing God — birth through us a new world order, a reign of justice and compassion, an era with honest politics and compassionate leaders. Move among this planet's palette of people until peace spills out. Nurture governments until they protect the cosmos and feed the children. Keep harmful elements away; halt dangerous toxins that threaten to destroy goodness.

Animating God — we understand ourselves to be formed in your image. But we get weary; our bones make us cry "ouch": disease overpowers our organs; loneliness makes us grouchy; jobs-without-meaning cripple our imaginations; cynicism diminishes our willingness to be good neighbors. Breathe new life into us again. Open our eyes to work that is satisfying for our minds and souls. Heal us and activate deep peace in our muscles. Amen.

Benediction (Leader)

As you leave the sanctuary to work and play,
Be aware that your cup of life is at least half full!
Notice that the roof over your home is strong.
Notice soft breezes, warm fires, and smiles of friends.
Take time to be grateful for who you are;
Check in with who you are becoming.
God, Animator of the Cosmos, is blessing you.
Go gently. Amen!

Music

Called As Partners In Christ's Service
Words: Jane Parker Huber, 1981
Music: John Zundel, 1870
BEECHER

Forth In Thy Name, O Lord
    Words: Charles Wesley, 1749
    Music: John Hatton, 1793
    DUKE STREET

God Of Grace And God Of Glory
    Words: Harry Emerson Fosdick, 1930
    Music: John Hughes, 1907
    CWM RHONDDA

O God Of Every Nation
    Words: William W. Reid Jr., 1958
    Music: Welsh hymn melody; harm. David Evans, 1927
    LLANGLOFFAN

Take My Gifts
    Words: Shirley Erena Murray, 1988
    Music: Colin Gibson, 1988
    TALAVERA TERRACE

The Voice Of Jesus Calls His People
    Words and Music: Joy F. Patterson, 1993
    THE VOICE OF JESUS

Proper 18
Ordinary Time 23
Pentecost 16

Jeremiah 18:1-11 or Deuteronomy 30:15-20   Philemon 1-21
Psalm 139:1-6, 13-18 or Psalm 1   Luke 14:25-33

If we love the Lord with all our hearts, minds, and strength,
we are going to have to stretch our hearts, open our minds,
and strengthen our souls ... God cannot lodge in a narrow mind;
God cannot lodge in a small heart. To accommodate God they must be palatial.

— William Sloan Coffin, *Credo*

Call To Worship

Leader: Good morning! It's great to be alive this early autumn day! School has begun; summer gardens are closing up; darkness comes sooner.

People: The earth seems to be slowing down and we know that winter comes soon enough.

Leader: What are you grateful for this morning?

People: In our conversations with God and with one another, we express thanks for joyful events, for cheerful hearts especially during difficult circumstances, and for friends who walk with us on life's journey.

Leader: I, too, appreciate our relationship and the vision we share of showcasing Divine Presence.

People: With open minds and souls, we express our experience with Holy Spirit in music and words and we anticipate God's thoughts coming to us!

Prayer Of Thanksgiving (Leader)

Creator of this Slowdown Season — you know us and this global village. You know what we think and why we behave as we do. Thank you for caring for us even when our minds are narrow and our hearts are hard and our prejudices stubborn. Thank you for staying with us wherever we go! In light and in darkness, we feel your watchfulness. During this hour, we diligently listen for your voice and intently pay attention to our inward responses. Amen.

Call To Confession (Leader)

Our human inclination is to do what we want when we want for the purpose we want. Then we tend to hide from the truth if it is not to our liking. The psalmist indicates that we cannot hide from Holy Mystery. For the next few moments, we invite the Spirit to examine us and reveal to each of us the "evil" that lurks within. The prayer starter is in unison. Join me.

Community Confession (Unison)

Heart-stretching Spirit — we want to be happy and we want to embody your grace.
We want to be like trees, firmly rooted in good soil nourished by living waters.

When ugliness and barrenness threaten, we often lose courage to confront evil.
Enliven our intuitions so we can discriminate between the advice of the world and the
wisdom of your voice. Amen.

Sermon Idea

Since Philemon, Psalm 1, and Psalm 139 speak of happiness, the sermon could explore "happiness" as a result of self-knowledge and relationship with Holy Presence. Luke 14:25 ff suggests that as we mature along our way with Holy Mystery, we must make some difficult choices, setting aside some of the relationships and material goods that appeal to us. As the days get shorter and the dark hours more numerous, we can take an inventory of what we are building, what we "fight" for, and how our decisions affect the global village. One observation from Luke 14:34 (not included in the lectionary passage) might be that when we are growing/maturing in ways to manifest God's love, we are like herbs, which add satisfying characteristics to the (culture's) mixture. The preacher also could explore the difference between "meaningful living" and happiness in contemporary parlance. In *Finding Meaning in the Second Half of Life* (James Hollis) suggests that in our culture, we have never learned to grow up. Psalm 139 might be used to illuminate the relationship between knowing oneself and knowing God, and between being known by God and accepting personal responsibility for learning to read one's own soul. If the congregation enjoys the sounds of different languages, someone might read portions of Psalm 139 in Hebrew. Note the anathema at the end of the psalm and comment that Christianity attempts loving neighbors and enemies rather than damning them as the psalms frequently do near the conclusion of the poems. A very challenging option would be to consider Jeremiah 18 and the idea that God can do anything he wishes with human beings. How does this idea fit with the Christian concept of a loving, gracious God? Is God bound by moral and ethical guidelines? Can Christians speak of "fate"? Do atheists have a point when they say that God hasn't managed humankind very well since greed and violence grow while justice seems to be missing? The preacher could hold a large ball of clay and shape it while s/he talks and then crush it or preserve it with all its imperfections. We are the clay; is God messing with us or intentionally shaping our experiences? What is our response — Jeremiah 18:12 or Luke 14:33-34?

Contemporary Affirmation (Unison)

God was and is;

    Holy Presence is apparent in Creation and in individual human development
        as we learn to know ourselves and respond to divine love.

God was and is;

    Jesus of Nazareth incarnated Holy Presence as he healed and mentored
        others for relationship with God.

    The Christ of God offers goodness and abundant life for all people.

God was and is;

    as Holy Spirit, God lives in us and inspires us to embody love, grace, and
        hope.

We are a group of people who acknowledge Divine Mystery;

    We aspire to live simply, hospitably, and gently so we can manifest
        compassion for the earth and its people.

    With one another we generate the courage to be in the world but not
        overwhelmed by it.

Offertory Statement (Leader)

This is the moment when we say to God:
   I have heard your voice; Here I am, use me and my resources
   to make this global village a safe neighborhood.
The baskets/plates are big enough to hold all of our tithes and offerings.

Doxology   Praise God From Whom All Blessings Flow, tune: OLD HUNDREDTH
(with inclusive language for God)

Praise God from whom all blessings flow;
Praise God, all creatures here below;
Praise God above, you heavenly hosts —
Creator, Christ, and Holy Ghost. Amen!

Prayer Of Thanksgiving (Leader)

Awesome God — thank you for your enthusing Spirit motivating us to work and play, to study and to relax with confidence about our lives. We are grateful, generous emblems of your grace right here. Amen.

Intercessory Prayers (Leader or Readers)

God of Leaders and Followers — the world has become a global neighborhood with governments, officials, and citizens. We pray for wisdom for each of our roles in society. We pray for people who get caught on the craggy edges of filibusters and votes, rebellions and power plays. Most of all, we yearn for an end to hatreds and wars. We pray for peace.

God of Foundations and Spires — we believe you ask us to love you more than anything or anyone. Grow us deep into the mysteries of heaven and earth; grow us outward with respect for creatures and all nature; grow us with thoughts and experiences to appreciate who you are shaping us to be. Some of us function as guides to others; give us discerning ears; give us artful tongues; guide us to compassionate responses.

God of Salads and Herbs — we crave happiness and health, satisfying days and comfortable nights. We pine for painless movement and cheerful attitudes. Jesus reminded his listeners to make plans, to make choices, and to be alert to the consequences of decisions. Amplify our minds so we can conceive of plans to nurture wholeness and honesty within ourselves, in our congregation, and in our neighborhood. Stretch our perceptions of the Holy so we respect people unlike ourselves. Expand our understanding of our roles in the culture.

God of Children and Adults — we pray for the next generation. We cannot envision the issues they will have to deal with. We cannot guess how they will deal with globalization and ethnic specialties. We cannot fathom how they will feed the world's population and keep the food chain safe. So we pray that you protect them from abuse of all kinds; guard them from subtle evils; help them to learn easily the information necessary for the future of civilization. Amen.

Benediction (Leader)

(Irish blessing, modified)
   Now as you leave this place —
   Be at peace with yourself and your neighbor.
   And —
   May the road rise to meet you

May the wind be always at your back
May the sun shine warm on your faces
And the rain fall gently on your fields.
Until we meet again,
May God hold you and you and you
    in those divine hands!
Amen!

Music
Draw Us In The Spirit's Tether
    Words: Percy Dearmer, 1931, alt.
    Music: Harold Friedell, 1957
    UNION SEMINARY

Faith, While Trees Are Still In Blossom
    Words: Anders Frostenson, 1960; trans. Fred Kaan, 1972
    Music: V. Earle Copes, 1960
    FOR THE BREAD

I've Got Peace Like A River
    Words and Music: African-American spiritual
    PEACE LIKE A RIVER

Mountain Brook With Rushing Waters
    Words: William W. Reid Jr., 1973
    Music: William Rowlands, 1905
    BLAENWERN

'Tis The Gift To Be Simple
    Words: Shaker song (18th century)
    Music: Shaker melody; arr. Margaret W. Mealy, 1984
    SIMPLE GIFTS

Weary Of All Trumpeting
    Words: Martin Franzmann, 1971
    Music: Hugo Distler, 1938; harm. Richard Proulx, 1975
    TRUMPETS

Proper 19
Ordinary Time 24
Pentecost 17

Jeremiah 4:11-12, 22-28 or Exodus 32:7-14   1 Timothy 1:12-17
Psalm 14 or Psalm 51:1-10   Luke 15:1-10

> *If we love the Lord with all our hearts, minds, and strength,*
> *we are going to have to stretch our hearts, open our minds,*
> *and strengthen our souls ... God cannot lodge in a narrow mind;*
> *God cannot lodge in a small heart. To accommodate God they must be palatial.*
>
> — William Sloan Coffin, *Credo*

Call To Worship

Leader: This is sanctuary! We've been busy all week losing and finding things, feeling successful and feeling inadequate!

People: **We are glad to be here! We're expecting to rest and relax, to be real, open, and receptive to divine grace.**

Leader: What shall we do to accomplish your expectations?

People: **Sing. Pray. Speak. Listen.**

Leader: Then, let us be fully engaged — mind and body — with Holy Presence.

Prayer Of Thanksgiving (Leader)

Innovative God — you've made us in your mold, like yourself! Thank you for all the opportunities to be creative and ingenious that come to us. Thank you, too, for setting precedence for "sabbath." As we take respite, here, from our daily activities, our psyches rest and are nourished. Move among us with bright clarity; illuminate our thoughts and illustrate our experiences. Amen.

Call To Confession (Leader)

In today's Hebrew scriptures, the theme is judgment. Human behaviors do have consequences within ourselves and for our communities. "God will get you" is the prophet's challenge. However you visualize your personal responsibility, make this moment one of microscopic reflection. What needs to be changed for you to feel clean, free, and empowered? Pray with me and then have your private conversation with God.

Community Confession (Unison)
God of Insightful Silence — we've settled in with one another.
We want to feel settled in with you.
We want to be nestled into your breath so we may be free from distractions.
When we stray from your best for our lives, bring us back.
When we get lost in the morass of politics, open our minds to the way out.
When Holy glow around us dims, brighten the path you set before us.

**When we let go of what is vital to our souls, sweep away the dust so we can see the real
thing. Amen.**

Sermon Idea

Though the lyrics to an old gospel song, "The Ninety And Nine," are dated, the melody with
some verbal interpretation makes a moving dance. The agricultural images are rarely vital for
city dwellers and the image of a real violent city in our world with judgments made 4,000 years
ago barely preaches. Nevertheless, the themes of "lostness" and external judgments and internal habits speak loudly for twenty-first-century human development savants. The common good
is only as good as the people who comprise the group. What is society's responsibility to those
lost, left behind? Is it appropriate for the church to assume responsibility for the ineptness of
governments to be honest and compassionate? Is it appropriate for the church to educate people
to participate in a particular culture? What is vanishing from the American dream that might
have been a light to other nations? Do we as Christians want to find what has been lost? Who
would describe what is missing from our national life? What would be the cost? Who in America
could use Jeremiah 4:23-29 as a dramatic reading? Who in the congregation? Temper the vitriolic condemnations with Luke 15.

Contemporary Affirmation (Unison)

We believe God cares for the cosmos that has been created;
  we believe God cares about creatures and us.
We know that Jesus of Nazareth incarnated divine wisdom
  as he lived and taught at the eastern end of the Mediterranean Sea
  2,000 years ago.
We experience the Holy Spirit coaxing us into relationship with the Holy One;
  we trust that the Spirit finds us when we are wandering among
  the culture's idols seeking satisfying days and nights.
As a community of faith, as friends, we encourage one another to listen for
  God's voice and to respond to it. We enjoy companionship and conversation
  about our journeys with Great Mystery. Together we explore ways to
  manifest Christ in our town and throughout the global village. Amen!

Offertory Statement (Leader)

We experience goodness in the midst of violence and suffering; one way to demonstrate
gratitude is to find ways to continue goodness here and elsewhere. We do that with our time, our
skills, and our money.

Doxology   Praise God From Whom All Blessings Flow, tune: OLD HUNDREDTH
Praise God from whom all blessings flow;
Praise God, all creatures here below;
Praise God above, you heavenly hosts —
Creator, Christ, and Holy Ghost. Amen!

Prayer Of Thanksgiving (Leader)

Thank you for finding us when we stray from your Spirit. Use us and our resources to
manifest your love and hopes for this world. Amen.

Intercessory Prayers (Leader or Readers)

Shepherding God — sheep and goats need flocks to belong to; they need to be guided to places, which can nurture them and provide fresh water. We're like that, too. Move among us healing and soothing, motivating and energizing. See where we hurt, where wounds don't heal, where joints ache, and hearts are scarred. See where we struggle to be our best selves in circumstances that do not encourage our decisions to be loyal to you. Strengthen us with your Spirit and with godly friends.

Fathering God — like our ancestors, we pray for peace; we pray for an end to hatred. We pray for global leaders who compromise and collaborate to end tribal disputes; we pray for renewed vision of neighborliness and hospitality. We long for wise men and women who will not enhance themselves at the expense of others. Empower us to be peace-makers, peace demonstrators, here on this street.

Mothering God — children and adults on every continent need care and protection from evil and abuse. Children and adults in every nation need nurture and healthy foods. Work among politicians and us to provide these basic necessities of life for those in need.

Beckoning God — we want to participate with your Spirit in ways that establish beauty and justice for all peoples. Use our hands and feet, our voices and our minds as instruments of wholesomeness in every sphere of life. Amen.

Benediction (Leader)

As you leave here —
Keep in mind the tranquility of this place;
Hold in your mind the ideas that inspire you;
Remember those with whom you have shared this hour.
May the creating God guide you to surprising places
    in the days ahead.
Go gently; feel generous and be infectious with joy!
Amen!

Music

Amazing Grace
    Words: John Newton, 1779; st. 4, anonymous
    Music: Virgina Harmony, 1831; harm. Edwin O. Excell, 1900
    NEW BRITAIN

God Of The Sparrow God Of The Whale
    Words: Jaroslav J. Vajda, 1983
    Music: Carl F. Schalk, 1983
    ROEDER

Mothering God, You Gave Me Birth
    Words: Jean Janzen, 1991, based on the writings of Julian of Norwich (14th century)
    Music: Brent Stratten, 1994
    JULIAN

A Woman And A Coin
    Words: Jaroslav J. Vajda, 1990
    Music: Carl F. Schalk, 1990
    NYGREN

Your Love, O God
    Words: Anders Frostenson, 1968; tr. Fred Kaan, 1972
    Music: V. Earle Copes, 1963
    VICAR

Proper 20
Ordinary Time 25
Pentecost 18

Jeremiah 8:18—9:1 or Amos 8:4-7   1 Timothy 2:1-7
Psalm 79:1-9 or Psalm 113   Luke 16:1-13

If we love the Lord with all our hearts, minds, and strength,
we are going to have to stretch our hearts, open our minds,
and strengthen our souls ... God cannot lodge in a narrow mind;
God cannot lodge in a small heart. To accommodate God they must be palatial.
                              — William Sloan Coffin, *Credo*

Call To Worship

Leader: Good morning! I hope you rested well last night and have come here to enjoy inte-
           grating tranquility, insistent inspiration, and lively conversation.

**People: We've come to celebrate, giving thanks to the Giver of Life, Living Water, and
           Spirit Fruits.**

Leader: God is Great Mystery, calling us to relish the beauty of creation and to live as citi-
           zens of benevolent society.

**People: From the east to the west, God moves among the rich and poor, inviting all
           humankind to collaborate in establishing justice.**

Leader: Let's accept God's invitation.

**People: We will pray aloud and silently; we will combine our voices in song. We will be
           active at home and in our neighborhoods seeking justice.**

Prayer Of Thanksgiving (Responsorial)

Leader: Holy One — in this sanctuary, we feel your love; in this place, we express our
           desires and our questions about you and about our lives.

**People: In this place, we remember that we are your people, your thankful and peace-
           making people.**

Leader: In this place, we turn our attention from the tangles of our lives to your gracious
           Presence.

**People: In the sanctuary of this space, we thank you for the breath of life, for the chang-
           ing seasons, and for the children growing up around us.**

Leader: In this place, we give you our undivided attention, expecting to hear your voice —

**People: expecting to hear your affirmations and challenges; and we expect to walk the
           path you set before us.**

Leader: Thank you for your love, for Jesus the Christ, and for the congregation you are
           crafting us to be. Amen.

Call To Confession (Leader)

The Bible readings until Advent are full of grief because of the degeneration of Jerusalem and the less-than-honest ethics of the Hebrew people. The prophets constantly reminded the people that the consequences of their actions would be tangible. Amos cautioned the people that devastation and exile were around the corner. He called them to be aware of the ways they betrayed the God of their ancestors. Although destruction was on the way, Amos already was looking forward to the restoration of a vital relationship between God and the people. Pray with me the printed prayer and then parley with the Holy One about your own attitudes and habits.

Community Confession (Unison)

God of Fire and Fruit — it's an old story: Honesty among shoppers and merchants is flexible.

The word "sale" seduces us to part with our money and sometimes our integrity.

We buy and sell trifling products; our debts haunt us at night.

Poverty is always outside our doors; cynicism robs us of cheerfulness; constant data about evil tarnishes our joy.

Fear steals our confidence.

With the fire of your Spirit, reveal the changes we need to make in order to be cocreators with you.

With fruits of your Spirit, nourish our souls so we can be benevolent people who care about the earth and the poor of the world.

Give us courage to travel the path you set before us. Amen.

Sermon Idea

Civilizations rise and fall. Often the "enemy issues" have to do with the morals, poverty, affluence, and apathy of the citizens. David and Solomon's Jerusalem/Israel is no exception. It is painful to read the prophets' and psalmist's perceptions of what was happening. Perhaps the distress current readers feel is because we see some of our own country's story mirrored on the pages of scripture. At the same time, today there are *millions* of perceptions of why the American dream is not more dependable for more people; there are *millions* of prescriptions for how to remedy the problems. Haranguing and guilt-tripping people are rarely effective ways to promote change in contemporary attitudes and behavior. Another approach might be to look at what happens when people gather for rites and rituals. Paul offers Timothy first-century options. Without judgmental tones, the sermon might explore fresh options that can be included in worship to inspire most of the people most of the time — remembering that for every idea there is an opposing one; for every option there is an alternative.

We are cocreators with God and we see evidence of change throughout all the seasons; we can expect changes in our internal timings and energy levels as well as in the ways we respond to the Holy Presence. Consider the foci for the liturgical seasons and all the arts. Compared with spring, we are in slow motion until the Thanksgiving/Advent gestation season begins. Though schools are busily in session, the earth's productivity in the northern hemisphere is slowing down, moving into dormancy. We can be shrewd/savvy managers of our time together for worship and at fellowship events.

Contemporary Affirmation

Leader: What do you think about Divine relationship with creation?

People: We believe God cares for the cosmos that has been created; we believe God cares about creatures and us.

Leader: What do you think about the man called *Jesus of Nazareth*?

People: We know that Jesus of Nazareth incarnated divine wisdom as he lived, healed, and taught at the eastern end of the Mediterranean Sea 2,000 years ago.

Leader: How do you understand *Holy Spirit*?

People: We experience Holy Spirit coaxing us into relationship with the Holy One; we trust that the Spirit finds us when we are wandering among the culture's idols seeking satisfying days and nights. We are inspired by the Holy Spirit to be creative in our work, in our relationships, and in our leisure.

Leader: What is the church for you?

People: This congregation, church, is a community of friends; we encourage one another to listen for God's voice and to respond to it. We enjoy companionship and conversation about our journeys with Great Mystery. Together we explore ways to manifest Christ in our town and throughout the global village. Together, we speak for justice, truth, nutrition, and peace.

Leader: Amen!

Offertory Statement (Leader)

It's a good day to give tithes and offerings, time and talents to God and to this church.

Doxology   Praise God From Whom All Blessings Flow, tune: OLD HUNDREDTH

Praise God from whom all blessings flow;
Praise God, all creatures here below;
Praise God above, you heavenly hosts —
Creator, Christ, and Holy Ghost. Amen!

Prayer Of Thanksgiving (Leader)

Living God — for all we have and are, thank you. For the gifts we receive and can share, we are grateful. Amen.

Intercessory Prayers (Leader or Readers)

God of Beginnings and Endings — we pray for peace — peace between Palestinians and Israelis, democrats and republicans, Americans and Iraqis. We pray for respect and gentleness, understanding and hospitality for this whole global village. We see that time reveals corruption and indoctrination, intentions and misinformation. We hear politicians and prophets coming and going, governments rising and falling. We ascribe to you, Holy One, the judgments and justice, the hardship and the victories. Help us to learn and to teach tolerance and collaboration.

God of Growing and Eldering — see our children shiver with excitement as they adventure into the world! Protect them from melancholy and overactivity. Help us mentor them in the journey to you. See our friends who struggle to pay their rent and mortgages and to put wholesome food on their tables. Give them strength, courage, and opportunity to do a job that is meaningful and pays well. See us who realize our bumpy days are numbered. Grace us to rest in your accompanying presence.

Hospitable God — this global village needs some "stone soup" — nourishing body and soul food served with conversation and hope. We hold before you the regions of this planet where famine and greed deny the necessities of life to people and animals. Do something we pray! Let wisdom provide for the common good and overtake selfish individualism in both hemispheres in all countries. Let the moon rise tonight giving light to dark minds; let the sun rise tomorrow and give new hope to those in need. Amen.

Benediction (Leader)

As you leave here —
Keep in mind the tranquility of this place;
Hold in your mind the ideas that inspire you;
Remember those with whom you have shared this hour.
May the creating God guide you to surprising places
    in the days ahead.
Go gently; feel generous and be infectious with joy!
Amen!

Music

For Each Day Of Life We Thank You
    Words: H. Glen Lanier, 1976, alt.
    Music: Amos Pilsbury, 1799; arr. Carlton R. Young, 1964
    CHARLESTOWN

God Of Freedom, God Of Justice
    Words: Shirley Erena Murray, 1980
    Music: Guthrie Foote (20th century)
    TREDEGAR

In The Bulb There Is A Flower
    Words and Music: Natalie Sleeth, 1986
    PROMISE

Wellspring Of Wisdom
    Words: Miriam Therese Winter, 1987
    Music: Miriam Therese Winter, 1987; harm. Don McKeever, 1987
    WELLSPRING

Proper 21
Ordinary Time 26
Pentecost 19

Jeremiah 32:1-3a, 6-15 or Amos 6:1a, 4-7   1 Timothy 6:6-19
Psalm 91:1-6, 14-16 or Psalm 146   Luke 16:19-31

> *If we love the Lord with all our hearts, minds, and strength,*
> *we are going to have to stretch our hearts, open our minds,*
> *and strengthen our souls ... God cannot lodge in a narrow mind;*
> *God cannot lodge in a small heart. To accommodate God they must be palatial.*
>
> — William Sloan Coffin, *Credo*

Call To Worship

Leader: Good morning, wealthy friends! You and I — we've brought nothing into the world and we'll take nothing out! But we've gathered again to be thankful for who we are and what we have.

People: **We are rich in spiritual things. We are content with God's Presence; the path we take to Holy Mystery satisfies our deepest longings. We are rich in Christ!**

Leader: On our paths with God, we strive to live in ways that honor God and manifest divine love so others may also be content.

People: **We strive for godliness, faith, love, endurance, and gentleness. We try to do good and to enjoy what God is doing among us.**

Leader: Together, we will express our thanks, ask our questions, listen for guidance, and appreciate this hour.

People: **We let go of the desires we came here with; we will pay close attention to our words, our thoughts, and the generative silence in our hearts.**

Prayer Of Thanksgiving (Leader and Unison)

Let's make our prayers audible.

Living God thank you for the Holy Spirit inspiring and blessing us in so many ways. Thank you that temptations are silenced as we listen for your voice. Thank you for your vivacious love, strengthening us to work toward making your reign a reality. Our minds and psyches are eager to be in conversation with you. Amen.

Call To Confession (Leader)

When the world seems to be falling apart, when evil seems dominant, when peace seems impossible, we implore the Holy Spirit to protect us. External and internal distress can be relieved as we trust Holy Mystery to strengthen us for this aspect of our human journey. Let's pray together and then let the silence take us individually to the heart of God.

Community Confession (Unison)

Holy One — we'd much rather be singing a happy song than grieving over the destruction of land, air, and creatures.

Yet, like the prophets of ancient times, we see warfulness in so many places. We see the
results of greed and recognize that justice is not succeeding for many people.
Search our minds and hearts for attitudes that defy your grace. Change our demeanors so
that we feel hospitable and happy. Open our ears to new songs! Amen.

Sermon Idea

Until something is so compelling, we tend to go about our lives with rather myopic vision.
In the gospel story, the nameless rich man is intent on his own preservation. He doesn't notice
that others are not as comfortable as he is. He doesn't see the poor man who has a name as well
as needs. Not until he is in great pain does he notice his predicament. Ancient Jerusalem/Israel,
too, did not take seriously its erosion and was overcome by Nebuchadnezzar of Babylon. The
best ideas and craftspersons were exiled to serve another civilization.

One intriguing exploration might be with how we identify ourselves and are known in
society. The rich man is known for his possessions and wealth. He is not given a specific name.
The poor man is known for his needs and has a name. How does our personal identity in society
promote the kingdom of God?

Advice and warnings are rarely helpful since there is already abundant information about
what causes personal spiritual harm as well as what diminishes a nation. One must intentionally, consciously assume responsibility for his/her own soul's well being. No one can force us
to nourish our souls or our relationships. God invites us to know and to act on the stories of
Jesus.

Contemporary Affirmation (Unison)

The Divine Imagination continues to be at work in the world;
  God breathes life and proclaims it good.
The Divine Worker was revealed in Jesus of Nazareth
  who moved among people healing, mentoring, feeding, and renewing.
The Divine Artist continues to create through us,
  inspiring us to exhibit the Christ in our choices and decisions.
In community, we encourage one another to explore who we
  can become as twenty-first-century friends of Jesus.
  Together, we can be honest, compassionate, and hopeful.
Let it be so. Amen!

Offertory Statement (Leader)

It is satisfying to see people being healed, restored, and contented as we use our talents and
moneys to make this world a more kind place. Share what you can.

Doxology   Christ, Whose Glory Fills The Skies (v. 1), tune: RATISBON
Christ, whose glory fills the skies, Christ, the true, the only light,
Sun of Righteousness, arise, triumph o'er the shades of night;
Dayspring from on high, be near; Daystar in my heart appear.

Prayer Of Thanksgiving (Leader)

Wondrous Light — we are alert to our responsibilities for our own souls and for establish-
ing goodness here. Thank you for skills and money that make our life together good and brighten
this corner of the world. Thank you for inspiring us to be kind and generous. Amen.

Intercessory Prayers (Leader or Readers)

Creating God — we see you continually creating and re-creating. We see evidence of your expansive imagination. We feel you busy among us, making things different from last year, refocusing our thoughts, and compelling us to expand our perceptions of divinity and humanity. We want to love you with our whole selves; revamp our souls to be palatial.

Midwifing God — birth through us a new world order, a reign of justice and compassion, an era with honest politics and compassionate leaders. Move among this planet's palette of people until peace spills out. Nurture governments till they protect the cosmos and feed the children. Keep harmful elements away; halt the dangerous toxins that threaten to destroy goodness.

Animating God — we are glad to be made in your image. But we are clay and we experience breaking fatigue. We get weary and our bones cry "ouch"! Our organs wear out and our attitudes turn grouchy. Sustain us through this earth journey. Don't let jobs-without-meaning cripple our imaginations. Lift us from cynicism to thoughts that make good neighbors. Breathe new life into us, again. Heal us and activate deep peace in our muscles.

Builder of the Universe and the Church — we are vulnerable to the wiles of profit seekers. Let us protect the earth and its resources. Let us teach our children to be frugal with water and oil and careful with foods. May we consciously harmonize what we do and what we say. Amen.

Benediction (Leader)

As you leave the sanctuary to work and play,
Be aware that your cup of life is at least half full!
Notice that the roof over your home is strong.
Notice soft breezes, warm fires, and smiles of friends.
Take time to be grateful for who you are;
Check in with who you are becoming.
God, busy animating the cosmos, is blessing you. Go gently. Amen!

Music

Creative God, You Spread The Earth
    Words: Ruth Duck, 1991
    Music: Traditional English melody; harm. Ralph Vaughan Williams
    KINGSFOLD

For The Fruit Of All Creation
    Words: Fred Pratt Green, 1970
    Music: Traditional Welsh melody; harm. Luther Orlando Emerson, 1906
    AR HYD Y NOS

We Are Not Our Own
   Words: Brian Wren, 1987
   Music: Brian Wren, 1987; arr. Fred Graham
   YARNTON

Wind Upon The Waters
   Words and Music: Marty Haugen, 1986
   WIND UPON THE WATERS

Proper 22
Ordinary Time 27
Pentecost 20

Lamentations 1:1-6 or Habakkuk 1:1-4; 2:1-4   2 Timothy 1:1-14
Lamentations 3:19-26 or Psalm 137:1-9   Luke 17:5-10

If we love the Lord with all our hearts, minds, and strength,
we are going to have to stretch our hearts, open our minds,
and strengthen our souls ... God cannot lodge in a narrow mind;
God cannot lodge in a small heart. To accommodate God they must be palatial.
                                        — William Sloan Coffin, *Credo*

Call To Worship

Leader: Autumn is coming. The land in the northern hemisphere is slowing down. The church calendar will soon conclude with celebrating "Christ as King." Today, we acknowledge that Christians in both hemispheres and on all continents read the same scriptures, ask many of the same questions, pray about many of the same things, and desire to work for justice.

People: **All around the planet, Christians seek guidance for manifesting peace throughout the global village.**

Leader: We are Christians anticipating the Holy Spirit to inspire us and to guide us with wisdom to make this world a hospitable home for all creatures.

People: **As God's people, we encourage one another, right here, to explore the questions of living, of divine action, and of endurance for the angst and contentment of the human experience.**

Leader: As part of the Body of Christ, we applaud each other as we live the teachings of Jesus in a way that establishes goodness in our homes and neighborhoods.

People: **As brothers and sisters on the journey to God, we give solace to one another in times of crisis.**

Leader: As friends of Jesus, we speak about our experience with the love of God; we promote truth-telling and we protect the goodness that has been entrusted to us.

People: **With music and dance, with prayers and silence, with thanksgiving and anticipation we celebrate the Holy Presence here and with God's people throughout the global village.**

Leader: There is enough Spirit, enough inspiration, enough goodness, enough bread and wine for everyone who is hungry and thirsty!

Prayer Of Thanksgiving (Unison)

Living God — thank you for all Creation — for the circle of the earth and its beauty. We admire the varieties of cultures, languages, and colors of humankind and animal kind. We appreciate the abundance of plants that nourish us. For bread and wine that sustain our souls and our bodies, we are grateful. We join our voices to express our delight in your creating presence! We savor our time together with you. Amen.

Call To Confession (Leader)

According to scriptures and recorded world history, evil and wickedness, terror and horrible things have always been present throughout the planet. The psalmist challenges us to do good in spite of injustice, to be unworried about exterior trouble, and to not respond in anger. Pray with me the community confession and then seek Holy guidance for your personal situation.

Community Confession (Unison)

God of Time and Eternity — we know the hopes of your people through the ages.

We, too, want justice and hospitality for us and all people.

Examine us and reveal the meanness that lurks within our minds and psyches.

Displace it with your compassion and empower us to participate in your reign on the earth. Amen.

Sermon Idea

Old Testament Habakkuk and Jeremiah (Lamentations) decry the violence and terror they see. They implore God to do something — something that will help kindly people survive, something that will restore beneficent leaders for the people. In our time, the Gaza strip has been vacated by Israel, but Arabs and Jews maintain the ancestral rivalry for land and holy places. Like Habakkuk, we sit in our pews and world leaders in their towers keep watching what will happen. We keep hoping the people who work for fairness and tolerance will win.

One direction the sermon might take is to acknowledge the inclination of humans to minimize others and aggrandize themselves. Then explore Paul's tactics with Timothy — that of affirmation, encouragement, and gratitude. This could be compared with Jesus' teachings in the Sermon on the Mount and his commandment to love God, self, and neighbor. The Coffin quote at the top of this section might be helpful: If we are to accommodate God, we must expand our minds, our psyches, and our experiences. Perhaps people seeking to manifest godliness are always in the minority.

If the Lord's Supper is shared, intinction at stations or around the table might promote a sense of closeness with the whole world family of God. Also, bread recipes from different countries might enhance the sense of unity. (If you use breads with hot spices, warn the people ahead of time.) Another suggestion: if juice is used rather than wine, use frozen juice only half diluted with sparkling water for a gentle surprise.

Contemporary Affirmation (Unison)

We believe God cares for the cosmos that has been created;
   we believe God cares about creatures and us.
We know that Jesus of Nazareth incarnated divine wisdom
   as he lived and taught at the eastern end of the Mediterranean Sea
   2,000 years ago.
We experience the Holy Spirit coaxing us into relationship with the Holy One;
   we trust that the Spirit finds us when we are wandering among
   the culture's idols seeking satisfying days and nights.
As a community of faith, as friends, we encourage one another to listen for
   God's voice and to respond to it. We enjoy companionship and conversation
   about our journeys with the Great Mystery. Together we explore ways to
   manifest Christ in our town and throughout the global village. Amen!

Offertory Statement (Leader)

The media of exchange in the world today are money and intellectual conceptions. The church around the world needs both. Give as you can.

Doxology   Praise God From Whom All Blessings Flow, tune: OLD HUNDREDTH

Praise God from whom all blessings flow;
Praise God, all creatures here below;
Praise God above, you heavenly hosts —
Creator, Christ, and Holy Ghost. Amen!

Prayer Of Thanksgiving (Leader)

God of the all the World — thank you for the abundance of our lives, for the ability to think and converse, for the skills to support ourselves and minister to others, and for companions on the journey to eternity. Amen.

Intercessory Prayers (Leader or Readers)

God of Jesus and Mary — we love the words of Jesus about life abundant; we long to hear promises of help in times of trouble; we want to emulate Mary's loyalty. Around this world this day, we pray that your Spirit would settle upon your people, animating all persons to boldly live as peace makers, as gentle neighbors, and as workers for candidness and equanimity.

God of Nations — once the world seemed so big; once the land Jesus walked seemed so far away; once the ends of the earth seemed to have an edge. Now, we know the earth is round and rotates around the sun; we know there are many peoples who call you "God." Now we know that airplanes and internet make us all like a close-at-hand village. Guide us to learn to live in close proximity with each other; enlarge our understanding of cultural differences; expand our curiosity and patience to take in what is different from our land and our kin.

Healing God — your human creatures everywhere on this planet grow old and die. On that trek from mothers' wombs to your arms, soothe us when we are in pain; mend our broken parts; heal our diseases; banish our cynicisms and lift our depressions. Renew our appreciation for the moment-by-moment breath of life. Thank you for the multiple expressions of your imagination in our minds and hearts. Amen.

Benediction (Leader)

As you leave here —
Keep in mind the vastness of the cosmos;
Keep in mind the smallness of the planet;
Keep in mind the tranquility of this place;
Hold in your mind the ideas that inspire you;
Remember those with whom you have shared this hour.
May the creating God guide you to surprising places
    in the days ahead.
Go gently; feel generous and be infectious with joy!
Amen!

Music

Guide Me, O Thou Great Jehovah
    Words: William Williams, 1745; tr. Peter Williams and the author, 1771
    Music: John Hughes, 1907
    CWM RHONDDA

Lord, You Give The Great Commission
    Words: Jeffery Rowthorn, 1978
    Music: Cyril V. Taylor, 1941
    ABBOT'S LEIGH

Many Are The Lightbeams
    Words: *De unitate ecclesiae*, Cyprian of Carthage, 252; tr. Anders Frostenson, 1972, 1986
    Music: Olle Widestrand, 1974; harm. A. Eugene Ellsworth, 1994
    MANY ARE THE LIGHTBEAMS

Praise, My Soul, The God Of Heaven
    Words: Henry F. Lyte, 1834; adapt. Ecumenical Women's Center and Ruth Duck, 1974
    Music: John Goss, 1869
    LAUDA ANIMA

Seed, Scattered And Sown
    Words: Dan Feiten, 1987
    Music: Dan Feiten, 1987; arr. Eric Gunnison and R. J. Miller, alt.
    SEED SCATTERED

Who Is My Mother, Who Is My Brother?
    Words: Shirley Erena Murray, 1991
    Music: Jack Schrader, 1991
    KINDRED

Proper 23
Ordinary Time 28
Pentecost 21

Jeremiah 29:1, 4-7 or 2 Kings 5:1-3, 7-15c   2 Timothy 2:8-15

Psalm 66:1-12 or Psalm 111   Luke 17:11-19

> *If we love the Lord with all our hearts, minds, and strength,*
> *we are going to have to stretch our hearts, open our minds,*
> *and strengthen our souls ... God cannot lodge in a narrow mind;*
> *God cannot lodge in a small heart. To accommodate God they must be palatial.*
> — William Sloan Coffin, *Credo*

Call To Worship

Leader: How wonderful! You've come back again! I'm glad to be in this house of God with you.

People: With our whole selves, we thank God for the freedom to gather and to support one another on this journey through life.

Leader: God is great Mystery and we yearn to experience being surrounded by God's infinite goodness.

People: Yes! We long to feel the ecstasy when God satisfies our deepest questions and gives meaning to the daily minutiae of our lives.

Leader: Then let us respond to God's goodness with silence, conversation, and art.

Prayer Of Thanksgiving (Leader)

God of Wonder — as we feel the history of this place, we are reminded that we too have been polished with percussive fire. As we look at the ocean, we remember that you continue to create and call your handiwork "good." We look at the mountains and know that the trees and rocks speak your name. Thank you for making humankind in your mold; we appreciate the opportunities to be cocreators with your Spirit. Refresh us this hour as we sing and pray and listen for your voice. Amen.

Call To Confession (Leader)

The theme of today's readings seems to be "thankfulness." Of ten lepers, one returned to express "thanks" to Jesus. After receiving a letter from King Solomon of Israel about building a temple and needing fine woods, King Hiram of Tyre responds with a kind letter of gratitude and collaboration. Jeremiah writes to the Jews exiled in Babylon urging them to settle in by marrying, birthing, and growing their own foods, always remembering the source of life. During these few moments, we step out of life's fast lane and reflect on the happenings of this past week. As we are still, we probably will notice times and circumstances where we neglected to express our gratitude, to respond to others with kindness, and to side with truth. Pray with me the printed confession; then have your private conversation with God.

Community Confession (Unison)

Living God — we get so busy that we forget to be kind; we get so involved with living that we forget to be thankful for what we have; we become so immersed in lunches and bedtimes that we neglect noticing your Spirit.

So now, bring to our minds the many times you have provided for us; remind us of the people who have blessed us; recall in our memories the times we have been amazed at the beauty of Creation.

Thank you for the wonder of being alive, for companions and for your animating Spirit. Amen.

Sermon Idea

Given current emphasis on human equality and mutuality, it is difficult to lift first-century Paul from the letter to Timothy and make sense of its concern with the placement of men and women in worship. Likewise, though the communications between Solomon and Hiram are in good "human relations form," it is hard to hear about conscripted labor — such as slavery. One theme the sermon might explore is how people of faith manifest their gratitude to God, to people, and to the earth. How many ways can we say/dance/sing/act/paint/cook, "Thank you"? Another approach with the texts is to ask: What do twenty-first-century people do with scriptures that make little sense in the post-modern world? Another question is: Where might modern Christians turn for inspiration if not the Bible?

Contemporary Affirmation (Unison)

We recognize God's creative imagination as we look up, around, and down;
we recognize God's love as we talk with and care for others;
we recognize God's presence as we pay attention to our daily tasks.
We know Jesus of Nazareth to be a wise teacher, mentoring disciples then and now
in *kingdom of heaven activities*;
we know Jesus to be light for the world!
We experience the Holy Spirit;
When we gather, we encourage one another to continue the journey with God;
we use all our senses to perceive holy guidance and to respond with gratitude;
we are not alone! The Spirit and one another's companionship sustains us.
Amen!

Offertory Statement (Leader)

The baskets come to you as opportunity to support ministry in this place with cheerful attitudes, talents, and money.

Doxology
Now Thank We All Our God (v. 3), tune: NUN DANKET ALLE GOT

All praise and thanks to God who reigns in highest heaven,
To Father and to Son and Spirit now be given.
The one eternal God, whom heaven and earth adore,
The God who was and is and shall be evermore.

Prayer Of Thanksgiving (Leader)

Awesome God — we thank you for shalom deep within our bodies; we thank you for peace deep in our souls; we thank you for life's provisions in our bank accounts, on our tables, in our entertainments, and in our services to society. With hopes of justice and goodness for all peoples, we share what we have. Amen.

Intercessory Prayers (Leader or Readers)

Maker of Sky and Air — how we marvel when nature pleases us with beautiful moons and glorious sunsets, bountiful harvests, and comfortable temperatures! We look from space and say, "Yes, indeed, there is an intelligent design to the universe!" Help us not to fritter away clean air or the ozone layer; give us wise and motivated leaders who respect the ecosystems that support planet life.

Crafter of Earth and Fire — we value fertile soil that provides our foods; we appreciate energy that keeps us warm in winter and cool in summer; we need oil and electricity to continue the pleasures we have come to think of as necessities. Help us not to squander the planet's resources. Provide leaders in our nation and in every nation who respect the earth's supply of oil and gas, forests and water.

Artist of Landscape and Seaside — there is so much beauty for us to appreciate and to enjoy. There are so many ways you've provided for our physical needs, so many ways you've invited us to participate with you in making this world hospitable for human endeavors! Move among all peoples till ownership is not the goal; move among us so collaboration and peace satisfy our minds. We pray for peace in families and between tribes throughout the global village. We pray for peaceful protection of the earth's productivity.

Designer of Hummingbirds and Kangaroos — thank you for the multiplicity of species. Help us to appreciate and protect the variety around us. We are glad you know how we are made for we get hurt and need healing; we experience disappointment and betrayal and need consolation; we lose partners and friends and need comfort. Wherever we are wounded — body and soul — heal us, we pray. We do thank you for your love and care. Amen.

Benediction (Leader)

May Great Mystery follow you around each day and night.
May the autumn moon increase your sense of wonder.
May clear skies encourage you to look beyond your self.
May empowering relationships send you to bless others.
Go from this sanctuary intent on your walk with God.
Go bearing peace-making words and hospitable attitudes.
Amen.

Music

Bless Now, O God, The Journey
    Words: Sylvia Dunstan, 1989
    Music: Swedish folk tune; harm. Lahrae Knatterud, 1983
    BRED DINA VIDA VINGAR

For Each Day Of Life We Thank You
    Words: H. Glen Lanier, 1976, alt.
    Music: Amos Pilsbury, 1799; arr. Carlton R. Young, 1964
    CHARLESTOWN

For The Beauty Of The Earth
    Words: Folliot S. Pierpoint, 1864
    Music: Conrad Kocher, 1838; arr. William Henry Monk, 1861
    DIX

Help Us Accept Each Other
    Words: Fred Kaan, 1974
    Music: John Ness Beck, 1977
    ACCEPTANCE

Let All Things Now Living
    Words: Katherine K. Davis, 1939, alt.
    Music: Welsh folk melody
    ASH GROVE

Proper 24
Ordinary Time 29
Pentecost 22

Jeremiah 31:27-34 or Genesis 32:22-31   2 Timothy 3:14—4:5

Psalm 119:97-104 or Psalm 121   Luke 18:1-8

> *If we love the Lord with all our hearts, minds, and strength,*
> *we are going to have to stretch our hearts, open our minds,*
> *and strengthen our souls ... God cannot lodge in a narrow mind;*
> *God cannot lodge in a small heart. To accommodate God they must be palatial.*
> — William Sloan Coffin, *Credo*

Call To Worship

Leader: I'm glad today is Sunday and we are here together.

People: We are grateful for sanctuary and for faithful friends.

Leader: God is with us as usual.

People: There's a poem we like to remember:
We lift our eyes to the hills;
From where does our help come?
Our help comes from God who made heaven and earth.
God, our protector never dozes or sleeps;
God guards us and is ever by our side.
The sun will not hurt us during the day
     nor the moon during the night.
God will protect us from danger and will keep us safe.
God is with us as we come and go, today and forever!

Leader: How good those words are — sweeter than honey; we gain wisdom and comfort from them.

People: Thanks be to God for divine wisdom!

Prayer Of Thanksgiving (Leader)

Gracious God — your word is light for our paths; your presence gives us strength for each day. Thank you. We open our minds to your voice this hour; speak so we can understand and live in ways to honor you. With our whole selves, we are alert for your guidance. Amen.

Call To Confession (Leader)

Every now and then, we find ourselves wrestling with God, like Jacob did at the River Jabbok. In these next few minutes, we make time to be introspective and notice what is weighing us down, hindering our smooth engagement with the Holy. Let's pray the printed prayer and then speak with God in the silence of our own hearts.

Community Confession (Unison)
Holy One — sometimes life seems so difficult.
Sometimes it seems as if no one cares enough to listen.
Sometimes our burdens seem too great to bear one more day.
Reveal to us the changes we need to make in order to be free from distress.
Remove the impediments of guilt and shame so that we can honor you with our decisions and our behavior, our attitudes and our hopes.
Set us on the path which gives us deep peace. Amen.

Sermon Idea

The theme of the texts seems to be that scriptures and relationship with God enable us to know ourselves and to get along in a corrupt environment. The readings again today challenge the preacher/interpreter to find the essence for divine-human relationship and for justice in human society. Several questions arise:

- How does one locate the Word of God for this generation?
- How does a preacher read the Bible and make the leap across the centuries from first-century cosmology to twenty-first-century understanding of the universe?
- Where is justice?
    Whose responsibility is it to make sure it happens?
    What has globalization done to the American sense of justice?
    Who has benefited from it?

While Psalm 121 gives us comfort as does Psalm 23, it is a jump from the spiritual/psychological truths of the poem to the practical economic ones. Perhaps that's the message: God is willing to hang in with our questions even though we can't possibly see the whole picture. God is willing to sustain us as we explore ways to "extract" justice for ourselves and for a world much bigger than the one with which Jesus spoke. Perhaps we personally and as a nation struggle with demons and with angels. The metaphor in Psalm 119:103 — God's instruction is sweeter than honey — can give way with an extension of the Psalm 119 reading and conclude with another metaphor: God's Word is a lamp to guide us and a light for our paths. God does appeal to all our senses!

Contemporary Affirmation (Unison)
We recognize God's creative imagination as we look up, around, and down;
we recognize God's love as we talk with and care for others;
we recognize God's presence as we pay attention to our daily tasks.
We know Jesus of Nazareth to be a wise teacher, mentoring disciples then and now
in *kingdom of heaven activities*;
we know Jesus to be light for the world!
We experience the Holy Spirit;
When we gather, we encourage one another to continue our journey with God;
we use all our senses to perceive holy guidance and to respond with gratitude;
we are not alone! The Spirit and one another's companionship sustains us.
Amen!

Offertory Statement (Leader)

With the shuffle of paper money and the clicking of coins, we make known our commitment to ministry in this place and to a "justice realm" throughout the global village.

Doxology   For The Fruit Of All Creation (v. 1), tune: EAST AKLAM

For the fruit of all creation, thanks be to God.
For the gifts to every nation, thanks be to God.
For the plowing, sowing, reaping, silent growth while we are sleeping,
Future needs in earth's safe keeping, thanks be to God.

Prayer Of Thanksgiving (Leader)

Living God — take our paper and our coins; take our checks and our talents and stretch them till we ourselves are fed; stretch them more till we share our daily bread. Amen.

Intercessory Prayers (Leader or Readers)

God of Earth and Sky — you have made us humans very smart; we can go and come from space; we can travel around the planet; we can feed millions; we can make weapons; we can build cities; we can decipher languages and write our histories. Help us also to be respectful and helpful neighbors. Help us also to parent our children with love and mentor them in ways that give them the tools they need to be healthy adults.

God of Air and Fire — we think we are more sentient than other creatures yet we malign the soil and the air with toxic substances. We think we deserve a feather in our caps for our ingenious inventions yet people in our cities are hungry and cold; our televisions display affluence yet there are not enough jobs in our towns to sustain our citizens with minimal skills nor to enable immigrants to begin a new, productive life. Let our hearts and minds imagine and develop other options of coexistence.

God of Peace — when we sit here together we think that peace is the absence of stress, violence, and greed. Here we enjoy tranquility and we easily think about how we might serve our neighbors. But as we listen for your voice, we recognize that peace is an attitude about ourselves in relationship to you; we recognize that peace is energy, generosity, and responsibility. Enter the human realm again and let peace overtake greed; let peace expand in America to include jobs for everyone that pays for shelter, food, and clothing; let peace weave its warmth and beauty to provide for people in every country and in every camp; let peace surround children of every color and language.

God of Sanity — our world seems so huge and yet so small. The issues out there are mountainous. So are our own problems. Our mortality gets to us and we feel cranky and cynical; our death-defying medicines and our antigravity cosmetics do little to free us from disease and atrophy. So we turn to you, our Maker, asking for strength to make it gracefully from the cradle to the grave. We turn to you asking you to soothe our discomforts and give us health for our psyches and bodies. Revive us with holy enthusiasm. Amen.

Benediction

Leader: May Great Mystery follow you around day and night.
People: The autumn moon expands our sense of wonder;
Leader: May clear skies encourage you to look beyond your self;
People: Empowering relationships send us to bless others;
Leader: Go from this sanctuary intent on your walk with God.

People: **We go bearing words of peace and hospitable attitudes.**
Leader: Amen.

Music
Come, O Thou Traveler Unknown
    Words: Charles Wesley, 1742
    Music: Trad. Scottish melody; harm. Carlton R. Young, 1963
    CANDLER

I To The Hills Will Lift My Eyes
    Words: *The Psalter*, 1912; alt. 1988
    Music: Scottish Psalter, 1615
    DUNDEE

Ours The Journey
    Words and Music: Julian B. Rush, 1979
    OURS THE JOURNEY

Proper 25
Ordinary Time 30
Pentecost 23

Joel 2:23-32 or Sirach 35:12-17   2 Timothy 4:6-8, 16-18
    or Jeremiah 14:7-10, 19-22
Psalm 65 or Psalm 84:1-7   Luke 18:9-14

> *If we love the Lord with all our hearts, minds, and strength,*
> *we are going to have to stretch our hearts, open our minds,*
> *and strengthen our souls ... God cannot lodge in a narrow mind;*
> *God cannot lodge in a small heart. To accommodate God they must be palatial.*
> — William Sloan Coffin, *Credo*

Call To Worship

Leader: It's a good time to gather, a good time to praise God for life!

People: **We love to be together in this place. With our whole selves we sing for joy!**

Leader: How happy we are when our souls are being nurtured!

People: **It is true; as we sing and pray, listen and respond to God's voice, we feel inspired, encouraged, and strengthened.**

Leader: God is here inviting us to explore the perplexing aspects of our lives.

People: **We eagerly accept the invitation! Let our exploration begin!**

Prayer Of Thanksgiving (Leader)

Holy One — our times are in your hands. We are grateful that you care for us and for all the earth. We do not understand why things are as they are, but we trust that you will never leave us nor forsake us. We are mindful of the intricate ways you bless us and call us to be our best selves. Thank you for your consistent love. Amen.

Call To Confession (Leader)

In these next few moments, we have opportunity to breathe deeply and feel in touch with the holy. Pray with me and then continue your private conversations with God.

Community Confession (Unison)

Spirit of God — we have received so many ideas and so many things from our ancestors.

Still we feel anxious.

Fill our empty spots.

We see the global village and its needs.

Erase our prejudices.

As we collect beautiful things and carefully lock our doors, we realize that we are afraid of not having *enough* and of not being *safe*.

Transform our attitudes about what is "enough" and help us live simply.
Surround us with happy friends who contently journey with us in things of the Spirit.
   Amen.

Sermon Idea

What does it mean to be the church *reforming*? What does it mean to be disciples of Jesus in the twenty-first century as compared with the sixteenth and seventeenth centuries? Eighteenth, nineteenth, and twentieth centuries? The gospel reading is a familiar *parable*. The sermon might explore the purpose and value of this literary form and consider why Jesus might have chosen it to carry his ideas. The question arises today: Do we need to distinguish between the parables Jesus told and his other "lectures"? What might be considered his "central" teachings? Another sermon approach would be to consider the directives Paul gives Timothy; what value do they have for young people today? Are we Christians or Paulians?

Contemporary Affirmation

Leader: We recognize God's creative imagination as we look up, around, and down; we recognize God's love as we talk with and care for others; we recognize God's presence as we pay attention to our daily tasks.

People: We know Jesus of Nazareth to be a wise teacher, mentoring disciples then and now in *kingdom of heaven activities*; we know Jesus to be light for the world!

Leader: We experience the Holy Spirit;

People: When we gather, we encourage one another to continue our journey with God; we use all our senses to perceive Holy guidance and to respond with gratitude.

Leader: We are not alone!

People: The Spirit and one another's companionship sustains us.

Leader: Amen!

Offertory Statement (Leader)

We are committed to ministry in this place, inside and outside these walls. Money, time, and skills are needed. Share what you can.

Doxology   For The Fruit Of All Creation (v. 3), tune: EAST ACKLAM

For the harvests of the Spirit, thanks be to God.
For the good we all inherit, thanks be to God.
For the wonders that astound us, for the truths that still confound us,
Most of all that love has found us, thanks be to God.

Prayer Of Thanksgiving (Leader)

We praise you, living God! We celebrate eternal life beginning now! We know you to be the I AM guiding us through our days and nights — the WAS, IS, and WILL BE! Amen!

Intercessory Prayers

(This can be a silent prayer or audible prayers from the congregation as topics are suggested by the leader. The response after each prayer is "Holy One, this is our prayer.")

Leader: God of Today and Tomorrow — we pray for this faith community, for this church.

People: Holy One, this is our prayer.

Leader:	Healing God — we pray for individuals who seek your touch.
People:	**Holy One, this is our prayer.**

Leader:	God of Yesterday — thank you for the men and women who have served you and the church through the ages.
People:	**Holy One, this is our prayer.**

Leader:	God of all People — we pray for peace.
People:	**Holy One, this is our prayer.**

Leader:	God of Children and Adults — we thank you for our children and those who teach them.
People:	**Holy One, this is our prayer. Amen.**

Benediction (Leader)

Be careful with what you see;
Be careful with what you hear;
Be careful with what you speak;
You and I are how God works grace and goodness in our homes and neighborhoods;
You and I are hands and feet, voice and hope of the living God!
Go with peace; engage others joyfully and receive Divine blessing.
Amen!

Music

God Is Here!
    Words: Fred Pratt Green, 1978
    Music: Cyril V. Taylor, 1941
    ABBOT'S LEIGH

Lead On, O Cloud Of Presence
    Words: Ruth Duck, 1974, rev. 1989
    Music: Henry T. Smart, 1835
    LANCASHIRE

We Are Not Our Own
    Words: Brian Wren, 1987
    Music: Brian Wren, 1987; arr. Fred Graham
    YARNTON

We Thank You, God, For Water, Soil, And Air
  Words: Brian Wren, 1973
  Music: William Rowan, 1985
  YOGANANDA

Additional Hymn Suggestions
  A Mighty Fortress Is Our God, Martin Luther
  Come, Great God Of All The Ages, Abbot's Leigh, Mary Jackson Cathey, 1990
  Come! Come! Everybody Worship, Natalie Sleeth, 1991
  Bring Many Names, Brian Wren and Carlton R. Young, 1989
  Ubi Caritas (Live In Charity), Jacques Berthier and the Taizé Community
  We Walk By Faith, Martyrdom, Alford and Wilson
  Jesu, Jesu, Fill Us With Your Love, Chereponi *(gently, use rhythm instruments and drum)*
  O For A World, Azmon, M. T. Winter and C. G. Glaser

Proper 26
Ordinary Time 31
Pentecost 24

Habakkuk 1:1-4; 2:1-4 or Isaiah 1:10-18   2 Thessalonians 1:1-4, 11-12
Psalm 119:137-144 or Psalm 32:1-7   Luke 19:1-10

> *If we love the Lord with all our hearts, minds, and strength,*
> *we are going to have to stretch our hearts, open our minds,*
> *and strengthen our souls ... God cannot lodge in a narrow mind;*
> *God cannot lodge in a small heart. To accommodate God they must be palatial.*
> — William Sloan Coffin, *Credo*

Call To Worship (Leader)

Welcome to this sanctuary! Take a deep breath and bring your whole self — body, mind, and psyche — to this place. Set aside the pain and troubles that you brought with you. Be aware of what gives you pleasure and be grateful. Be aware of how and when you feel God's presence. Listen to the psalmist:

Happy are those whose wrongs are erased;
Happy are they who feel at home with God.
God is our hiding place and lifts us from trouble.
We honor God with our living as expression of our gratitude!

Prayer Of Thanksgiving (Leader)

Living God — thank you for guiding us day by day. We sing and dance our gratitude. In this hour, speak to us again so we may hear your hopes for our lives; speak again so we can answer you with gracious attitudes and hospitable habits. We are alert for your loving guidance. Amen.

Call To Confession (Leader)

Most of us want something to be different so we can be happy. Not many of us are conscious moment by moment that happiness, like peace, begins and is sustained internally. Some of us experience happiness when we feel connected to the Holy One. I think that happiness shows up as contentment with life; happiness is a result of attitudes, relationships, and work that have credibility with our souls. Pray with me the printed prayer and then have your personal conversation with the Holy One.

Community Confession (Unison)

Yahweh — ancient "commandments" are clearly printed in our Bibles.
We read them and ask what is "reasonable" and "applicable" for these times.
With our minds we ask for guidance on this journey we call life.
With our souls, we yearn for freedom from fears; we long to feel secure in our relationships and in our homes.
We want to be happy.

265

Reveal to us the hindrances that lurk in us and inhibit our inner peace.
Open us to what is good and honest, what is just and lovely; help us walk in that path.
Amen.

Sermon Idea

Civilizations rise and fall; vital and fierce leaders come and go. We say we are God's people because we believe that Jesus lived, taught, and died so we might live. We keep on teaching the Golden Rule and the Sermon on the Mount but human greed and violence don't go away. Old Testament prophet Habakkuk articulates our current questions:

- How long must we call for help before God takes some action?
- How can God endure the violence and destruction?
- Why is it that evil gets the better of righteousness?
- Why is justice not done and mercy not practiced?

Since these questions have no *real* answers, the sermon might explore the major themes of the prophets and explicate how Jesus falls in line with them and how he extends expectations. Consider how the concept of sin changes and how the concept of manners and acceptability change. When Jesus ignores popular opinion and goes home with Zacchaeus, he sets up a new etiquette for his followers. A sermon title might be: Etiquette for Friends of Jesus.

Contemporary Affirmation (Unison)

We believe that God is, was, and will be;
   we call God *Mystery, Creator, Holy, I AM*....
We believe that God was in Jesus of Nazareth, teaching and healing;
   we call Jesus *Light for the World, Lily of the Valley, Bread of Life*....
We believe that God's Spirit — the Holy Spirit — lives through us as
   self-control, gentleness, patience, hope, and compassion.
We experience God's presence in many ways, and in many settings.
   Here, we gather with individuals who intentionally journey with us
      toward God's reign on this earth and in eternity.
We are not alone! Thanks be to God!

Offertory Statement (Leader)

Even though we may have complaints about the weather, about our leaders, or about our programs, we have this opportunity to express our gratitude to God and to those who walked this way before us by providing money, skills, and talents to make ministry vital on this street corner. The baskets are big enough to hold whatever you can share.

Doxology   Now Thank We All Our God (v. 1), tune: NUN DANKET ALLE GOTT
Now thank we all our God with heart and hands and voices,
Who wondrous things hath done, in whom this world rejoices;
Who from our mothers' arms, hath blessed us on our way
With countless gifts of love and still is ours today.

Prayer Of Thanksgiving (Leader)

Holy One — we are grateful for what we have and who we are becoming. Work with us and through us to make this world a good place to live. Amen.

Intercessory Prayers (Leader or Readers)

God of Prophets — we watch to see what you will do with our questions. We pray for an end to rivalry and destruction. We wonder how long we must endure terror and greed, ignorance and arrogance. We wonder how long humankind will fight over what name is your *real name*. We wonder if humans will ever walk with Jesus and be gracious and respectful to people different from ourselves, who live by an etiquette different from our own. We pray for tolerance and collaboration throughout the global village.

God of Jesus — thank you for the first-century man whose friends included women and children, outcasts and higher-ups. Thank you for Jesus who gave his life for what he believed. His Sermon on the Mount and his people skills guide us today. His *human interest* stories reveal bits of our own stories. Help us to recognize the Zacchaeus in ourselves and to respond to your active presence as he did.

God of Saints — thank you for the leaders in this congregation. Open their minds to options and opportunities; awaken their hearts to service and beauty. Thank you, too, for the men and women of past generations who taught and worked to keep these doors open and the space welcoming. Thank you for each person sitting here now. As our souls commune with you, heal our wounds; soothe our griefs; relieve our pains; strengthen our immune systems so that our discomforts are few.

Living God — we think with words and we express our thoughts and our hopes with the language we understand. Make fresh for us the intentions of Jesus as we pray his prayer: Our Father ... Amen.

Benediction (Leader)

We have heard what God has done;
    Be alert for what God is doing now.
We have heard how Jesus accepted individuals for who they were;
    Be aware of how you interact with people you meet.
We have heard how Habakkuk the prophet questioned God about the politics of his day;
    Pray for our global village:
        Be gracious and merciful in our own times, God, even when you are angry.
        Let justice envelop all peoples!
Go from this place cradled in divine love and empowered to be God's hands, feet, and voice
    in your daily activities.
Strong contentment be yours.
Amen.

Music

For All The Saints
    Words: William W. How, 1864, alt.
    Music: Ralph Vaughan Williams, 1906
    SINE NOMINE

Give Thanks For Life
    Words: Shirley Erena Murray, 1986
    Music: Ralph Vaughan Williams, 1906
    SINE NOMINE

Let Hope And Sorrow Now Unite
    Words: Brian Wren, 1979, rev. 1983
    Music: Bohemian Brethren's *Kirchengesänge*, 1566
    MIT FREUDEN ZART

Mountains Are All Aglow
    Words: Ok In Lim, 1967; trans. Hae Jong Kim, 1988; versification Hope Omachi-
        Kawashima
    Music: Jae Hoon Park, 1967
    KAHM-SAH

O God Of Vision
    Words: Jane Parker Huber, 1981
    Music: *Erneuerten Gesangbuch*, 1665
    LOBE DEN HERREN

Proper 27
Ordinary Time 32
Pentecost 25

Haggai 1:15b—2:9 or Job 19:23-27a   2 Thessalonians 2:1-5, 13-17
Psalm 145:1-5, 17-21 or Psalm 98   Luke 20:27-38
  or Psalm 17:1-9

> *If we love the Lord with all our hearts, minds, and strength,*
> *we are going to have to stretch our hearts, open our minds,*
> *and strengthen our souls ... God cannot lodge in a narrow mind;*
> *God cannot lodge in a small heart. To accommodate God they must be palatial.*
> — William Sloan Coffin, *Credo*

Call To Worship

Leader: I'm glad we're here. In our hemisphere, winter is settling in and we know that there is only a double-digit count until Christmas Day.

People: It's true — the days come and go; the years pass quickly. Holidays take flight almost before the sun goes down.

Leader: All the while, we say our prayers and sing our songs; we hope for better tomorrows and restful nights.

People: The year is coming to an end. Another calendar will lead us to Epiphany, Lent, and Easter.

Leader: Each week we come here to recall where we've been and who we are; each Sunday we rest from the culture's claims on our time; our bodies and our brains have a chance to be refreshed.

People: Each Sunday, we make time to refresh our souls with music, conversation, and prayers; we listen for God's voice and we yearn to be enfolded in Great Mystery.

Leader: Today is Sunday. Now is the time to set aside your cares and open yourself to Holy Presence. Let yourself be immersed in beauty and grace.

Prayer Of Thanksgiving (Leader)

Ingenious God — with a sense of awe, we acknowledge your Presence and our needs. With gratitude we remember how you care for us. With appreciation for this holy space, we open ourselves to your love. With anticipation, we listen for your guidance. Amen.

Call To Confession (Leader)

The theme in the lections for this morning is about continuity. Occasionally we are exiled from the best part of ourselves or from the Holy or from our families. Occasionally we realize that we have allowed something or someone to detour our journey to God. Occasionally, we read the Bible and literalize its principles, only to find ourselves estranged from harmonious living. We journal our thoughts and feelings and on rereading them, we recognize that God is leading us to something different from what we thought. The challenge is to remain constant in our intention to walk with the Spirit and to remember what went before and to dream what we hope to be. Pray with me the printed prayer; then have your own discourse with God.

Community Confession (Unison)
Living God — like peoples before us, we have experienced exile — being separated from the best and loveliness of life.
Like Job, we have been accused of improper thoughts.
Like Sadducees, we worry about who will marry whom in eternity. We get caught-up in right words and miss opportunities to be good neighbors.
Straighten out our priorities and clear up our thinking.
Free us from unwholesome habits and refresh us with joy.
Lead us in the path of everlasting life. Amen.

Sermon Idea
Haggai encouraged people to remember the temple prior to exile. He coaxed them to build a new one by dreaming of its beauty and the way God would bless all the people; that is how they would continue worshiping the God of their ancestors. The psalmist talks about honoring God with new songs in vital worship. Jesus finds himself engaged in a discussion about life after life, that is how human property and progeny would continue. Paul speaks about guarding what has been received and passing it on with gratitude, maintaining a continuity of ideas, dogma, and doctrine. At this point in the liturgical year, perhaps the "new song" idea would preach easily. We have followed the Reformed Tradition for fifty Sundays; we have listened to the same Bible stories all our lives; we have sat in the same pew for five decades. Now, before we begin the liturgical year again with all the familiar symbols of Advent and Christmas, we could try some new forms of praise, try a different order for our prayers, learn some new hymns, and experiment with different words to express our faith. The sermon might include looking at today's liturgy and noting how it is different and what about it remains consistent with the received traditions. Co-mingling the Old and the New might work for a title, using Haggai as the primary scripture with a large dose of the psalm's "new song."

Contemporary Affirmation (Unison)
Jesus of Nazareth had the courage to challenge the institutions of his day.
He had the strength and wisdom to make heaven a viable option.
In spite of suffering and death, he was faithful to his vision;
his teachings have influenced all the world.
He imaged God as divine Parent, divine and benevolent Ruler,
and as Creator of all the world.
We believe that God is still creating and welcomes us
to participate in making heaven available on earth.
Through life and death, God is with us.

Offertory Statement (Leader)
Share what you can to make this a beautiful and functioning place. Share what you can to make this global village a safe home with provisions to sustain life.

Doxology Praise God From Whom All Blessings Flow, tune: OLD HUNDREDTH

Praise God from whom all blessings flow;
Praise God, all creatures here below;
Praise God above, you heavenly hosts —
Creator, Christ, and Holy Ghost. Amen!

Prayer Of Thanksgiving (Leader)

God of Yesterday and Tomorrow — today, we join our voices in expressing our gratitude for what we have and for the opportunities to serve our neighbors. Amen.

Intercessory Prayers (Leader)

God of Beginnings and Endings — we like to think that some day we'll have our lives all well ordered and then we will feel less anxious. We like to think that some day soon we will have meaningful jobs, which will more than provide for our needs. We like to think that we are moving toward a simple lifestyle that will allow us creative leisure activities. We like to think that peace — personal and for the world — is on the way. As this year ends and we again celebrate your birth in human form, we pray for all the world: for lots of peace, enough food, enough space, enough clean water, enough clean soil, and enough willingness to share power.

God of the Middle — so much happens between the beginning and the ending. Sustain children and adults through the midsections of their lives. Keep their minds full of good thoughts; protect their bodies from harm; give them dreams of satisfying tomorrows. We pray for nations that struggle to mature and be independent in the turbulent world marketplace. Provide wise and seasoned, honest and fair leaders to guide the process toward collaboration and neighborliness throughout this global village.

God of the Seasons — thank you for all the times of the year when we focus on how you have been with humanity since time began. Thank you for Jesus who carried divinity through his world, teaching justice and compassion, healing the broken and setting the oppressed free. We are glad for the invitation to participate in cultivating a new way to be in the world — to help make the kingdom of heaven a reality. Through each season of the year and of the church, we are grateful for your presence. We ask that we learn something new about ourselves and about you as we go about the tasks of living. Come again to humankind and birth holiness, goodness, beauty, and hope. Empower us to be your strong voice and your gentle hands and feet. Amen.

Benediction (Leader)

Life is not a dead end.
It is a surprising journey to God.
Say "Yes" to life.
Laugh each day and unwind the threads of the world.
Notice new life around each corner.
Make new dreams and cultivate a glad heart!

Music

Cantad Al Señor
    Words: Brazilian folk song; tr. Gerhard Cartford, b. 1923
    Music: Brazilian folk melody

Lead On, O Cloud Of Presence
    Words: Ruth Duck, 1974, rev. 1989
    Music: Henry T. Smart, 1835
    LANCASHIRE

Sing My Song Backward
    Words: Brian Wren, 1974, rev. 1994
    Music: Ann Loomes, 1974
    HILARY

Proper 28
Ordinary Time 33
Pentecost 26

Isaiah 65:17-25 or Malachi 4:1-2a   2 Thessalonians 3:6-13
Isaiah 12 or Psalm 98   Luke 21:5-9

If we love the Lord with all our hearts, minds, and strength,
we are going to have to stretch our hearts, open our minds,
and strengthen our souls ... God cannot lodge in a narrow mind;
God cannot lodge in a small heart. To accommodate God they must be palatial.
                                        — William Sloan Coffin, *Credo*

Call To Worship

Leader: Good morning! I'm glad we're here together on this November Sunday. There's excitement in the air as we make family plans for Thursday and continue the count-down to Christmas Day.

People: **We're here to enjoy each other and to praise God for life!**

Leader: Have you brought your guitars? Harps? Trumpets? Flutes?

People: **No! But we have brought our voices and we can make fascinating harmonies. We can sing new songs to God!**

Leader: Sing with joy to God! Sing with enthusiasm. Clap your hands!

People: **Let the whole neighborhood hear our rejoicing!**

Prayer Of Thanksgiving (Leader)

Energy of the Cosmos — eagerly we expect to sing and pray; joyfully we express our appreciation for life and its beauty. Expectantly we listen for your voice. Refresh us for this day and the week ahead. Inspire us to be gentle and hospitable every day within our own house-holds as well as at work and at play. We are alert for your Spirit's movement. Amen.

Call To Confession (Leader)

In the hush of these few moments, we can survey our attitudes and actions. Anything that impedes godly behavior can be noted and transformed. The printed community prayer can lead us into our private conversations with God. Pray with me.

Community Confession (Unison)

Loving God — we work hard every day — work at our relationships, our homes, our jobs, and here at church.

Yet something is missing.

Search us until we know ourselves intimately; shine in us until we see the attitudes and hesitations that block your creativity in us.

Satisfy our hearts with abundant gifts of Spirit; free us from guilt and shame.

Satisfy our minds with fresh insights from the life of Jesus.

Flow through our bodies as hope and justice for our world. Amen.

Sermon Idea

Isaiah, centuries before Jesus, looked forward to forgetting about the horrors of his nation's past trauma in the violence of war and exile. He dreamed of Jerusalem, God's city, being free and full of happy people. Isaiah heard God say that elements of nature would become compatible. History repeats itself; cities come and go in power and prestige. The gospel writer had the disciples in conversation with Jesus about the temple (in Jerusalem). Jesus talked about the beauty being destroyed and about hard times to come. He went on to say that they should decide to trust his Spirit for wisdom to defend themselves. The sermon might explore the current global political situation with the intent of being grateful for the beauty of autumn and winter, for dependable food supplies, for the opportunities to communicate long distance with family and friends, for adequate water and fertile land. Perhaps the question might be: Is human nature so flawed with self-aggrandizement that we can only *dream* of peace on earth, only *imagine* Jerusalem undivided and tranquil, only *hope* for honesty in American politics, and wise education for our children? Jesus' teachings about the kingdom of God — heaven on earth — seem to be the antidote for cynicism, incivility, religious violence, racial strains, and sexual biases. Thanksgiving time and on through the New Year holiday is opportunity to notice the *real* aspects of biblical hopes within our homes, church, and nation.

Contemporary Affirmation

Leader: How do you pray?

People: We pray believing the Creating God responds by listening to and inspiring us.

Leader: Do you experience the Holy Spirit empowering you, creating through you?

People: God's Spirit enthuses and inspires us to do what needs to be done, to speak truthfully, to appreciate our companions, to care for the earth, and to share what we have with individuals who seek food, shelter, and clothing.

Leader: Are your words consistent with your behavior?

People: We aspire to embody the "commandments" of Jesus of Nazareth: we love God; we love ourselves; we love our neighbors; and we are learning to value our enemies. Day by day, we speak and act hospitably, graciously, and honestly within our homes, church, and communities.

Leader: How do you express your relationship with God?

People: We sing and pray; we dance and draw; we listen and converse! We make music and write poems; we snuggle babies and massage grandparents.

Leader: Are you thankful people?

People: Yes! We thank God:

for the planet and we are respectful of its systems;
for the sky, air, land, water, and fire;
for the varieties of wholesome foods;
for children and their curiosity;
for the generations before us;
for the freedoms our country promotes;
for Jesus whose teachings give eternal life.

Leader: Amen!

Offertory Statement (Leader)

Thankful people are generous people!

Doxology   Now Thank We All Our God (v. 1), tune: NUN DANKET ALLE GOTT

Now thank we all our God with heart and hands and voices,
Who wondrous things hath done, in whom this world rejoices
Who from our mothers' arms, hath blessed us on our way
With countless gifts of love, and still is ours today.

Prayer Of Thanksgiving (Unison)
Eternal God — thank you for your Spirit working among us. We give you ourselves. With our best and our not-so-good, create a global village where your creatures can live together in peace. Amen.

Intercessory Prayers (Leader or Readers)
(This list could be distributed among the congregation.)
Creating God — like men and women through time, we pray for:

- peace within ourselves and in the world.
- strength sufficient for each day.
- relief from pain and disease,
- safety for our children,
- wisdom for our parents,
- enough food and water for every creature, and
- wise leaders in every country.

Amen.

Benediction (Leader)
Go from this place with a song on your lips,
    with gratitude as your dominant attitude.
Go with a lilt in your step and a sparkle in your eyes!
Feel the Spirit of the Living God
    guiding you each step and each word along the way!
Be content at least part of each day.
Happy Thanksgiving!

Music
Come Down, O Love Divine
    Words: Bianco of Siena (15th century); tr. Trichard F. Littledale, 1867, alt.
    Music: Ralph Vaughan Williams, 1906
    DOWN AMPNEY

Creative God, You Spread The Earth
   Words: Ruth Duck, 1991
   Music: Trad. English melody; harm. Ralph Vaughan Williams
   KINGSFOLD

Gather Us In
   Words and Music: Marty Haugen, 1981
   GATHER US IN

Immortal, Invisible, God Only Wise
   Words: Walter Chalmers Smith, 1867, alt.
   Music: Welsh folk melody
   ST. DENIO

Joyful, Joyful, We Adore Thee
   Words: Henry van Dyke, 1907, alt.
   Music: Ludwig van Beethoven, 1824; arr. Edward Hodges, 1864
   HYMN TO JOY

Christ The King (Proper 29)
Ordinary Time 34

Jeremiah 23:1-6   Colossians 1:11-20
Luke 1:68-79 or Psalm 46   Luke 23:33-43

> *If we love the Lord with all our hearts, minds, and strength,*
> *we are going to have to stretch our hearts, open our minds,*
> *and strengthen our souls ... God cannot lodge in a narrow mind;*
> *God cannot lodge in a small heart. To accommodate God they must be palatial.*
> — William Sloan Coffin, *Credo*

Call To Worship (Leader)

Today is the last Sunday in the church year. Next Sunday we initiate a new liturgical calendar: Advent 1. Next week we will decorate this space with symbols of pregnancy and birth, with ornaments of love and peace, with wreaths and garlands, with purples and reds, blues, greens, and golds. Today, we consider how the Christ of God lives among us. Take a gentle, deep breath and be fully present in this place. Take a deep, gentle breath and be aware of God's Presence. Take a breath that fills your body with energy. Notice what holds your attention. Notice how you spend your time. Notice how you use your resources. Jesus the Christ speaks of the kingdom of heaven coming to earth. We image Jesus as our hero, our king, our CEO, our guide. We imagine participating in God's kingdom, a Holy Reign on earth. In this hour, we sing and pray, thankful that God is and will be. In these sixty minutes, we determine to place all our loyalties with the Holy God and plan again to embody the principles of kingdom living. In these minutes, we express our appreciation to the God who lives among us.

Prayer Of Thanksgiving (Unison)

God of Jesus and Us — we are aware of your creative imagination as we look at the world and the people throughout this global village. We know Jesus of Nazareth dreamed and taught that you would set up on earth a new, humane, and godly government and culture. We long for that to happen! And so we gather as your hopeful people, intent on being available to your Spirit, intent on being willing to live honestly and hospitably. Thank you for inviting us to be cocreators with you. We listen for your voice, and we respond with our voices and our actions. Amen.

Call To Confession (Leader)

An Old Testament poem (Psalm 46) says:

> God is our shelter and strength,
>   always ready to help in times of trouble.
> Even when the seas roar and the hills shake
>   we will not be afraid.

The reality is that we find ourselves in many situations when we are afraid, for good reason. There are times when we have no control over situations and the environment. But there are times when our decisions or our lack of decisiveness sets up consequences that are painful. Sometimes our *heart positions* cause ripple effects that demean our lives and those we love. In these few moments, we can assess our heart/psyche/souls and seek freedom from attitudes that are destructive to ourselves and to others. Pray aloud with me, then continue your personal conversation with God in silence.

Community Confession (Unison)
God of Poets and Pray-ers — we open ourselves to your examining Spirit.
Reveal the negative and the harsh that lurk in us.
Highlight the aspects that reflect your hope for our lives.
Set us free from the enslaving elements of our culture and transform our expectations and
**   our priorities.**
Guide us to the river of life, which brings you joy and satisfies our longings. Amen.

Sermon Idea
The scriptures for today hope/dream for a reality we do not experience in America or in any other part of our global village. The sermon might explore the necessity for and benefits of hopefulness when humans are immersed in unfair, unjust, and unhealthy real situations. Poets, musicians, and artists often lift us out of our gutters and help us hope for better times. Consider *The Peaceable Kingdom* and Tavener's *Funeral Ikos*, Rita Dove's poetry, and writings of Wendell Berry. Attention can be called to the encouraging passages of scripture like Psalm 46, John 6:25-35, 63. Musicians, dancers, and artists in the congregation could be invited to demonstrate hopefulness with works of their own crafts and with a one sentence description of their thoughts.

Contemporary Affirmation (Antiphonal)
All:	**We know we are mortal and that life often seems too short.**
Right side:	**We believe that God, the Creator, made the universe and declared it "good."**
Left side:	**We believe that God wants goodness and mercy to surround us day and night, even when we must endure difficult situations.**
All:	**We see the love and hopes of God clearly apparent in Jesus of Nazareth whose life and teachings manifested God's life-giving principles, which he called "the kingdom of God."**
Right side:	**We experience the Holy Spirit inspiring us with enlivening and innovative ways to bring God's Reign to our twenty-first-century technological and profit-driven environment.**
Left side:	**As a household of God, a part of the Body of Christ, we are present to one another on every part of our journey to God.**
All:	**We are not alone! Thanks be to God!**

Offertory Statement (Leader)
We participate in the kingdom of God by combining and spending our resources wisely.

Doxology   Now Thank We All Our God (v. 3), tune: NUN DUNKET ALLE GOTT
All praise and thanks to God who reigns in highest heaven,
To Father and to Son and Spirit now be given.
The one eternal God whom heaven and earth adore
The God who was and is and shall be evermore.

Prayer Of Thanksgiving (Leader)

Energy of the Cosmos — thank you for the talents gathered in this place — steady bank accounts, a wealth of education, a richness of sounds, a bevy of skills, a colorful palate of people, eager souls.... Conduct us as a "benefit concert" within your reign of peace and justice. Amen.

Intercessory Prayers (Leader or Readers)

Creator of the Universe — we see the natural world and appreciate its systems, which sustain life. We look at the sky and marvel at the blue and sparkle, knowing that we are very tiny beside the stars and planets. Thank you for holding it all in place. Open our eyes and our minds to ways we can use the land and its creatures, the waters and its life forms, the air and its gases without violence or polluting.

Emperor of People — we pray for peace. Begin your reign now. Move among leaders and disciples in every religion. Walk with humankind and make a garden of our chaos. Raise up leaders who are aware of the Holy Spirit and mercy and justice. Bring forth men and women who catch the imaginations of the rest of us to make this and every country a hospitable living environment. The world seems so close; let compassion reign where terror provokes fears and violence maims the children. Work through us in our neighborhoods and through our votes for honest public officials.

Majesty for our Lives — thank you for not abandoning us human creatures. We carry many scars. Our psyches have been abused. Our minds are cluttered. Our bodies are out of tune. Heal us; relieve our distress and free us from dis-ease. Give us strength for each day and rest for each night.

God of Jesus and Mary — expand your Spirit in us. We give you our loyalty as did Jesus and Mary. Order our priorities to manifest your claim on our living. Empower us with *Sermon on the Mount Ethics* and *Kingdom Decision-making*. Help us live "forgive as we are forgiven" and "love others as we love ourselves." Let it be so! Amen.

Benediction (Leader)

You are a child of God!
A "chip off the divine block"!
You carry the genes of the Creator.
You are talented to participate in peace-making,
     teaching, healing, and feeding individuals through out this global village.
The words of Jesus provide you with wisdom.
Go into this *realm* called life with a cheerful attitude, with a keen sense of responsibility,
     and with the ability to share the justice of the living God!
Be contented with life, at peace with yourself, and with everyone you meet! Amen.

Music

Cantemos Al Señor

  Words: Carlos Rosas; tr. Roberto Escamilla, Elise S. Eslinger, and George Lockwood,
    1983, 1987
  Music: Carlos Rosas; arr. Raquel Mora Martinez
  ROSAS

Come, Ye Thankful People, Come

  Words: Henry Alford, 1844
  Music: George J. Elvey, 1858
  ST. GEORGE'S WINDSOR

Lift Every Voice And Sing

  Words: James Weldon Johnson, 1921
  Music: J. Rosamond Johnson, 1921
  LIFT EVERY VOICE

Mountains Are All Aglow

  Words: Ok In Lim, 1967; trans. Hae Jong Kim, 1988; versification Hope Omachi-
    Kawashima
  Music: Jae Hoon Park, 1967
  KAHM-SAH

All Saints

Daniel 7:1-3, 15-18
Psalm 149

Ephesians 1:11-23
Luke 6:20-31

If we love the Lord with all our hearts, minds, and strength,
we are going to have to stretch our hearts, open our minds,
and strengthen our souls ... God cannot lodge in a narrow mind;
God cannot lodge in a small heart. To accommodate God they must be palatial.

— William Sloan Coffin, *Credo*

Call To Worship

Leader: It's a good day to praise God! It's a good time to remember how God has been with us.

People: It's the right time to be grateful for the women and men who have blessed us through the years — whose faith has been an example for us.

Leader: We thank God for the Holy Spirit in us and revealed in others.

People: How powerful are the blessings God gives us!

Leader: The power working in us is the same power that raised Jesus to life.

People: Hallelujah!

Prayer Of Thanksgiving (Leader)

Great God — we know that the church is the Body of Christ. We are glad to be part of that Body! We are glad to be in a long line of faithful people who have sought to honor you and make something of your reign apparent on this earth. With hearts and minds, we articulate our gratitude for this place and for all the people who have offered us bits of wisdom on our journey to you. For all the saints who have led us on our way, thank you. Amen.

Call To Confession (Leader)

Jesus taught his disciples to do for others what they wanted done for themselves. We call this saying the "golden rule." Notice in your own mind and psyche where you have difficulty living by these words. Pray with me the printed prayer and then make your own prayer to God.

Community Confession (Unison)

God of Time and Eternity — we hear Jesus say that kindness begins with us, that respect begins with us, that hospitality begins with us.
Some days we easily live by the words of Jesus. Sometimes, we fall sadly short of that goal. Reveal to us the times and places we can more graciously embody the wisdom of Jesus. Help us notice multiple options for sharing the love we have received. Amen.

Sermon Idea

Lead the people on a guided meditation to times and people who have listened non-judgmentally, who affirmed them at various stages of development, and who offered bits of wisdom for the soul as well as the body. Invite them to light a candle for each person who was present for them.

(Light the Christ candle as the source of fire, making sure there is safe and easy access to the candles and to the "eternal flame." A wick from the acolyte's lighter works well and dips easily into votive holders.)

When everyone has returned to her/his seat, invite one sentence of thanks for the saints who blessed them along the way.

(If the gathering is small, this may take only a few moments; if there is a large crowd, the candlelighting and statement of thanks may take a long time. Be sensitive to what is happening and don't let the time become a negative drain. You might plant a person or two who are willing to initiate the sharing.)

Some congregations appreciate gentle music in the background; others enjoy the silence. Conclude the meditation time with the hymn (perhaps only v. 1), "For All The Saints."

Prayer Of Thanksgiving (Leader or Unison)
Eternal God — we remember so many people who have been our saints through the years.
Thank you for their liveliness, for their patience, and for all their gifts of Spirit.
May our memories of them continue to encourage us and to honor them.
Empower us to mentor and bless those around us so we, too, may be saints for this time and
    place. Amen.

Benediction (Leader)
It's a good day (or night) to praise God!
A good day (or night) to be aware of our blessings!
A good day to recall how others have guided you and me toward the Mystery of God.
A good day to bless others on their way toward Holy Living.
The peace of God that is beyond human quietness sustain you all through this day and night.
Amen.

Music
Rejoice In God's Saints
    Words: Fred Pratt Green, 1977
    Music: attr. William Croft, 1708
    HANOVER

Let Hope And Sorrow Now Unite
    Words: Brian Wren, 1979, rev. 1983
    Music: Bohemian Brethren's *Kirchengesänge*, 1566
    MIT FREUDEN ZART

For All The Saints
  Words: William Howe, 1864, alt.
  Music: Ralph Vaughan Williams, 1906
  SINE NOMINE

Awake, My Soul, And With The Sun
  Words: Thomas Ken, 1695, alt.
  Music: François Hippolyte Barthélémon, 1785
  MORNING HYMN

Give Thanks For Life
  Words: Shirley Erena Murray, 1986
  Music: Ralph Vaughan Williams, 1906
  SINE NOMINE

In The Bulb There Is A Flower
  Words and Music: Natalie Sleeth
  PROMISE

Reformation Day

Jeremiah 31:31-34   Romans 3:19-28
Psalm 46   John 8:31-36

Who is this king
that forms another king out of the ground,
who for the sake of two beggars
makes himself a beggar?
> *Who is this with his hand out*
> *saying, Please, give just a little*
> *so I can give you a kingdom.*
>> *He heals. He enlivens.*
>> *He tells the water to boil*
>> *and the steam to fade into the air.*
>>> *He makes this dying world eternal ...*
>>> *He gives the soul a house ...*
>>> *He descends into dirt*
>>> *and makes it majesty.*
>>>> *Be silent now.*
>>>> *Say fewer and fewer praise poems.*
>>>> *Let yourself become living poetry.*
>>>> — Rumi, "Soul Houses," *Bridge to the Soul*

Call To Worship

Leader: It's Sunday again! As before, we gather here because we believe that truth sets us free. We are followers of Jesus and children of God.

People: In Christ, we are set free from the power of sin.

Leader: The Holy One promises to write divine law in our hearts and to be our God.

People: We will be forgiven and freed from guilt.

Leader: This is cause for rejoicing! Let us sing beautiful words, praising God!

Thanksgiving Prayer (Leader)

Living God — what a day! Autumn is everywhere! And we are aware that winter chill and dormancy are sliding into our days and nights. We are grateful for the multiple aspects of your creativity. We are aware, too, that we humans create things, changing what we think and how we know, what we eat and where we sleep. Made in your image, we are cocreators with you. In these moments of quiet, we acknowledge your presence and we open ourselves to your love. We speak and sing our gratitude. Amen.

Community Confession

Leader: It is good to be still and to be aware of what we have done well and where we might have behaved or thought differently. In these moments we confess generalities; then silently, make your conversation with God personal and let the Spirit free you from shame.

All: From time to time, God of the Mountains, we neglect to behave as your children. Now and then we are hurtful to the earth, to humankind, and to other creatures. Reset our attitudes; refocus our minds on compassion and peace, and lift our spirits from despair. Amen.

Silence

Assurance Of Grace (Leader)

All of us sin. All of us seek relief from guilt and shame. All of us are freed when we recognize the attitudes and behaviors that block divine affirmation. God offers us the gift of forgiveness. Receive this gift and be at peace with yourself and your neighbors.

Congregational Response   Behold The Goodness Of Our God (Psalm 133), tune: CRIMOND
Behold the goodness of our God; How blest it is to be
A company of God's beloved, In holy unity.

Sermon Idea

Martin Luther, John Calvin, Ulrich Zwingli, and others intentionally set about to make the church a more orderly and a more up-to-date social and religious institution. Each one had specific ideas he emphasized hoping to make city and society open to being God's kingdom on earth. As scholars, they gave society a fresh look at Jewish/Christian heritage. Men of the scholastic and enlightenment eras, they used the prevalent power patterns and explored alternative ways to be the church and to honor God. As with all paradigm shifts, as change agents, they were criticized for one thing or another. Reformation Sunday offers an opportunity to recognize heroes in our past and to consider how we can keep the Reformation alive and vital for today's seekers after Holy Presence. Thirteenth-century Jelaluddin Rumi suggests that words and rituals don't quite suffice in any era; instead, the self must be the poem and the action. John Spong, a twenty-first-century change agent, speaks of bringing our God-concepts into sync with science; Bart Ehrman talks of acknowledging the thousands of manuscripts of scriptures and the biases with which they are translated. The church is continually being reformed! We might even say that we are experiencing *quantum spirituality* along with quantum physics and quantum mechanics!

Contemporary Affirmation (Unison)

We believe the Holy Presence surrounds us, creating this whole planet; this has always been true.

We think God dwells in us, using our minds to care for the earth and all its creatures in ways consistent with current information.

We feel Christ urging us to be neighborly, feeding the hungry, caring for the ill, and crafting peace.

We acknowledge Holy Spirit in us and in others; our lives are the poems and the perfumes that make grace tangible in this world.

Intercessory Prayers (Leader or Readers)

(This could be time to name members of the congregation who have died the past year. A bell, chime, or short arpeggio can be used to emphasize and separate spoken names.)

God of Reformers — thank you for the women and men who through the centuries have articulated your presence. We are grateful for their insights and diligence that have urged society to learn compassion and kindness. We are glad they struggled for justice. We're glad, too, that we are not bound and boxed by their perceptions, for we hear you calling us to fresh experiences of hospitality, fairness, and equality. We remember those we loved who have joined you in eternity: (names of deceased members).

God of Change Agents — sometimes we are weary of being change agents in our cities; our culture seems to thrive on power-gathering, vulgarities, and media sound-bites; our voices seem so quiet. Still, we pray for the determination and insights to relieve oppression and poverty, homelessness and hunger. We want this global village to have contented people, abundant clear air, sparkling waters, and fertile land. We are frightened as we hear of planetary warming and desertification, of inadequate and impure food sources, of predatory money lending, and schemes to rob people of their livelihood. Like poets and prophets before us, we pray for leaders whose vision is big enough for the big problems of humankind. We pray for divine wisdom and safety.

God of Peace-makers — the terror of war is such a maiming way to deal with boundaries and religious differences! We, and our children, never quite recover from the spiritual and psychological wounds. So we pray for peace. Let it begin in our homes and in our country, among different ethnic groups, among restless youth, among adults who speak with barbed words. Let words mediate conflict without hurtful actions. Where the past has set up patterns of violence and disrespect, let compassion and hope overwhelm political ineptitude so goodness has a chance.

God of Wholeness — all your people seek a sense of being close to you. We all want to be pain and disease free. We all want to enter eternity easily. But that is not the way the world is designed. So we pray for strength and courage to live the life that comes to us. We pray for minds that are open to your healing grace. We pray for souls that grow gentle and full as the calendar counts our years. And we pray for the next generation. Protect our children from evil ways; keep them from harm; help them to learn information and to be wise citizens of this world and the life beyond this one. Amen.

Benediction (Leader)
May the dreams of the reformers inspire you;
may God who empowers men and women in each generation touch you;
may Jesus be your teacher;
may the Holy Spirit encourage you day by day.
And until we meet again,
may your life be a lively song, a thoughtful poem, a joyful dance — a colorful piece of art!

Music
Immortal, Invisible, God Only Wise
Words: Walter Chalmers Smith, 1867, alt.
Music: Welsh folk melody
ST. DENIO

Let Us Talents And Tongues Employ
  Words: Fred Kaan, 1975
  Music: Jamaican folk melody; adapt. Doreen Potter, 1975
  LINSTEAD

Holy Spirit, Truth Divine
  Words: Samuel Longfellow, 1864, alt. 1987
  Music: Orlando Gibbons, 1623, alt.
  SONG 13

Thanksgiving Day

Deuteronomy 26:1-11
Psalm 100

Philippians 4:4-9
John 6:25-35

I am an adventure-er on a voyage of discovery,
ready to receive fresh impressions, eager for fresh horizons ...
to identify myself in and unify with universal rhythms.
— Edward Weston, photographer, 1886-1958

Call To Worship   **A Litany Of Thankfulness**
(Words that imply thankfulness are in italics.)

Leader: It's Thanksgiving Day! Winter is settling in and the earth's production around us is slowing down. Our *gratitude* today is clear and palpable. We *thank* God for what we have and who we are. God is good and divine faithfulness sustains us day by day.

People: Through all our human adventures, we experience God's Spirit as our guide.

Leader: Each day, we receive fresh impressions of Divine Presence and we make time to *appreciate* how the Holy One is among us.

People: We *acknowledge* that God made us — made us in the Divine mold! We *treasure* opportunities to be cocreators with the Creator of the whole cosmos!

Leader: We are alert for the subtle voice of the Holy One drawing our attention to this planet and its resources.

People: We *respect* the land and the waters and *cherish* their life-sustaining qualities.

Leader: Don't forget the variety of wholesome foods that *please* our palates!

People: Red and yellow, green and purple, large and small, sweet and sour, seeded and smooth — all the vegetables and fruits that provide for the intricate needs of our physical bodies — we are *grateful* for them.

Leader: We are *grateful* for the meat we have so we can *enjoy* barbecues and marinated succulence, salted and herbed!

People: We *savor* time and conversations with our kin and friends who accompany us on this adventure we call life.

Leader: Recall the men and women who prepared the way for us.

People: We *applaud* the courage and audacity of the pilgrims who longed for space and privilege to explore religious options, to carve a government that would protect the common good and provide for those needing help, and to encourage individual prosperity that would enhance the whole community.

Leader: Well said! We *value* our country and the women and men who wear US uniforms around the world to foster democracy and freedom in order that everyone can participate in the rhythms of the culture.

People: We *admire* the individuals who use their training and experience to govern our country. We thank God for their gifts and we pray that they use their power wisely.

Leader: So we gather today to be aware of *blessings* that surround us and sustain us.

People: We are *contented* with living, *satisfied* with our journey toward God! So let us make a joyful noise — loud enough, for a few moments, for our neighbors to hear! We relish life!

Leader: Is there anything else we want to add to our thanksgiving list?

(Allow time for people to name their items.)

I *thank* God of the next generation — for our children. Together, you and I are mentors for them, teaching them to be hopeful, collaborative, responsible, and compassionate individuals.

People: *Thanks* be to God for our children and for the beauty and goodness surrounding us all!

Thanksgiving Prayer (Leader)

God of Yesterday, Today, and Tomorrow — empower us with the Holy Spirit so we may consciously pass on the *blessings* we hold dear. Liberate us from baggage that weighs upon us but no longer promotes health, sanity, graciousness, and gladness. We open ourselves to your light; we want to *enjoy* our adventure on this earth with you. Amen.

Sermon Idea

The Old Testament reading sets up ways to express personal gratitude within the context of the gathered community. Philippians speaks of personal mental health, which benefits the family and the whole community. The fourth gospel lection adds another dimension to our thinking:

- what we take into our bodies sustains us physically,
- what we take into our minds shapes our thoughts and attitudes,
- what we take into our psyches shapes our personalities, and
- our ability to appreciate others and our response to the universe.

What nourishes our psyche/souls?

- Not television, not game boys, not sports, not cars, not clothes, not houses.
- Not rules, not a specific vocabulary, not a particular church.
- Bread from heaven is available; elixir of life is at hand.
- Abundant living is an attitude, which is a result of a relationship with the Holy One.

Nourishment for the psyche comes from awareness of beauty and truth that are experienced in the Great Mystery we call God/Christ/Holy Spirit. Jesus shows the way.

Benediction

Leader: Are you grateful people?

People: **Yes. We are thankful and generous people!**

Leader: Are you intentional about manifesting your attitude of gratitude?

People: **Yes. We share what we have.**

Leader: Will you consciously pass along your contentment with life?

People: **Yes. We will listen non-judgmentally; our conversations will be respectful.**

Leader: Will you be alert for the Holy Presence throughout this whole day?

People: **Yes! We are God's thankful, compassionate, and hopeful people, nurtured by bread and by wine that give life!**

Leader: I thank God for you! Go, nestled in the arms of Caring Presence!

Music

Let All Things Now Living
Words: Katherine K. Davis, 1939, alt.
Music: Welsh folk melody; descant Katherine K. Davis, 1939
ASH GROVE

For The Fruit Of All Creation
Words: Fred Pratt Green, 1970
Music: Trad. Welsh melody; harm. Luther Orlando Emerson, 1906
AR HYD Y NOS

Over My Head
Words and Music: African American spiritual; arr. Horace Clarence Boyer
REEB

Now Thank We All Our God
Words: Martin Rinkart, 1636; trans. Catherine Winkworth, 1858, alt.
Music: Johann Crüger, 1647; harm. Felix Mendelssohn, 1840
NIN DANKET

Come, Sing A Song Of Harvest
Words: Fred Pratt Green, 1976
Music: Melcior Vulpius, 1609
CHRISTUS, DER IST MEIN LEBEN

Additional
Materials

A Brief Skit About Friendship
Proverbs 31

Characters
Reader 1 — male or female
Reader 2 — female, older than Reader 1
Reader 3 — male or female

Reader 1: *(to Reader 2)* I'm new in this area, and I'm lonely. I wish I could find a good friend, maybe a partner.

Reader 2: What kind of friend or partner are you looking for — an extrovert? Rich? Assertive? Educated?

Reader 3: *(to Reader 2)* Aren't you being a bit personal?

Reader 2: Yes. When I look for a friend there are some qualities I am quite sure about.

Reader 1: For example?

Reader 2: I want friends who are loyal and self-reliant.

Reader 3: Oh, so you make a list of "friendship traits"?

Reader 2: There are all kinds of lists....

Reader 1: I like to be with people who are aware of what they think and feel.

Reader 3: Well, my mother always told me to avoid crowds, that boredom is a frame of mind, and that idle hands would get me into trouble.

Reader 2: The best lists I know come from literature — like the Bible.

Reader 1: Like "Don't commit adultery" or "Don't say vulgar words"?

Reader 3: That's important to me.

Reader 2: Okay, let me think. There are several lists of character traits in the New Testament: loving, joyful, peace-making, patient, kind, good, compassionate, humble, self-controlled....

Reader 3: Oh, all those things! I can remember a few — don't be obligated to anyone (Romans 13:8), be strong in faith, don't be jealous.... You hear those at weddings all the time.

Reader 1: All I can remember are "don'ts."

Reader 2: My favorite list was probably written by a city leader in Palestine, maybe 2,500 years ago! The church has usually used it to keep women in line. It's written in a positive style — an acrostic on the Hebrew alphabet so everyone, especially boys, memorized it saying, "A good wife is hard to find...."

Reader 3: Yeah? Recite it for us.

Reader 1: Is this going to help me feel less lonely?

Reader 2: It might guide your search for friends.

Reader 3: Well, go on. The suspense is killing me.

Reader 2: It goes something like this:

> It's hard to find a capable friend;
>   that person is worth far more than jewels!
> Family members and neighbors put their confidence in that person;
>   they feel very rich!
> The capable friend does only good;
>   never does a friend bring harm!
> Friends work and play and never get bored, nor seek trouble.
> A capable friend brings surprises from out-of-the-way places;
>   that friend gets up early to help do what needs to be done.
> A capable friend is strong, industrious, careful with money, and
>   values people, animals, and things....

Reader 1: I bet that kind of person is generous with people who are in need.

Reader 3: I think friends aren't afraid; they think ahead and plan for the unexpected.

Reader 1: I bet capable friends are appreciated by everyone.

Reader 2: Respect — a worthwhile friend is respected for wisdom and kindness.

Reader 1: Yeah. I'm looking for friends like we've described. Know any?

Reader 2: I like to think that I am becoming a better kind of friend and partner as each day comes and goes.

Reader 3: I'm working on it. But right now, I'm hungry. Let's go to my place and make a pasta salad.

Hanging Of The Greens Service

(This is a "hanging of the greens" service for worship. Everyone remains seated throughout the hanging of the greens, except leaders and persons placing decorations. The congregation reads the bold-faced print.)

Prelude

Welcome
    The peace of God be with you.
    And also with you.

Chimes

Call To Worship

Leader 1: Today we celebrate God manifesting divine graciousness to people who seek to be in relationship with the holy. Since ancient times of Judah and Israel's King David, God has invited people to do what is just and right with neighbors and within the whole country. Today we begin counting the days within the faith family until we relive God's coming to earth in human form, in the baby who grew to be a man — Jesus of Nazareth.

People: **We know this story:**
    A shoot will come from the stump of Jesse;
    From his roots a branch will bear fruit.
    The Spirit of God will rest on him —
        the Spirit of wisdom, understanding, and power.
    With fairness he will judge the needy;
        he will care for the poor of the earth.
    The root of Jesse will delight in God —
    In that day the wolf will live with the lamb,
    The leopard will lie with the goat,
    The lion and the calf will walk together
        and a Child shall lead them.

Leader 2: This time is Advent — a time of preparation, of penance, and of waiting. We make our hearts and homes ready for celebration with symbols of divinity being birthed with humanity.

People: **We know this part of the story, too:**
    For unto us a child is born; to us a child is given
    And the government shall be upon his shoulders
    And he will be called Wonderful Counselor,
    Almighty God, Everlasting Father, and Prince of Peace.

Leader 1:   We are being intentional about celebrating God among us — again! God, showing up in unexpected places like barns and pastures, homes and churches.

People: Thank God for living among us, for filling our minds and hearts with signs of holy things and with awesome imagination.

("We Three Kings" is played in the background.)

Leader 3:   This is a time for giving and receiving gifts. As far back as written history, we know that during winter, people gave each other gifts — especially helping the homeless and poor make it through the cold months. St. Nicholas and many other legends describe the generosity of the wealthy caring for persons in need. Americans have Santa Claus.

**People: We know that part of the Bible story!
The wise men from the East — the magi took gifts
     to the child of Mary and Joseph.
We call him the Christ Child.
When the wise men saw the star in the East, they were overjoyed.
They followed the star until it stood over the stable where the child lay.
They opened their treasures and presented him gifts —
     gold, frankincense, and myrrh.**

Leader 4:   People who claim Jesus as God's Son are known for generosity. *Christians* share what they have with others as a gesture of love for God.

**People: We are friends of Jesus the Christ.
We know the whole story in poetry and prose, dance and song.**

Carol   O Come, O Come, Emmanuel
(performed with liturgical dance)

Confession
Leader 3:   It's a wonderful story of God's coming. Our ancestors cherished giving simple gifts. But, today, our story of God's generous living among us has been taken over by merchandising and profiteering.

**People: God, we confess that we are seduced by our culture's
          Christmas Machine.
Open our ears to your voice and to angel sounds
          and to bells calling us to action.
Today, we choose to unplug the *Christmas Machine*
          and enjoy sharing who we are with family and friends.
God, in this hour, we ask that our love
          for you be refreshed. Amen.**

Word Of Grace
Leader 1: The good news is that when we name the truth within, we receive deep peace.
People: Thanks be to God!

Proclamation
Leader 1: We make this space festive with music and beautiful things.
People: Let's put up an evergreen tree. Christians have been decorating trees for over 1,000 years. Even Martin Luther in Germany in the 1500s is said to have placed candles on a tree to simulate the stars in the sky above the place of Jesus' birth.

Carol   O Christmas Tree
(The tree lights are plugged in. Begin hanging the Advent/Christmas ornaments. These words to "O Christmas Tree" are a blend of several versions.)

O Christmas tree, O Christmas tree, how faithful is your color!
O Christmas tree, O Christmas tree, how faithful is your color!
So fresh and green in summer's breeze,
Still deeply green through winter's freeze.
O Christmas tree, O Christmas tree, how faithful is your color!

O Christmas tree, O Christmas tree, your steadfast green can teach me.
O Christmas tree, O Christmas tree, your steadfast green can teach me —
Of strength and hope, fidelity, of comfort and stability.
O Christmas tree, O Christmas tree, how lovely are your branches.

Leader 2: Hanging greenery goes back to ancient times. Evergreen ropes and wreaths were hung in homes and on public buildings as a sign of victory. Holly and ivy, rosemary and fir, cedar and pine — these are symbols of eternal life.

(People hang garlands over the front rail or pew.)

Carol   The Holly And The Ivy
(People place Advent/Christmas ornaments on the tree while singing this carol and the next one.)

The holly and the ivy when they are both full grown
Of all the trees in the wood, the holly bears the crown.
The holly bears a prickle as sharp as any thorn
And Mary bore sweet Jesus Child on Christmas day in the morn.
O the rising of the sun and the running of the deer,
The playing of the merry organ, sweet singing in the choir.

Leader 3: Let's place red and white poinsettias around this sanctuary. This flower originated in Central America as the "Flower of the Holy Night." Its star shape suggests the Bethlehem star.

(People place poinsettias on the chancel steps, under the cross, and beside piano.)

Leader 4: One legend says a child picked the red flower and gave it to the Christ Child as a gift. Another says that the white poinsettia represents the purity of Christ.

Leader 1: The legend adds that the star-shaped white blossom turned red when Jesus was killed. So the red and white flowers remind us of the holy night and point us to Good Friday.

Carol   Lo, How A Rose E'er Blooming

Leader 2: We've given symbolic meaning to many things — flowers, ornaments, colors — all to remind us of how God is among us.

Affirmation (Unison)

People: **We are grateful for the visual story around us. We are anticipating Christmas Day when we with Christians around the world celebrate the incarnation of God in human form. We, too, watch for signs of holy activity among us. Wise people still follow the star, which points to God's surprising presence. We are among the wise ones. The Christ will be born anew among us — a bright morning star! God is ... God loves ... God gives life!**

Carol   'Twas In The Moon Of Wintertime (Huron Carol)

Offering

Leader 1: We who follow the star, offer our gifts to God — gifts of money, ideas, strength, and skills.

Carol   In The Bleak Mid-Winter

Thanksgiving

Leader 2: Light of the World — thank you for inner peace that comes to us as we give you our whole selves and our resources. Use our hands and feet, our minds and voices to make this world a safe and hospitable place. Amen.

Doxology   Gloria In Excelsis Deo

Lighting The Advent Wreath   Bring A Torch, Jeannette Isabella
(Hymn plays in the background.)

Leader 5: No longer do we walk in darkness. We see the light of God!

Leader 6: Like people through the ages, we've made a wreath — a complete circle — and place flames among its branches to remind us of divine light for us and for the world to see. The fire burns and glows among us for six weeks. Like Old Testament prophet Jeremiah, we long for God to send us a good ruler. We want to live in safety, like the ancient Hebrew people of David's lineage. This wreath is a symbol of God's endless love for all Creation.

Leader 7: The three purple candles represent the darkness of the world. When they are lighted, they signify hope, peace, and love available for our lives.

Leader 8: The pink candle, lighted the third week of Advent, calls forth our joy! The center white candle we light on Christmas Eve is the Christ candle.

298

Leader 5:   Today is the first Sunday of Advent, 25 days until we celebrate the birth of Jesus. We light one candle.

(One purple candle is lit.)

Carol   People, Look East

Benediction (Leader)
We are full of emotion during this holiday season.
Be aware of all your feelings — happy and sad.
Gather often with friends so that your heart is glad some of the time.
Every chance you get, let the Spirit of Christ into the world.

Choral Response   Hope Of The World (Mary's Child ...)

Leader 1:   Thank you for taking part in this service of visual symbols of the Holy Presence among us. We pray that you will experience the inspiration of the Spirit. Introduce yourself and let us get to know you. If you are looking for a church home that values diversity and creativity, perhaps you have found an approximation of what you seek.

Postlude

Christmas Eve Skit
Coffee Shop Christmas Eve

Characters
Rebecca
Lucy
Sarah
Gail
Jeff
Grandma
Lee
Robert
Max
Curt
Ryan
Jeanne
Carolers (choir members)

Props
Three small bistro tables
Chairs
Three candles (one on each table, one for everyone in the congregation)
Coffee cups
Manger with puppet animals and doll
Shopping bag
Loaf of bread
Christmas Tree

Theme
A holiday evening is both tiring and inspiring. Children and adults express real interests while aware that Christians around them are telling an ancient story of angelic messages, pregnant women, and a baby born in a barn. Not wanting to go to church, they tell the story for each other in the coffee shop, strangers no more.

Plot
Children, parents, and one grandparent are tired from their shopping and looking at beautiful things. They resist joining others already at church for "traditional" Christmas Eve celebrations. Yet they tell the parts of the story they each remember and sing the carols they recall. The waiter is a narrator of sorts, reminding his customers that he wants to go home yet he wants to help tell the story of God and love and birth, of angels and shepherds, and important messages.

(Inside a coffee shop, loud music is playing — "Chestnuts roasting...." One family is already seated: Rebecca, Lucy, Sarah, Gail, Jeff, and Grandma. Another family approaches.)

Rebecca: I'm thirsty. I want a "splash."

Sarah: Me, too.

Lucy: Me, three.

Gail: I'd like a cup of coffee.

Jeff: It's 5:00.

(They seat themselves at a table.)

Jeff: We could have a snack now and drop by church for the Christmas program on the way home.

Grandma: I'd like that.

Rebecca: I don't want to go to church. I'm tired of songs about trees and snow and babies.

Jeff: Who wants what? Here comes the server.

Lee: Hi. I'm Lee. What can I get you?

(Everyone orders.)

Lee: Be back in a couple.

Rebecca: *(to waiter)* Hurry. I'm wilting!

(Rebecca goes to explore the manger in the back of the shop; "Chestnuts roasting ..." is still playing.)

Lucy: We've heard this song in a zillion different versions today!

Sarah: Heh! We could write a new song! *(music fades out)*
　　Smell the coffee beans.
　　Get a whiff of chai tea.
　　Shake a leg; clap your hands
　　I gotta go....

Grandma: Uh, uh.

Jeff: I have to keep reminding myself that this is a holiday.

Rebecca: *(returns to the table)* What holiday?

Sarah: We can tell the story. I'll start.

Rebecca: I want to start. Once upon a time ...

(Lee returns with the beverages.)

Lee: 'Twas the night before Christmas and all through the house ...

Rebecca: No! *(laughs)*

Lee: Not a creature was stirring, not even a louse ...

Lucy: No!

Sarah: Mary and Joseph were pregnant ... *(stands up to demonstrate)*

Lee: And they were traveling but they wanted to be at home — like me.

Sarah: They needed to stay overnight.

Gail: So they looked for a motel.

Jeff: But "no vacancy" signs were everywhere: No room!

Lucy: So they got desperate and creative ...

Jeff: Joe and Mary asked the barn animals if they could stay with them.

Rebecca: *(gets a puppet from the manger in the back of the shop)* "Moo-sure," said the cow.

(People at the other table join the storytelling.)

Robert: *(gets a puppet from the manger)* "Baa, baa-sure" says the sheep.

Max: *(gets a puppet from the manger)* "Sure, braaa," said the donkey.

Curt: I think it would have been very smelly!

Max: But the animals liked having company.

Jeff: The straw was softer to lay on than the sidewalks.

Sarah: You mean "lie on." The hay was nicer to "lie on."

Jeff: Good call.

Waiter: *(approaches table; to Sarah)* Mary, dear, may I put more ice in your drink? *(to Grandma)* Gran'ma, sweet, may I warm your coffee? *(to Curt)* Sir, may I add some cream to yours? The next line of your story is "Waaaa!" A human baby was born with the animals watching — *(to the children)* usually it's the other way around.

Ryan: Okay, so a baby was born —

Jeanne: I wonder how many babies are being born tonight ...

Robert: That baby was named Jesus.

Rebecca: His whole name was Jesus Immanuel Counselor Peace-maker Teacher.

Lee: That's too long. I think of him as "Friend at your service."

Sarah: You mean like "God with us"?

Lee: Yeah.

Jeanne: Where do you suppose the baby got that name?

Gail: From some old poet-prophet named Isaiah, I think.

Lucy: There's a boy in my class named "Isaiah."

Gail: Is he a poet, too?

Lucy: Sometimes.

Lee: What's the next part of our story?

Rebecca: There was a star. *(sings)* There's a star in the East on Christmas morn, rise up shepherds and follow!

Ryan: There were shepherds.

Sarah: And astronomers.

Max: And nifty gifts!

Lee: And more travel, this time to Egypt!

Sarah: Ah, the Sphinx.

Lucy: I bet Jesus loved to crawl up the paws of the Sphinx!

Lee: I bet they just wanted to be at home — like me.

(Jeanne gets loaf of bread out of her shopping bag, takes a piece and passes it to the others.)

Grandma: Umm, this would be especially good with a cup of hot chocolate.

Lee: House special. Coming right up. *(goes to get hot chocolate)*

(Carolers pass front of shop singing "Silver Bells.")

Curt: It's almost church time.

Rebecca: *(whines)* I don't want to go to church.

Sarah: I like our version of the story, don't you?

Gail: Have we left out any important parts of the real story?

Jeanne: We didn't mention God or love ...

Rebecca: Or Gabriel flying in wearing combat boots.

Grandma: We didn't tell the part about Mary being overwhelmed by the Holy Spirit.

Jeff: Nor did we name Joseph who probably wondered if he was crazy!

Lee: *(delivers the hot chocolate)* My grandmother sang the story to me:
C is for the Christ Child born upon this day
H for herald angels in the night
R is our Redeemer
I means Israel
S is for the star that shone so bright
T is for three wise men they who traveled far
M is for the manger where he lay
A is for all he stands for
S means shepherds came
And that's why there's a Christmas Day.

Ryan: We know *that* story.

Jeanne: Here it is, the night before Christmas ...

Lee: And I want to go home.

Max: Me, too. I want to open a gift.

Jeanne: Gold, frankincense, and myrrh ....

Sarah: I hope for ballet slippers.

Ryan: I want a new soccer ball.

Robert: I want a longer violin bow.

Curt: I want healthy, happy children!

Jeff: Look at us; we missed church.

Lee: Look what time it is!
    'Twas the night before Christmas
    And here in this shop
    We told the old story
    Amid coffee, tea and, soda pop ...

Grandma: We shared our time and broke some bread
    Strangers now friends — with our story —
    Sipped tea and soothed our heads
    Truth about birth and love, about God and hope.

Rebecca: 'Tis the night before Christmas
    And songs filled our minds ...

Jeanne: While we talked of gifts
    To please us and waiting for a new day's sun to shine.

Sarah: We've shared our time with hot chocolate and bread ...

Gail: It's dark now and only hours before
    We celebrate divinity coming to our door.

Curt: 'Tis the night before Christmas and we must go
    Knead the St. Lucia braid and finish the tree ...

Jeff: Morning will come and evening, too
    Of the day we've waited all year to see;
    Soon we will have only memories and gifts
    From you and me.

Lee: It's been good. Thanks for telling the story.
    Put your cups on the counter when you're through.
    Would you sing "Silent Night/Night Of Silence" as I close up the shop?
    Blow out your candles.

Rebecca: Oh, may I carry this one so we can see our car?

(The lights go out except for the one candle.)

Lucy: One candle is very bright with the darkness all around it!

Grandma: The Christian story says Mary's baby Jesus, God's Child is light for all the world to see.

Max: Come on.

(Everyone stands and heads for the door.)

Lee: Where's the candle? I need it to see the lock in the shop door.
Hold the candle so I can see.

(Rebecca holds the candle so Lee can see.)

Ryan: Is it soon morning?

Max: Did we tell the whole story?

Robert: Can I open a gift?

(Door is locked — Lee and Curt walk up the center aisle lighting the candles at the ends of each pew; each person passes on the light.)

Lee: *(to everyone/no one in particular)* The Christ Child brings light into our world.

(The choir begins to sing, "We Wish You A Merry Christmas...." One family exits left; the other family exits right. At the end of the song, the lights come up for the rest of the service.)

---

1. "C-H-R-I-S-T-M-A-S" words by Jenny Lou Carson and Eddy Arnold, 1961. Can be found in *The Reader's Digest Merry Christmas Songbook* (Pleasantville, New York: The Reader's Digest Association, Inc., 1981).

About The Author

Julia Ross Strope serves on the ministry staff of Church of the Covenant (Presbyterian) in Greensboro, North Carolina. She previously served Abington Presbyterian Church in Abington, Pennsylvania, St. John's Presbyterian Church in Durham, North Carolina, and Binkley Baptist Church in Chapel Hill, North Carolina. In addition to her pastoral work, Strope is an educator and counselor. She is a graduate of Houghton College (B.A.), Duke University Divinity School (M.Div.), and Union Theological Seminary at Richmond (D.Min.), where her doctoral thesis (Sacrotherapy: Healing Through the Visual and Tactical Arts) explored using the arts as ways to experience and articulate adventure with the Holy. Julia Ross Strope serves on the ministry staff of Church of the Covenant (Presbyterian) in Greensboro, North Carolina. She previously served Abington Presbyterian Church in Abingdton, Pennsylvania, St. John's Presbyterian Church in Durham, North Carolina, and Binkley Baptist Church in Chapel Hill, North Carolina. In addition to her pastoral work, Strope is an educator and counselor. She is a graduate of Houghton College (B.A.), Duke University Divinity School (M.Div.), and Union Theological Seminary at Richmond (D.M in.), where her doctoral thesis (Sacrotherapy: Healing Through the Visual and Tactical Arts) explored using the arts as ways to experience and articulate adventure with the Holy.

Leandra Merea Strope, who provided the hymn suggestions and drew the Celtic knot, is the minister of music at Binkley Baptist Church in Chapel Hill North Carolina. She earned her degrees in Flute Performance from Meredith College (B.M.), in Choral Conducting from the Yale School of Music (M.M.), and has done doctoral work in Choral Conducting and Literature at Indiana University. She has directed ensembles at Meredith, Yale, and IU as well as at numerous churches, and for five years she directed the choral program at Abington Friends School in Abington, Pennsylvania. Leandra also served as the lead teacher of choral music at the Governor's School of North Carolina in Winston-Salem from 1996 until 2005.

Melanie Bassett, who contributed the hand drawings on the section heading pages, is an artist and art teacher who lives and works in Greensboro, North Carolina.

US/Canadian Lectionary Comparison

The following index shows the correlation between the Sundays and special days of the church year as they are titled or labeled in the Revised Common Lectionary published by the Consultation On Common Texts and used in the United States (the reference used for this book) and the Sundays and special days of the church year as they are titled or labeled in the Revised Common Lectionary used in Canada.

Revised Common Lectionary	Canadian Revised Common Lectionary
Advent 1	Advent 1
Advent 2	Advent 2
Advent 3	Advent 3
Advent 4	Advent 4
Christmas Eve	Christmas Eve
The Nativity Of Our Lord/Christmas Day	The Nativity Of Our Lord
Christmas 1	Christmas 1
January 1/Holy Name Of Jesus	January 1/The Name Of Jesus
Christmas 2	Christmas 2
The Epiphany Of Our Lord	The Epiphany Of Our Lord
The Baptism Of Our Lord/Epiphany 1	The Baptism Of Our Lord/Proper 1
Epiphany 2/Ordinary Time 2	Epiphany 2/Proper 2
Epiphany 3/Ordinary Time 3	Epiphany 3/Proper 3
Epiphany 4/Ordinary Time 4	Epiphany 4/Proper 4
Epiphany 5/Ordinary Time 5	Epiphany 5/Proper 5
Epiphany 6/Ordinary Time 6	Epiphany 6/Proper 6
Epiphany 7/Ordinary Time 7	Epiphany 7/Proper 7
Epiphany 8/Ordinary Time 8	Epiphany 8/Proper 8
The Transfiguration Of Our Lord/ Last Sunday After The Epiphany	The Transfiguration Of Our Lord/ Last Sunday After Epiphany
Ash Wednesday	Ash Wednesday
Lent 1	Lent 1
Lent 2	Lent 2
Lent 3	Lent 3
Lent 4	Lent 4
Lent 5	Lent 5
Sunday Of The Passion/Palm Sunday	Passion/Palm Sunday
Maundy Thursday	Holy/Maundy Thursday
Good Friday	Good Friday
The Resurrection Of Our Lord/Easter Day	The Resurrection Of Our Lord
Easter 2	Easter 2
Easter 3	Easter 3
Easter 4	Easter 4
Easter 5	Easter 5
Easter 6	Easter 6
The Ascension Of Our Lord	The Ascension Of Our Lord
Easter 7	Easter 7
The Day Of Pentecost	The Day Of Pentecost
The Holy Trinity	The Holy Trinity
Proper 4/Pentecost 2/O T 9*	Proper 9
Proper 5/Pent 3/O T 10	Proper 10
Proper 6/Pent 4/O T 11	Proper 11
Proper 7/Pent 5/O T 12	Proper 12
Proper 8/Pent 6/O T 13	Proper 13
Proper 9/Pent 7/O T 14	Proper 14

Proper 10/Pent 8/O T 15   Proper 15
Proper 11/Pent 9/O T 16   Proper 16
Proper 12/Pent 10/O T 17   Proper 17
Proper 13/Pent 11/O T 18   Proper 18
Proper 14/Pent 12/O T 19   Proper 19
Proper 15/Pent 13/O T 20   Proper 20
Proper 16/Pent 14/O T 21   Proper 21
Proper 17/Pent 15/O T 22   Proper 22
Proper 18/Pent 16/O T 23   Proper 23
Proper 19/Pent 17/O T 24   Proper 24
Proper 20/Pent 18/O T 25   Proper 25
Proper 21/Pent 19/O T 26   Proper 26
Proper 22/Pent 20/O T 27   Proper 27
Proper 23/Pent 21/O T 28   Proper 28
Proper 24/Pent 22/O T 29   Proper 29
Proper 25/Pent 23/O T 30   Proper 30
Proper 26/Pent 24/O T 31   Proper 31
Proper 27/Pent 25/O T 32   Proper 32
Proper 28/Pent 26/O T 33   Proper 33
Christ The King (Proper 29/O T 34) Proper 34/Christ The King/
                Reign Of Christ

Reformation Day (October 31)   Reformation Day (October 31)
All Saints (November 1 or   All Saints' Day (November 1)
 1st Sunday in November)
Thanksgiving Day   Thanksgiving Day
 (4th Thursday of November)   (2nd Monday of October)

*O T = Ordinary Time

Breinigsville, PA USA
06 October 2009
225348BV00001B/1/P